A
TORAH
COMMENTARY
FOR OUR
TIMES

A
TORAH
COMMENTARY
FOR OUR
TIMES

VOLUME III: NUMBERS AND DEUTERONOMY

HARVEY J. FIELDS

Illustrations by
GIORA CARMI

UAHC PRESS · New York, New York

Library of Congress Cataloging-in-Publication Data
(Revised for volume 3)

Fields, Harvey J.
   A Torah commentary for our times.

   Includes bibliographical references.
   Contents: v. 1. Genesis—v.2. Exodus and
Leviticus—v. 3. Numbers and Deuteronomy.
   1. Bible. O.T. Pentateuch—Commentaries. 2. Bible.
O.T. Pentateuch. I. Karmi, Giyora, ill. II. Title.
BS1225.3.F46 1990   222'.1077   89-28478
ISBN 0-8074-0511-6 (v. 3)

Feldman Library

THE FELDMAN LIBRARY FUND was created in 1974 through a gift from the Milton and Sally Feldman Foundation. The Feldman Library Fund, which provides for the publication by the UAHC of selected outstanding Jewish books and texts, memorializes Sally Feldman, who in her lifetime devoted herself to Jewish youth and Jewish learning. Herself an orphan and brought up in an orphanage, she dedicated her efforts to helping Jewish young people get the educational opportunities she had not enjoyed.

In loving memory of my beloved wife Sally
"She was my life, and she is gone;
She was my riches, and I am a pauper."

"Many daughters have done valiantly,
but thou excellest them all."

Milton E. Feldman

For
SYBIL

partner, wise critic, eyes,
and love of my life

Contents

THE TORAH PORTIONS OF DEUTERONOMY

Acknowledgments

With this volume of *A Torah Commentary for Our Times* completed, I look back upon the past five years of research, study, and writing with great satisfaction. Pondering the unique and profound interpretive tradition of Torah throughout Jewish history has transformed me. "How incredible!" I have often muttered to myself as amazement and pride congealed at the discovery of a new and novel jewel of wisdom offered by commentators. Their humanity, art, and reverence continue as a challenge, a model of intellectual and spiritual excellence. Orchestrating their arguments and differing opinions, "speaking" with them, sometimes through them, leaves me enriched and a whole lot wiser—I hope.

Thanks to hundreds of students who have studied Torah with me during these past years. They have all helped to shape the form and substance of these pages. It was Aron Hirt-Manheimer who urged this project upon me. I am indebted to his wise advice, critical suggestions, and constant friendship. I am also deeply grateful to Rabbi Howard I. Bogot, Rabbi Shelton Donnell, and Rabbi Steven Z. Leder for their thoughtful reading and reactions to this volume. My work here has been blessed by the devoted and careful editing of Annette Abramson and by the production expertise of Stuart L. Benick.

My wife, Sybil, has sifted each volume of this commentary with her keen understanding of Jewish tradition and her devotion to clarity and excellence. I dedicate this volume to her out of gratitude, respect, and love.

Harvey J. Fields

TREASURES OF TORAH

"Words of Torah," say the ancient rabbis, "are like golden bowls. With golden bowls, the more you polish and rub them, the more they shine and brighten the faces of those who look at them. So it is with words of Torah. The more they are studied, explored for meaning, discussed, and used as a guide for action, the more they brighten the faces of those who love them." (*Avot de-Rabbi Natan* 31:34b)

Within Jewish tradition, "enlightenment" and "wisdom" are synonymous with knowing and practicing the words of Torah. The author of Psalm 19:8–9 has this in mind when commenting: "The Torah of God is perfect, renewing life; the teachings of God are enduring, making the simple wise; the laws of God are just, rejoicing the heart; the commandments of God are clear, giving light to the eyes."

This view of Torah as the vital source of Jewish enlightenment and the guide for ethical and ritual behavior is established within the Torah itself. Moses constantly reminds the Israelites that God has made a covenant, a sacred agreement, with them. The teachings and commandments of Torah have been given to them so that they may become a "holy" people. Indeed, the possession, understanding, and practice of Torah justifies Jewish existence. Moses warns the Israelites: "See, I set before you this day life and prosperity, death and adversity. . . . Choose life—if you and your offspring would live—by loving *Adonai* your God, heeding God's commands, and holding fast to God." (Deuteronomy 30:15–20)

It is not surprising that the study and interpretation of Torah became an obsession of Jews. Rabbinic commentators see in its tales, history, poetry, and laws more than an ordinary library of information. They compare Torah to a "lifeline," praise it as "the medicine of life," refer to it as a "map of existence," or as "fine wine that strengthens and soothes the spirit." The Torah, they say, "adds beauty to Israel." It prevents evil thoughts from seizing and distorting human powers for goodness, truth, justice, and love. For the Jewish people, Torah is a spiritual "homeland." Those who study and practice its teachings are never alienated from themselves or from their people.

Contemporary interpreter Rabbi Jacob Neusner does not exaggerate when he defines Judaism as the unique expression of Torah. Bearing in mind centuries of comment, passion, and intellect devoted to understanding Torah, Neusner concludes that "Judaism consists of the religious tradition enshrined in the holy books, expressed by the holy words, deeds, way of living, principles of faith, subsumed under the word 'Torah.' " (*Song of Songs Rabbah* 1:15; *Numbers Rabbah, Shelach,* 17:6; *Sifre Deuteronomy, Ekev,* 82b; *Pesikta de-Rav Kahanah* 102a; *The Way of Torah: An Introduction to Judaism,* p. 91)

These attributions of power and meaning to Torah all demonstrate its essential role in the history and destiny of the Jewish people. Each generation of Jews has evolved its understanding of itself through its struggle to decipher and apply the values and laws of Torah to its time. In our own age, as we have amply seen in Volumes One and Two of *A Torah Commentary for Our Times,* the exciting challenge of grappling with the meanings of Torah goes on. In this third and final volume, we turn attention to the Torah books of Numbers and Deuteronomy, where we encounter that continuing effort.

Reviewing Genesis, Exodus, and Leviticus

The first book of Torah, Genesis, deals with "origins." It presents the beginnings of life, humanity, the covenant with Abraham, and Isaac and Jacob establishing the relationship of the Jewish people to its land and God. The book ends with Joseph leading the family of his father, Jacob, to the safety and shelter of Egypt.

Exodus chronicles the rebirth of the Israelites. Joseph dies, his contributions to Egypt's survival forgotten by a new pharaoh who enslaves the Israelites. In the darkest moment of their captivity, Moses arises to lead them out of Egypt. Liberated, they live in the Sinai desert, where they are given the Torah; organize themselves as a community; and build a sanctuary. Punctuating the narrative of Exodus are the constant complaints of the people about living conditions in the desert. While Moses ascends Mount Sinai to bring them the Torah, they betray him and God by building a golden calf. God threatens to punish them with destruction for their breach of faith. Moses intervenes and saves them.

The Book of Leviticus contains directions for guiding the people and the priests in offering sacrifices to God. While it reads like a manual of ritual discipline, it includes an articulation of ethical commandments matched only by the Ten Commandments found in Exodus and Deuteronomy. Interpreters encounter many challenges in making Leviticus relevant to their times. Their discussions range from questions about the meaning of prayer and sacrifice to concerns about sin, ancient diseases, slander, and scapegoating. Within its dense rules about the slaughter of sacrifices and care for those afflicted with disease, interpreters discuss care for the poor, justice for the oppressed, and the challenge of creating a society based on the moral precept of "love your neighbor as yourself."

The Book of Numbers

In contrast to the first three books of the Torah, *Bemidbar,* literally translated as "in the desert," but commonly known as "Numbers," is a narrative of the Israelite people's forty years of wandering across the Sinai desert. The name "Numbers" is attached to the book because the first four of its thirty-six chapters deal with taking a census, or "numbering" the people, just one month after their liberation from Egypt.

Numbers captures the young community emerging out of oppression and organizing its leadership, institutions, and resources for reconquering its homeland. In a way, the book reveals the people of Israel during its difficult and awkward years of adolescence. Camping in forty different places, they face the natural obstacles of a barren and hostile desert. As a new and evolving community they forge laws with which to govern themselves and a military readiness for repossessing their land.

Like Exodus, Numbers combines narration with legislation. Concern for the purity of the community and its special relationship to God is addressed by laws dealing with nazirites, the suspected adulteress, oaths, blessings of priests, wearing of fringes, inheritance of land, the ritual offering of the red heifer, and concern for the safety of those guilty of manslaughter. All of these laws are meant to prepare the people for their administration and possession of the land of Israel.

Ironically, the tales woven into Numbers often feature the theme of rebellion. The people are constantly complaining about their plight in the desert. They question the leadership of Moses and Aaron, at times even demanding a return to Egypt. They whine about the tasteless manna, gripe about the lack of water. When Moses sends spies into the Land of Israel to bring back a report meant to guide the people in conquering the land, the majority of the scouts spread the lie that victory over its inhabitants will be impossible. At another point, Korah and his followers foment a rebellion against Moses and Aaron. Exasperated by the people's lack of faith, even Aaron and Moses turn against God. As a result of complaining and disloyalty, the entire generation freed from Egypt, including Moses and

Aaron, is condemned to die in the wilderness. Only Joshua and Caleb are permitted to survive and lead the new generation of Israelites into the Land of Israel.

The story of Balak, king of Moab, calling upon Balaʾam son of Beor in Pethor to curse the Israelites seems to rescue the demoralized people. The foreign prophet, promised great wealth by Balak if he will pronounce the destruction of the people, refuses to be bought. Instead, he praises them. Three times he blesses them, predicting that "no harm is in sight for Jacob, no disaster in view for Israel" and concluding: "How beautiful are your tents, O Jacob, your dwellings, O Israel."

Numbers concludes with a rush of preparations for reconquering the Land of Israel. A new census is taken. A detailed description of sacrifices for holy days is given. Division of the land is discussed along with the rights of women to inherit. The book concludes with Moses and the people standing on the steppes of Moab at the Jordan River near Jericho in readiness for the journey and battles ahead.

Through the generations, interpreters of Numbers have dealt with a number of issues. Attention is given to the meaning of "counting" the Israelites, to the peculiar ceremony for examining the claim against a suspected adulteress, to the significance of nazirite vows. Commentators examine grievances of the Israelites, probe the spies' report about the Land of Israel, ask about the justification of Korah's rebellion against Aaron and Moses, and pose the question: Why was Moses, so devoted a servant of God, not allowed to crown his career of leadership by bringing the people into the Land of Israel?

Matters of ritual and law also attract the attention of interpreters. They explore the importance of *tzitzit*, or "fringes," commanded to be worn by Israelites; probe the peculiar ceremonies surrounding the sacrifice of the *parah adumah*, or "red cow"; review the dangers of fanaticism raised by Pinchas's execution of Zimri and a Midianite woman; and grapple with the importance of the process of justice in society.

The discussion of these issues within this volume illustrates the wide variety of views held by interpreters of the Torah, who often clash with one another. An insight overlooked for centuries may be discovered and "polished up" for a "new" argument by a contemporary commentator. As sifted and critically discussed by interpreters, the trials facing the Israelites as they trek across the wilderness for forty years, maturing as a people, are still relevant. In many ways, Numbers reflects the uncertain and adventurous human journey of every generation.

The Book of Deuteronomy

As commentators have noted for centuries, the Book of Deuteronomy differs in its structure and in the character of its language. The English title "Deuteronomy" is derived from the Greek word that means "second law," which is the translation of the Hebrew expression *mishneh ha-Torah* (Deuteronomy 17:18), or "a repetition of the law." The Hebrew name for the book is taken from its second word, *devarim*, meaning "words." Those various titles of the book provide a clue into its style and contents.

Commenting on the unique nature of the Book of Deuteronomy, Nachmanides notes that "in this book Moses explains to the generation that is about to enter and conquer the Land of Israel many of the commandments that he believed required repetition and elaboration . . . as in the many instances against idolatry. He repeats the laws to impress the people with the serious consequences of not observing them." Don Isaac Abravanel agrees with Nachmanides. However, he adds another dimension, claiming that "Moses composed the Book of Deuteronomy on his own, commenting and interpreting what he understood to be God's purpose in giving the commandments to the people of Israel."

Both Nachmanides and Abravanel locate what seems to differentiate Deuteronomy from the other books of the Torah. Its narrative and laws are all a part of a personal reflection of Moses. The leader is portrayed at the end of his career. A new generation of Israelites, led by Joshua and Caleb, is poised to enter the Land of Israel. Moses gathers them together and for the last time addresses them. Deuteronomy contains his final three speeches to the people. It is a collection of his recollections, reflections, and interpretations forged over forty years.

In the first speech Moses reminds the people of their experience at Mount Sinai and of God's warnings against idolatry. He tells them that their parents were not allowed to enter the land because of their constant unfaithfulness to God.

In the second speech he repeats the Ten Commandments and many of the laws already found in Exodus. Loyalty to God's commandments, Moses promises, will assure the people's survival; unfaithfulness will bring punishment and destruction. Ritual and ethical commandments are treated with equal importance. Observing the Sabbath; caring for the poor, the stranger, and the hungry; not cooking a kid in its mother's milk; dispensing justice in the courts; caring for trees in time of war; prohibitions against wearing cloth woven of a mixture of linen and wool; marriage and divorce; and appropriate and inappropriate sexual relations are among the varied subjects Moses interprets for the people.

In his final speech Moses speaks of the *berit,* or "covenant," that God made with the people at Mount Sinai. He reminds them that it applies to all generations of Israelites and that all its commandments are possible for anyone to fulfill. They are "in your mouth and in your heart, to observe." He warns against rejecting the covenant, telling the people: "I have put before you life and death, blessing and curse. Choose life—if you and your offspring would live—by loving *Adonai* your God, heeding God's commands, and holding fast to God."

Deuteronomy concludes with a record of the end of Moses' life. He blesses the people with words of poetry and then calls Joshua forward to receive the authority of leadership. At one hundred and twenty years of age, Moses ascends Mount Nebo in the land of Moab. From there he can see the Land of Israel. He dies on Mount Nebo, but his burial place is unknown. "Never again," says the Torah, "did there arise in Israel a prophet like Moses—whom *Adonai* singled out, face to face. . . ."

As we might suspect, commentators engage in their exploration and study of Deuteronomy with the same critical vigor we have seen demonstrated in their interpretations of the other books of Torah. They rivet their attention on such subjects as the fair dispensation of justice, the tension between arrogance and gratitude, sin and repentance, and evil and goodness in the world. The regulations for the slaughter of animals, care for the environment, returning lost property, and the responsibility of handing on leadership from one generation to the next—all concern them. So does the interpretation of the *Shema,* what we can mean by "loving God," and how to understand Moses' claim that the people of Israel is an *am segulah,* or "a treasured people."

Hidden treasures

While Deuteronomy repeats many of the laws and commandments found in the earlier books of the Torah, interpreters do not overlook the significant variations in text or the drama of this book as the last teachings of Moses to his people. The artistry and differing style of Moses' testimony and motives provide a lively and compelling insight into some of the most important aspects of Jewish tradition.

It was Rabbi Pinchas, living in fourth-century Babylonia, who drew a comparison between looking for lost money and searching for the meanings and lessons of Torah.

It is strange, he said, how human beings will kindle hundreds of wicks and lamps to find a few coins that have been lost. So much effort and determination for such a small reward! So much work for so little profit!

However, continued Rabbi Pinchas, there is an important message here. If you seek after an understanding of the words of Torah, as if they were lost and hidden treasures, you will be greatly rewarded. Light many hundreds of wicks and lamps. For the Torah is a treasure that provides life in this world and in the world to come. Its exploration invigorates the mind and challenges the intellect and spirit to pursue deeds of goodness, justice, and love. (*Song of Songs Rabbah* 1:9)

THE
TORAH
PORTIONS
OF
NUMBERS

PARASHAT BEMIDBAR
Numbers 1:1–4:20

The second book of the Torah, Exodus, concludes with a description for setting up the sanctuary on the first day of the first month of the second year after the Israelites leave Egypt. The fourth book of the Torah, known in Hebrew as *Bemidbar,* or "in the desert," or in English as Numbers, begins with God commanding Moses to take a census of the entire Israelite community. The commandment is given on the first day of the second month of the second year after the Israelites' departure from Egypt. All males over the age of twenty are counted, and it is reported that there is a total of 603,550. This number excludes 22,000 Levites, who are exclusively responsible for all services of the sanctuary and are to camp around the sanctuary at all times. After counting all firstborn Israelite males over the age of one month, Moses is instructed to compare their number of 22,273 with the total of 22,000 Levites and to charge a redemption tax for the additional 273. It is to be paid to Aaron and his sons for service to the sanctuary. Moses also lists and counts the Kohathites separately from the Levites since the Kohathites are responsible for lifting and carrying the sacred objects of the sanctuary. They are not to be present when the sanctuary is either dismantled or set up.

OUR TARGUM

· 1 ·

One month after setting up the sanctuary "in the desert" *(bemidbar),* Moses is instructed by God to number all Israelite males over the age of twenty, all who are able to bear arms. The census is taken according to the tribal houses of the Israelites: Reuben; Simeon; Judah; Issachar; Zebulun; the sons of Joseph, Ephraim and Manasseh; Benjamin; Dan; Asher; Gad; and Naphtali. Moses and Aaron register all the males. Their total is 603,550.

The Levites, the sons of Levi, are not counted in the census since they do not bear arms but are exclusively responsible for the sanctuary and its

rituals. They are commanded to camp around the sanctuary at all times and to assist Aaron the priest in all the rituals.

· 2 ·

Moses counts the Levites from the age of one month. The total comes to 22,000. He also numbers the firstborn males among the Israelites. That total comes to 22,273.

God tells Moses that the Levites will carry out the work of the sanctuary and free the rest of the Israelites from such ritual responsibilities. However, since there are an additional 273 firstborn Israelites, a special tax of five shekels per head is to be paid as a donation, freeing them from their sanctuary duties. The money is given to Aaron and his sons to be used at their discretion.

· 3 ·

Dismantling and preparing the sanctuary for movement from place to place is to be done, exclusively, by Aaron and his sons. All objects of the sanctuary, the screens, curtains, ark, bowls, lampstands, are to be covered with dolphin skin or special cloths.

· 4 ·

Moses and Aaron are told to take a count of the Kohathites, the descendants of Kohath, one of the three sons of Levi. Those between the ages of thirty and fifty are assigned to lift and carry the sanctuary parts when they are moved from place to place.

THEMES

Parashat Bemidbar contains two important themes:

1. The meaning of *midbar,* or "desert," in Jewish tradition.
2. The significance of counting the Israelites.

PEREK ALEF: *Why Does So Much of Such Importance in Jewish History Happen in the Midbar—in the Desert?*

In 1838–1839, the famous Scottish artist David Roberts (1796–1864) journeyed throughout the Middle East. His pictures and personal diary are valuable records of what he saw and experienced. Traveling by foot and camel caravan through the Sinai desert, Roberts and his party encountered searing heat by day and shivering cold at night. His diary describes the ragged peaks, the black, rugged, desolate summits, "the dark frowning front of Mount Sinai," and the barren desert.

Commenting on his climb through the pass toward Mount Sinai, Roberts says, "Although I had crossed the most rugged passes of the Alps and made from Chamouny the whole circuit of Mount Blanc, I never found a path so rude and difficult as that which we were now ascending." Another member of his party writes, "I had never seen a spot more wild and desolate." (David Roberts; Nachman Ran, editor, *The Holy Land,* Wellfleet Books, New York, 1982, pp. V-27 - V-35)

Those who have traveled through the triangular-shaped Sinai peninsula, situated between Egypt's Gulf of Suez and the Gulf of Eilat, know its variegated landscape. In the north, along the Mediterranean Sea, one finds endless stretches of high, shifting sand dunes. Further south are jagged limestone cliffs and mountains relieved by vast rocky plateaus. In the southern area are tall granite mountains, valleys, and gorges eroded from the melt of winter rains and snow and imbedded with rich veins of copper and turquoise. Even today, there are fewer than one hundred thousand inhabitants in this arid and unfriendly region.

It is into the desolate landscape of the Sinai desert that the newly liberated Jewish people wander and remain for forty years. Students of Jewish history and Torah literature have constantly asked through the centuries, "Why did they stay so long?" Why after bitter years of Egyptian oppression did Moses not lead them directly to the Land of Israel? Indeed, why is the Torah given to the people of Israel in such a hostile environment rather than in the comfort of the Promised Land flowing with milk and honey? Finally, why does the Torah devote the entire book of *Bemidbar* and much of Deuteronomy to the Israelites' struggle for survival in such an inhospitable place?

Torah commentators offer various answers.

In our own times, historian and Israeli statesman Abba Eban suggests that the liberated Israelites were locked in the Sinai for strategic reasons. They had intended to return to the land of their ancestors, but they were few in number and incapable of taking on the Philistine armies, which controlled the shorter, more direct, northern route to Canaan, or the Canaanite armies along the Negev border. Eban explains that it took forty years of wandering "from oasis to oasis" before they were strong enough to reconquer their land. (*My People: The Story of the Jews,* Random House, New York, 1984, pp. 15–16)

While he does not disagree with Eban's observation, Israeli historian Nachman Ran sees more in the desert experience than a forced period of wandering and building strategic strength. The desert experience, says Ran, was a time of nation building and religious development. "To a people whose entire living generation had seen only the level lands of Egypt, the Israelite march into this region of mountain magnificence, with its sharp and splintered peaks and profound valleys, must have been a perpetual source of astonishment and awe. No nobler school could have been conceived for training a nation of slaves into a nation of freemen or weaning a people from the grossness of idolatry to a sense of the grandeur and power of the God alike of Nature and Mind." (*The Holy Land,* p. V-27)

For Ran, the *midbar* is a "school" where the Israelites mature out of slavery and idolatry into a free, powerful people. Within its unique, barren, and dangerous environment they learn respect for the wonders of nature and the importance of each person to the community. No longer slaves, they must now bear the burden of their survival. Their desert journey teaches them mutual dependence and loyalty to one another and to the ethical and ritual commandments that are meant to uplift life with sacred meanings. In Egypt they were condemned to live by the will of others. In the *midbar* they become free human beings responsible to God and to themselves for every choice they make.

Other commentators believe that the experience of the Israelites in the desert toughened them for all the trials they would face in the future. They suffer hunger and thirst, are attacked by enemies seeking to destroy them, and are forced to endure discomfort and constant danger. Their suffering strengthens their will to survive. It gives birth to a conviction that, no matter how oppressed or beaten, they will ultimately emerge victorious over those who threaten their destruction.

This desert experience later becomes a model for Jewish behavior. During times of persecution Jews would look back upon their wanderings across the hostile Sinai desert. Recalling its trials and triumphs, they would draw inspiration and determination to overcome all forces set against them.

Rabbi Akiba stretches this lesson about the importance of Israelite suffering in the desert to include another dimension. Their trials and suffering, he says, "allowed them to merit receiving the priceless gift of Torah." Akiba's assertion is a bold one: The experience of pain and disappointment brings special rewards. (*Sanhedrin* 101a)

Writer Helen Keller, blind and deaf from childhood, may have been saying the same thing when she commented, "I thank God for my handicaps for, through them, I have found myself, my work, and my God." Her rewards grew out of her striving to surmount her disabilities.

Sometimes the reward of our own suffering is a greater appreciation of the pain of others and the determination to do something to relieve it. Bearing distress often enlarges our sympathy. It provides a new wisdom and perspective from which to disarm violence and injustice with the pursuit of compassion, truth, cooperation, and peace. One of Akiba's best friends, Simeon ben Azzai, might have had this in mind when he taught that "the reward for doing a mitzvah is the opportunity to do another mitzvah. (*Avot* 4:2)

On the other hand, Akiba may have had in mind the reward, or sense of satisfaction, that comes from suffering for the sake of a righteous cause. Jews have often been persecuted for loyalty to their faith and people. Akiba himself was tortured and died a martyr's death at the hands of the Romans. Yet, even in the midst of his agony, he whispered to his students, "Now I understand the words, 'You shall love *Adonai* your God with all your heart, all your soul, and all your power.'" In the midst of his painful death, he reached the conclusion that his reward for suffering was the knowledge that he was giving his life for the sake of his people and faith.

Why in the wilderness?
Philosopher Philo explains that the Torah was given in the wilderness because cities are filled with corruption, luxury, idolatry, and other evils. He also argues that, for one to be pure and ready to receive the Torah, one must be separated from all the vices of the city. (On the Decalogue, I)

Torah was given in the desert to teach that we must consider ourselves open like the midbar *in order to learn Torah. (Nedarim 55b)*

Just as the desert contains nothing but layers of sand, so, too, the human body is composed of nothing but dust. But, just as the desert was transformed into a holy place by the appearance of the Divine Presence, so, too, with human beings. They become a source of greatness if they allow their spiritual spark to dominate their actions. (Rabbi Mordechai Katz, Lilmod Ul'lamade: From the Teachings of Our Sages, *Jewish Education Program Publications, New York, 1978, p. 129)*

Several early rabbinic commentators disagree with Akiba's claim that the Israelites were rewarded for their suffering in the desert with the gift of Torah. Instead they argue that God deliberately chose the desolate *midbar* as the most appropriate environment for giving the Torah. In supporting their contention, they cite a number of reasons.

The barren *midbar*, say the rabbis, belongs to no one. It is no-man's-land. For that reason God selects it as the best place for giving the Torah because the Torah is for all peoples. Like the desert, the Torah is open and free, accessible to everyone. It is neither a secret doctrine nor an exclusive one. Anyone at anytime is welcome to accept it and make it one's own. This, say the rabbis, explains why the Torah is given in no-man's-land. It is a gift to all human beings. (*Mechilta, Bachodesh* and *Yitro*)

Another teacher suggests that the Torah was given in the *midbar* and not in the Land of Israel to prevent arguments among the people of Israel. Had it been given in the territory of one tribe, that tribe might have said, "Look at us. We are superior to all other tribes since the Torah was given on our land." To prevent such claims and the jealousy and misunderstandings that might have resulted from them, God presents the Torah to the people of Israel in the *midbar*, which belongs to no one. In this way they are taught that no Jew is superior to another and that all Jews have responsibility for carrying out the commandments of the Torah. (*Numbers Rabbah, Chukat,* 19:26)

Other commentators believe that the Torah was given in the wilderness of Sinai to teach that, as the desert is open to all influences, those who wish to make the Torah their own must also be open to all its various teachings. In other words, the best students are not those who close their minds or have no patience for the views of others but rather those who make themselves like the desert. They are receptive to new ideas, willing to consider new perspectives. They take time to examine and experiment with novel views, unafraid to try innovative suggestions. "If people are not as free as the desert," one interpreter says, "then they are not worthy to receive the Torah." (*Pesikta de-Rav Kahana* 107a)

Modern interpreter Rabbi M. Miller of Gateshead, England, claims that "of all the places in the world, it was just in a place of drought and desolation, of barrenness and blackness, that God was welcomed with honor." Miller's view is that the desert was the appropriate place for the spiritual message of Torah because the desert is not corrupted by previous growth and development. It remains desolate, wild and pure, without need of alteration.

Miller's point is that "the Torah is given to those who make themselves as a wilderness, who purge themselves of impure influences and desires, of all aspirations and interests that are incompatible with the spirit of the Torah." Such influences, he explains, may include selfishness, the urge to covet what others possess, the corruption of friends or family, vicious habits, impatience, or cruelty to others. All of these influences block the attainment of "higher levels of moral and spiritual greatness." Preconceived ideas and prejudices blind us to new ideas and cripple us with dangerous habits. (*Shabbat Shiurim,* 5729, pp. 215–221)

Rabbi Miller's contention that the giving of the Torah in the desert contains a significant spiritual and ethical lesson is shared by Rabbi Morris Adler. However, Adler makes a different point. He argues that we live "in a desert age." The "voice of God does not sound clear and true in such a time." Confusion over right and wrong, faith, and reason prevails. In such a time it feels as if God were absent.

The reminder that the Torah was given in such a wilderness, says Adler, teaches that "there is no human condition . . . so dark that it can completely shut out God." Quite the opposite is the case. "God speaks, and sometimes . . . speaks most clearly in the wilderness." Often, explains Adler, people find themselves in difficult situations, overwhelmed by worries, stress, and pain. They are treated unjustly and feel themselves "succumbing to a sense of hopelessness." Precisely at such times it is helpful to remember that God gave the Torah in the desert, not in the lush land of milk and honey. "Whatever your particular desert, I say to you, 'Listen. Listen, for even there God speaks. . . .'" (*The Voice Still Speaks,* Bloch Publishing Company, New York, 1969, pp. 265–269)

Peli

Expanding Adler's insight, Pinchas H. Peli sees the desert as a metaphor, describing the psychological and spiritual realms of human existence.

There is a "wilderness" within each person, a "desert" where selfish desires rule, where one looks out only for one's own needs. No person is ever satisfied in the desert. There is constant complaining about lack of food and water, the scorching hot days and bitter cold nights. Anger, frustration, disagreements, and hunger prevail. The Torah is given in the desert, Peli argues, "to conquer and curb the demonic wilderness within human beings." The lesson here is that, "if human beings do not conquer the desert, it may eventually conquer them. There is no peaceful coexistence between the two. . . ." (*Jerusalem Post,* June 1, 1985, p. 17)

Why does so much of such importance in Jewish history happen in the desert? As we have seen, there are many answers to that question. One more suggests itself.

According to Jewish tradition, when you see the *midbar,* you are to say, "Be praised *Adonai* our God for the wondrous works of creation." The wilderness has always inspired awe and respect. Its quiet is mysterious and invites contemplation. One goes to the wilderness, as Moses did, to find new perspectives on life, to deepen spiritual awareness, and to gain clearer insights into moral concerns. Perhaps that is why the desert plays such a significant role in Jewish tradition. The *midbar* is the place where liberated Israelites receive the Torah, clarify their strategies for entering the Promised Land, and bond together as a people ready to face their uncertain future.

PEREK BET: *Why Count the Israelites?*

Bemidbar, or the Book of Numbers, opens with a date. We are told that, on the first day of the second month in the second year following the Exodus from Egypt, Moses was commanded to gather the Israelites together. A year has passed since they were liberated. They have wandered in the desert and stood together at Mount Sinai to receive the laws of God. Now, on the first day of the second month, a year after leaving Egypt, Moses is told to take a census of the people.

Interpreters who study the words of the instruction given to Moses call attention to their peculiarity. The words *seu et rosh* may be translated "take a census," but literally they mean "lift up," or "mark the head." As a result, their true meaning remains unclear.

Furthermore, commentators point out that this census at the beginning of Numbers differs from another census previously mentioned in Exodus 30:12–15. There we are given no precise date of the counting. Instead Moses is told to record the names of each person twenty years or older and to require payment of a half-shekel as an offering to God. By contrast, in the census of Numbers, no payment is mentioned or required.

Several questions arise: Why this numbering of the Israelites a year after the Exodus? What is the meaning of the words *seu et rosh?* Why does the Torah provide two versions of the census? What, if any, is the relationship between them?

For purposes of clarity, let's begin by answering the last question first. Early rabbinic commentators maintain that God commands Moses to number the people of Israel at least four times: once just after leaving Egypt (Exodus 12:37); another time after they build the golden calf; once again to protect them from the spread of a plague (Exodus 30:11); and a year after they depart from Egypt and are wandering in the desert (Numbers 1:1ff.)

Why are the people counted so many times?

The answer, say the rabbis, is to demonstrate God's love for the people of Israel. God, they explain, is like a king who possesses a fabulous treasure. He adores it. Each day he takes it in his hands and caresses it. He counts it to make sure that nothing is lost. So it is, say the rabbis, with the people of Israel. God loves to count them and, with each counting, declares, "I have created all the magnificent stars of the universe, yet it is Israel who will do My will." (*Numbers Rabbah* 2:19)

Rashi

Building upon this interpretation, Rashi explains that each census is a sign both of God's love for and reliance upon the people of Israel.

Just as we count those things or persons important to us and "count" upon them to care for us and, if necessary, defend us, so God counts upon every Jew to be a partner in the task of *tikkun olam,* or "improving and enhancing the world." Each census is a loving analysis of God's agents—or of God's "treasure." What we have here is a sign that God not only loves us but needs us. God is "counting" upon us to carry out our part of the covenant-partnership. (Commentary on Numbers 1:1)

Rashi's grandson, Rashbam, disagrees. He contends that the census has nothing to do with God's love for the Jewish people. Instead he argues that the counting of all those over the age of twenty years is a strategic matter. "They are preparing to enter the Land of Israel and require an army ready to go forth into battle." The census is taken to determine how many soldiers are eligible for the military challenge facing them. (Commentary on Numbers 1:1)

Ramban (Nachmanides)

Agreeing with Rashbam's view, Nachmanides explains that the census is an illustration of the Torah's warning against relying upon miracles. The people must fight to reclaim their land. It will not be handed to them by a miracle. The census is a means of organizing and enlisting them. It makes it clear that victory depends on each of them and on the coordination of their talents and efforts.

People are assets: rules for successful companies
Treat people as adults. Treat them as partners; treat them with dignity; treat them with respect. Treat them—not capital spending and

---

automation—as the primary source of productivity gains. These are the fundamental lessons from excellent companies. . . . In other words, if you want productivity and the financial reward that goes with it, you must treat your workers as your most important asset. (Thomas J. Peters and Robert H. Waterman, Jr., In Search of Excellence, *Harper and Row Publishers, Inc., New York, 1982, p. 238*)

Rabbi Jacob J. Weinstein enlarges Rashbam's interpretation. He points out that the census was "a model for large scale administrative competence." Moses asks for and records the name of each person. He organizes the census by tribe, separating the responsibilities of the Levites, who care for the services and security of the sanctuary. Each tribe, organized by family groups, is divided into four sections and assigned its own standard with a special identifying symbol.

What we have in the census is not simply a call-up for military service but the creative organizing of a community. The census is a practical necessity. It enables the Israelites to identify individual talents and abilities—the important assets of leadership required for victory. Through the process of counting the people, Moses is building an organizational structure and creating a design and purpose to Israelite society, even as it wanders in the Sinai desert. (*The Place of Understanding,* Bloch Publishing Company, New York, 1959, pp. 97–99)

Seu et rosh
Nachmanides notes that the words seu et rosh, *usually translated "take a census," literally translate as "lift up the head. . . ." These words are meant to teach us that "we are to honor those who are pious and generous and criticize those who are not."* (Commentary on Numbers 1:1)

Rabbi Pinchas teaches that there is a secret meaning in the words seu et rosh. *They are also the words used by an executioner who says, "Take off so and so's head." In the Torah these words teach that, if the people of Israel are*

> *worthy in good deeds, they will keep their heads and live; if not, they will loose their heads and die.* (Numbers Rabbah *1:11*)

In contrast with the practical organizing function of a census, Nachmanides suggests a psychological purpose. The people of Israel know their history. The patriarch Jacob has led them to Egypt with only seventy people. There they suffer oppression, sickness, plague, and death. To bolster their morale and build a sense of confidence in their strength, Moses calls for a census. Through it he demonstrates to them that, while they went to Egypt with only 600 people, they are now a force of 603,550 ready to defeat any army that threatens them.

Furthermore, Nachmanides explains, the census is conducted by Moses in a special manner. Instead of just numbering the people, those taking the poll are instructed by Moses "to do so in a manner that will give honor and importance to each person." Thus, says Nachmanides, Moses tells the poll takers, "Do not ask the head of each family for the number of people in the family. Rather, invite each person to pass before me. Take down that person's name, and let each one feel honored to be part of the census." By numbering each person, Moses encourages pride and feelings of self-worth. (Commentary on Numbers 1:45)

Leibowitz

Contemporary interpreter Nehama Leibowitz underscores the importance of Nachmanides' approach. She points out one of the great social dangers of our times: political, social, economic, and religious ideologies "that subject the individual to the mass and see the individual as a cog in the machine of the state, assuming that if one human being is destroyed there is always another one to take his place." Instead, Leibowitz continues, "Nachmanides emphasizes that the census was personal and individual . . . impressing on us the value and critical worth of each and every

soul, which is a unique creation of God and a world of its own." (*Studies in Bemidbar,* World Zionist Organization, Jerusalem, 1980, pp. 12–15)

Each is important
They are not just like animals or material objects, but each one has an importance of his own like a king or priest. Indeed, God shows special love toward them, and this is the significance of mentioning each one of them by name and status. They were all equal and individual in status. (Isaac ben Moses Arama, Akedat Yitzhak)

The census brings home the message to each and every one. Each sees that one does not stand alone but is a part of the totality of things. Yet, the entire world is dependent on each individual. . . . By being counted, we know our place in and our worth to the community at large. (Yehuda Nachshoni in Studies in the Weekly Parashah, *quoting the view of Shaloh from his* Shenei Luchot ha-Berit)

Hirsch

Rabbi Samson Raphael Hirsch argues that the census was more than a means of bolstering Israelite morale or of assuring each person's importance to the community. It is not enough, Hirsch points out, to have your name listed on a register or to take your place in a line behind a standard.

In Hirsch's view, the significance of the census is twofold.

First, as indicated in Exodus 30:12, a mandatory payment of a half-shekel is required from every person for the upkeep of the sanctuary. "Through this contribution," explains Hirsch, we learn that "a Jew is only 'counted' as belonging [to the people] by *doing something* for the sanctuary."

Payment of the half-shekel as a tax is the way

in which each Israelite demonstrates support for the community. The funds are pooled and used to finance schools and synagogues, to care for the aging, and to provide for the poor and homeless, the sick and needy. A Jew is "counted" upon by the community for support and is only a part of the census—of those who count—when *doing something* to benefit the entire community.

Second, Hirsch sees more than a lesson of community responsibility and generosity in the ancient Israelite census. He notes that the census is arranged as a valuable model of community organization. "The individuals first group themselves into families, the families into tribes, and finally the tribes into one common 'house of Israel.' "

Hirsch points out that, while each individual is unique, so, too, are the family and the tribe. All are linked "by a common inner factor, and each one of them must feel itself to be . . . a concrete and important part of this unity." In the census each person stands out with a name, family connections, and tribal affiliation, yet each feels a part of the whole community. "The greatest diversity of tribal and family specialties . . . and dispositions was diligently and carefully nurtured," explains Hirsch, yet "every tribe in its specialty and every family in its own peculiarity have to work at the common task of the house of Israel. . . ."

The census, therefore, is a model of community responsibility for the people of Israel and all humanity. Essentially, it underscores not only the importance of preserving and promoting individual rights and creativity but also strengthens the bonds of family, diverse religious, social, political, and economic associations as the means of ensuring a secure human future. Hirsch concludes that "every member of the family is counted by name, so that each one joins the whole, conscious of the importance of his personality to the nation." (Commentary on Numbers 1:1–2)

For Jewish interpreters the ancient census of the Israelites a year after the Exodus from Egypt was much more than an ordinary numbering of people. They elaborated upon its method and meanings, underscoring lessons about the role and responsibilities of each individual to family, nation, and all of humanity. Their creative views provide us with lasting insights to ponder.

QUESTIONS FOR STUDY AND DISCUSSION

1. Do problems, suffering, and hardships really help to "strengthen" a person or a people? What have they contributed to Jewish survival throughout the ages?

2. Poet T.S. Eliot, using the metaphor of the desert, once referred to contemporary society as a "wasteland." Would you agree? Why would Jewish tradition claim that the Torah was given in the desert, in a "wasteland"? What do we learn about coping with modern life from the ancient experience of the Israelites in the desert?

3. What are the lessons we can draw from the census of the Israelites? How can they be applied to our responsibilities to family, community, nation, and the whole human family?

PARASHAT NASO
Numbers 4:21–7:89

Parashat Naso concludes the census begun in the first chapters of Numbers with a counting of the Gershonites, Merarites, and Kohathites and a description of their work in the sanctuary. It also includes instructions for removing from the Israelite camp those suspected of disease or those who may have become impure by touching a dead body. Moses explains how to seek forgiveness for wrongdoing and what to do if a husband suspects his wife of adultery. The practices of the nazirite are repeated together with a description of the ritual for completing a nazirite vow. The portion concludes with the threefold priestly blessing for the people of Israel and with a description of the offerings brought by the twelve tribal chieftains to the sanctuary dedication ceremony.

OUR TARGUM

·1·

Moses takes a census of the Gershonite clans. Recording those between the ages of thirty and fifty, he notes a total of 2,630. They are responsible for carrying the sanctuary coverings, hangings, cords, accessories, and the altar. Ithamar, Aaron's son, is to supervise their work.

Moses also counts Merarite clan members between the ages of thirty and fifty. Their duties, like those of the Gershonites, have to do with moving the sanctuary. Under the direction of Ithamar, they are to carry the planks, bars, posts, sockets, pegs, and cords. The Merarites total 3,200.

Moses also records the number of Kohathites, whose work is connected with transporting parts of the sanctuary. Their total is 2,750, bringing the number of Levites caring for the sanctuary to 8,580.

·2·

The people are told that anyone who has an oozing open sore or who may have touched a corpse is to be removed from the Israelite camp.

·3·

Moses instructs the people that, if one person wrongs another, confession and restitution are required. If one steals property, its worth plus 20 percent is to be restored to the owner. If the owner has died, restitution is to be made to the sanctuary priest along with a ram offering of repentance. Such offerings belong to the priests.

·4·

Moses informs the people that, when a husband is jealous and suspects his wife of unfaithfulness, but there is no witness to prove his accusation, she is to be brought before the sanctuary priest. He will uncover her head and ask her to place her hands upon the altar of the meal offering. He is then to prepare a mixture of water, earth, and ashes from the meal offering. This mixture, known as the "water of bitterness," is meant to induce a trance.

The priest will then say to her: "If no man has had intercourse with you and you have not been unfaithful to your husband, be immune from this water of bitterness. If you have been unfaithful, then may God curse you with sagging thighs and belly."

After the priest writes the curse, the woman will drink the water of bitterness. If she falls into a trance, she is guilty; if she does not, she is innocent.

·5·

Moses reminds the people that those who vow to be nazirites are not to cut their hair or drink wine or any other intoxicants. Nor are they to have contact with a corpse. Contact with a corpse annuls the nazirite vow. The vow may, however, be resumed by shaving the head on the seventh day and by bringing offerings of turtledoves, pigeons, and a lamb to the sanctuary priest.

The nazirite term concludes with a sacrifice of a male lamb in its first year, a ewe lamb in its first year, a ram, a basket of unleavened cakes with oil mixed in, and unleavened wafers spread with oil, along with meal and libation offerings. The nazirite delivers these offerings, shaves his or her hair, and places the offerings upon the altar. The priest then places the shoulder of the ram and one unleavened cake and wafer into the hands of the nazirite. He waves them before the altar, accepting them as a donation. Upon conclusion of this ritual, a person is considered a former nazirite and may drink wine.

·6·

Moses gives Aaron and his sons the formula for blessing the people: May *Adonai* bless and guard you. May *Adonai* deal kindly and graciously with you. May *Adonai* bestow favor upon you and grant you peace.

·7·

On the day after the sanctuary is completed, Moses consecrates it and all its furnishings. During each of the subsequent twelve days, the tribal chieftains bring a special offering to the Levites for use in the sanctuary.

·8·

After the sanctuary dedication, whenever Moses wishes to speak with God, he enters and listens to the voice reaching him from above the ark cover between the two lionlike cherubim.

THEMES

Parashat Naso contains two important themes:

1. Eliminating suspicion and restoring trust.
2. Abstention as a way to holiness.

PEREK ALEF: *The Case of Suspected Adultery: Can We Move from Suspicion to Trust?*

The Book of Proverbs contains a number of valuable insights into human behavior. About "patience" and "jealousy" it teaches: "Patience results in much understanding; impatience results in foolishness. A calm disposition assures physical health, but jealousy rots the bones." (14:29–30) By drawing a parallel between impatience and jealousy, Jewish tradition provides a context in which to understand the case of a *sotah,* a wife suspected by her husband of adultery.

What does the Torah tell us?

Two situations are described. The first is the case of a wife who has had sexual relations with another man and keeps the matter a secret from her husband. The husband suspects her, but he has no witness. His jealousy grows against her. What shall he do? The second situation is of the wife who has not had sexual relations with another man. Her husband, however, suspects her. Though he has no witness, he is wild with jealousy. How is she to be protected from the "foolishness" of her husband?

Within ancient society, such cases were handled through "tests" or "ordeals." For example, the Babylonian *Code of Hammurabi* (about 1750 B.C.E.) states that a wife suspected by her husband of infidelity is to prove her innocence by throwing herself into a river. If she survives, she is innocent; if she drowns, she was guilty. Other cultures also record harsh measures for suspected wives. They could be thrown out of the house by their husbands, divorced, publicly humiliated, beaten, or killed. Some societies used trials by fire or, as in the Torah, the drinking of a ritual mixture prepared by priests.

Clearly, women suffered at the hands of jealous husbands, and their treatment was often cruel. There was, however, no similar "trial" for husbands who might be suspected, justly or unjustly, by their wives of infidelity. Such "equal" justice did not exist in ancient times. However, the Torah does offer a significant advancement in the protection of women. So do its interpreters.

In *Sotah,* an entire section of the Talmud dealing with the subject of a "suspected adulteress," rabbinic authorities carefully prescribe a process that a jealous husband must follow. If he suspects his wife of having an affair with a specific man, the husband must warn her in the presence of two witnesses about meeting secretly with him. Then, only if he has two witnesses who testify that she secretly spent time enough to have sexual relations with the man, can her husband request that she be forced by the court to drink the "water of bitterness." The case may not be heard by a local court, but it must be taken to the Supreme Court, or Sanhedrin, in Jerusalem. Only the Supreme Court has the power to order a wife to drink the "water of bitterness." However, if the man has been unfaithful to the woman, either before or after their marriage, or if she is disabled, he has no right to bring such charges against her. (*Mishnah Sotah* 1:1–4)

So many conditions (e.g., the warning about a specific man; the presence of two witnesses to testify to the time spent secretly with that specific man; the husband's record of fidelity; the necessity to hear the case before the Supreme Court in Jerusalem) were spelled out that women were protected from the fury of jealous husbands who might treat them unjustly. Even a woman under suspicion could not legally be thrown out of her home, divorced, or physically harmed. Rabbinic law assured her right to a fair inquiry and trial.

Protecting women
In ancient times, the life of a wife suspected of being unfaithful could be terminated abruptly without investigation. Judaism, however, required that a very thorough investigation be made before any action could be taken. This requirement was intended to safeguard the woman's good name and to protect her from merciless prosecution. (Sefer ha-Hinuch, Mitzvot 365–367)

By the time the Temple is destroyed and the Supreme Court, or Sanhedrin, ceases to function in 70 C.E., the use of the ordeal of the "water of bitterness" for the *sotah* is no longer practiced. For many commentators, however, other questions about the treatment of the suspected adulteress remain. Why would a wife, or for that matter a husband, become unfaithful? How should jealousy, envy, anger, and abuse be handled by courts of law? What is so unique about the relationship of husband and wife that the matter of suspected adultery requires not only an elaborate ceremony of proof but also attention from a Supreme Court in Jerusalem?

In exploring these questions, the rabbinic commentators speculate on what might cause a wife to seek a sexual relationship with a man other than her husband. Quoting the wisdom of Proverbs: "A person who commits adultery is devoid of sense; only a self-destructive person does such a thing," the rabbis draw a parallel between "insanity" and "infidelity." In another discussion they boldly declare that "every moral lapse is also a mental one." In other words, no person sins without losing a grasp on reality. Harmful decisions are made by those who fail to understand the consequences of their actions.

Specifically, the rabbis suggest that there is no difference between a man using a woman as a prostitute or a woman having an extramarital affair. Both, say the rabbis, "have lost their reason." They are choosing a course of action without rationally calculating the dreadful consequences for themselves and their loved ones. Neither men nor women indulge in sexual relationships outside of marriage unless "a spirit of folly possesses them." (*Sotah* 3a; *Numbers Rabbah* 9:6)

By placing the behavior of a husband or wife who commits adultery or may be suspected of marital infidelity into the category of "folly" or "loss of reason," the rabbis seek to expose the *cause* of the trouble. For them the issue is not simply the adultery but the factors precipitating it. What could lead a person to seek love and sex outside of marriage? Could it be loneliness, constant arguments, serious differences of interest, abuse, insensitivity, or mental instability? Understanding causes introduces the possibility of curing the problems. It opens opportunities for seeking reconciliation between husband and wife.

Rabbi Meir and his wife, Beruriah, known as a woman of great wisdom, serve as a model of mutual respect and caring. Rabbi Meir makes several psychological observations about human behavior and marriage. Teaching students during the second century C.E., he observes that there are three kinds of personalities: the type of person who sees a fly fall into his cup, flicks it out, and drinks the contents of the cup (such a man may see his wife gossiping with neighbors and relatives, male and female, and, because he trusts her, leaves her alone); the type of person who sees a fly fluttering over his cup and immediately throws away the contents of the cup without tasting them (such impulsive behavior is evil; it is typical of a person who will suddenly decide, without cause, to divorce his wife); and the third type of person who finds a dead fly in his cup, takes it, sucks it, and then drinks the contents of the cup. Such a crude person, observes Rabbi Meir, will, without protest or warning, allow his wife to become intimate with her servants, go out into the marketplace dressed immodestly, and wash herself where men bathe. In his lack of caring or genuine commitment to her, he will callously use her and then find a reason to discard her.

> ### On the treatment of wives
> *A husband should advise his wife to be modest; he should be flexible, not domineering; he should never resort to force or terror; he should not promote domestic strife by constantly arguing and criticizing; he should not speak out of jealousy but out of commitment and love; he should be easygoing, always honoring his wife above himself. In this way he will never drive her away or into immorality. (Based on Num-*

bers Rabbah 9:2; also Y. Nachshoni, Studies in the Weekly Parashah, Bemidbar, Mesorah Publications Ltd., Jerusalem, 1989, pp. 945–948)

Rabbi Meir's point is that temperament and neglect can drive a wedge between husband and wife. If a husband observes his wife entering into inappropriate relationships or a wife feels abandoned or compromised by her husband's relationships with other women, such misunderstandings require open and immediate discussion between husband and wife. Their feelings must be expressed. Unless they care enough about each other to articulate what bothers them and what they deem acceptable behavior, suspicions will eventually drive husband and wife to acts of immorality. Rabbi Meir uses the example of the *sotah* as an opportunity to explore and explain the challenges facing the fragile relationship of marriage. (*Numbers Rabbah* 9:12)

Peli

While modern commentator Pinchas Peli does not disagree with Rabbi Meir's psychological observations or with the causes of stress between husband and wife, he does offer a different view about the strange ceremony of the "water of bitterness." He speculates that "it is possible that Torah devised the best way under the circumstances to save this marriage by removing the mutual psychological distrust" between husband and wife. That is to say that "the *sotah* ceremony is an extreme remedial measure for a troubled marriage. . . . Jealousy, overpossessiveness, and similar emotions can be destructive and explosive in any husband-wife relationship. The *sotah* ritual brings to us one painful remedy." (*Jerusalem Post* May 28, 1988, p. 22)

Peli's point is that sometimes bitterness, suspicion, anger, and pain nearly destroy a marriage. In such situations one needs to drink the "water of bitterness" to restore trust, mutual respect, and understanding. Radical "medicine" is the only cure. In ancient times that meant the wife's submission to the ritual for a suspected adulteress. In our own time it can mean that both husband and wife seek counseling and learn how to drain the bitterness of misunderstanding from their relationship, restoring their love and trust for each other.

The issues raised in the case of the *sotah* in ancient times are significant today, not only for husbands and wives, but for all relationships based on mutual commitment. Friendships, business partnerships, and family ties are also ruined by suspicion, selfishness, and misunderstanding. How do we repair and strengthen such relationships? Ironically, those who neglect faltering relationships may find themselves drinking a home-cooked brew of the "water of bitterness."

PEREK BET: *The Case of the Nazirite: Can Abstention Guarantee Holiness?*

The Torah assigns several different categories of responsibility for the people of Israel: chieftains of tribes, priests, carriers of the ancient *mishkan,* or "sanctuary." All these jobs are designated by God and passed on from generation to generation. By contrast, the Torah informs us that any person, male or female, can freely choose to become a nazirite.

Becoming a nazirite entails a commitment of service for a minimum of thirty days. One is prohibited from cutting one's hair, drinking or eating grapes, raisins, vinegar, grape husks, or grape kernels. Like a priest, a nazirite is forbidden contact with a dead body. According to the Torah, "throughout one's term as a nazirite one is consecrated to God." (Numbers 6:8)

Commentators disagree on the role and institution of the nazirite in Jewish tradition. Nine chapters and sixty sections of the *Mishnah* and one hundred and thirty pages of *Gemara* in the Talmud present varying and often contradictory views on the subject. Even now, interpreters of Torah both praise and condemn the *Torat Nazir,*

or the "Nazirite's Code of Behavior," while few Jews actually practice it.

 Rashi

On the basis of *Targum Yonatan,* Rashi explains that the word *nazir,* or "nazirite," comes from the root meaning "to separate oneself" and refers to those students of Torah who "keep themselves separate from the ways of the common people." Extending Rashi's view, David Kimchi praises the nazirites for providing "a way for young people to distance themselves from worldly pleasures and passions." Others approve of the practice, especially of abstaining from wine, because it allows one "to serve God with a clear mind." (See Rashi, Kimchi, and *Tze'enah u-Re'enah* on Numbers 6:1ff.)

In his eleventh-century book of philosophy and ethics, *Hovot ha-Levavot,* "Duties of the Heart," Bachya ben Joseph ibn Pakuda praises nazirite practice and discipline. He argues that God places human beings on earth to test their souls and to make them as pure as angels. They battle for such purity against all physical needs, temptations, and desires. Often worldly pleasures appear harmless, but frequently they lead to excesses that overwhelm our powers of reason and seduce us into habits of self-destruction.

Nazirites, explains Bachya, are "physicians for the souls of human beings." Serving as models of abstention, they teach moderation. "All people," Bachya continues, "should work only enough to support themselves and to avoid being a burden on others; they should limit their conversation and restrain their envious eyes and ears. They should control hunger, should be satisfied with a single meal each day, viewing it as necessary medicine, and should fast one day during each week." The commitment of the nazirite leads people to appreciate this modest way of life.

Bachya's championing of the nazirite and the life of abstention is supported by commentator Moshe Chaim Luzzatto in his popular seventeenth-century textbook, *Mesillat Yesharim,* "Pathway of the Righteous." "True abstinence," explains Luzzatto, "means making use of only those things that some natural demand has rendered indispensable." For example, we need to nurture our body with a minimum of liquid each day. One should drink only the minimum required. Such control is not for the average person, however, but rather it is the gift of a disciplined spiritual minority capable of seeking holiness before God.

Luzzatto describes the ideal behavior of such a minority. This minority holds itself aloof from society, does not look beyond its own needs, ignores and disdains all pleasures of life. Seeking solitude and saintliness, it chooses to do more than the laws of Torah require. Luzzatto concludes that the nazirites are revered teachers and sources of inspiration because of their exemplary behavior.

Other commentators disagree, finding the nazirites' life of abstention nothing less than "sinful." Rabbi Eleazar Ha-Kappar, who lived during the second century and was a good friend of Rabbi Judah who composed the *Mishnah,* held that, by abstaining from wine and denying themselves the enjoyments of life, nazirites neglected the commandments of Torah and were "sinners." This, Rabbi Eleazar points out, explains why, at the conclusion of their nazirite vow, they must bring a sin offering to the sanctuary. Having deliberately abstained from the potential joys that God prepares for all human beings, they must seek forgiveness. This, remarks Rabbi Eleazar, is why God demands such an offering. (*Ta'anit* 11a)

Demonstrating strong disapproval of nazirite vows, which are meant to deny the pleasures of life, rabbinic authorities living in the Land of Israel during the second and third centuries argue that such vows are self-destructive. They are compared to "taking a sword into your own hand and thrusting it into your heart." Rabbi Yitzhak teaches that, if you are present at the time another person is considering such a vow, you must shock him to his senses by asking: "Are not all the restrictions and laws of Torah enough for you? Why do you insist on restraining yourself from that which the Torah permits you to enjoy?" Others claim that, when each human being

comes before God on the Day of Judgment, God will ask, "Why did you deny yourself pleasure from all that your eyes beheld?" (Jerusalem Talmud, *Nedarim* 9:1; 30:3)

Rambam (Maimonides)

Philosopher and commentator Moses Maimonides also opposes the choice of abstinence and self-denial. "The Torah," he writes, "advocates no mortification of the body. Its intention was that a person should follow nature, taking the middle road. One should eat in moderation and live uprightly and faithfully within the society of others not in the deserts and mountains. One should not afflict the body by wearing wool and hair. Because the Torah forbids such abstention from the joys of life," concludes Maimonides, "it warns us with the example of the nazirite."

In his classic discussion of Jewish law, the *Mishneh Torah,* Maimonides, on the subject of the nazirite, warns against the self-righteous tendency of concluding that all forms of bodily pleasure lead to sin and, therefore, should be avoided. He counsels that if people foolishly decide, because passion, envy, and pride are evil, to separate themselves from others and abstain from eating meat, drinking wine, marrying, living in comfortable homes, or wearing fine clothing, they should be told that they are choosing "an evil path." Our tradition, argues Maimonides, "forbids us from denying to ourselves any of the joys permitted by Torah." (*Shemonah Perakim and Mishneh Torah, Deot* 3:1)

The chasidic teachers frowned upon the nazirite practice of self-denial or abstinence. Human beings, they taught, were born to enjoy life, to breath in the sweet fragrances of flowers, taste crisp, delicious delicacies, wonder at the magic of majestic mountains and green forests, and fulfill the powerful surge of sexual desires in the mysterious realm of love. For the Chasidim, enjoying life was a way of praising God. Rabbi Pinchas Shapiro of Koretz holds that "joy atones for sins because it is the gift of God." Rabbi Moshe Leib of Sassov comments that "joy is better than tears . . . for it breaks through all the gates of heaven."

Rabbi Baruch of Medzibozh, grandson of the Ba'al Shem Tov, the founder of Chasidism, captures Jewish tradition's enthusiasm for all the delights of life and its disdain for withdrawal or self-denial when he comments that "one should take into one's heart three things: the love of God, the love of Israel, and the love of Torah. One does not need to engage in ascetic practices. It is sufficient for the average person to understand that in all things, physical and material, there is holiness." (*Sefer ha-Hasidut,* p. 60a)

Modern commentator Simeon Federbush is critical of the nazirites, not simply for their rejection of "worldly privileges and possessions," but also for their "antisocial attitude toward the community." Federbush condemns the practice of nazirites because it "separates one from the benefits of life" and removes one from "striving for the perfection of the human race." He argues that "any chain is only as strong as its weakest link. If one denies oneself to provide for one's own wants, who will take care of the needs of others? . . . Those who are occupied with ascetic indulgence will have no concern for the needs of their neighbors." (*Ethics and Law in Israel,* p. 166, quoted in B.S. Jacobson, *Meditations on the Torah,* Sinai Publishing, Tel Aviv, 1956, p. 213)

Learning to limit one's appetites
Sforno points out that the self-denial of the nazirite is limited. "One is told to refrain from drinking wine only; one is not allowed to cause pain and suffering to oneself by other restrictions or self-affliction. The Torah aims at decreasing desires, not eliminating them entirely." In learning to limit one's appetites, one becomes "holy to God." (Y. Nachshoni, Studies in the Weekly Parashah, Bemidbar, *p. 956)*

Aharon Halevi, the author of *Sefer ha-Hinuch,* approaches the case of the nazirite from a positive but guarded perspective. Human beings, he explains, are born with great spiritual and intellectual potentials that are placed within frail bodies full of passions and drives. The challenge of each person is to control the demands and temptations of the body and to rise toward holiness. By abstaining from wine and not cutting their hair, nazirites overcome vanity and begin a climb toward holiness. They work at ruling their inclination for self-indulgence and seek to place themselves in a position where they can pay scrupulous attention to what the Torah and God demand. However, says Halevi, nazirites must be warned against going too far and dangerously tipping the delicate balance toward the soul at the expense of the body. Like Maimonides, Halevi emphasizes moderation, yet he praises nazirites for their choice to seek the will of God. (*Mitzvot* 368–377)

Ibn Ezra

Ibn Ezra seizes the notion of "overcoming vanity" through abstinence and claims that nazirites symbolize by their self-denial the important virtues of self-control and discipline. He points out that the word *nazir* is actually associated with the Hebrew word for "crown" and stands for those who, like powerful monarchs, rule their dangerous passions and destructive temptations by constantly curbing them. While ibn Ezra may not have understood the power of addiction to smoking, drinking, and drugs, it is clear that he sees in the vow and discipline of the nazirite a means of achieving "control" over such deadly influences.

Sixteenth-century interpreter and philosopher Moses Isserles takes ibn Ezra's explanation to a logical conclusion. Also citing Maimonides' ideal of "the middle road," or moderation in all human choices, Isserles points out that nazirites are to be praised for realizing that they "have a weakness for worldly pleasures" and difficulty "diverting their evil inclinations from extremes to the middle way." By taking on the nazirite vow, such people push themselves to excessive self-denial and then "find the way back to the ideal of moderation." In other words, nazirites realize their impulse for indulgence and choose to overcome it by training themselves in self-denial. Eventually they master their inclinations and achieve the satisfaction that comes from living a life of moderation.

Jewish tradition remains deeply divided over whether to praise or condemn the nazirites' abstention from wine and the cutting of hair and their refusal to touch a dead body. On the face of it, the nazirite vow and practice seem remote from any modern application. Yet debating whether to praise or criticize the nazirite tradition may miss the essential meaning of the nazirite commitment and behavior.

Perhaps, for moderns, the real lesson to be drawn from the example of the nazirite deals with the challenge of introducing the discipline of "yes, I will" or "no, I will not" into our lifestyles. Temptations of alcohol, drugs, smoking, overworking, and overeating are everywhere. Reviewing the Torah's description of the nazirite vows and practice may offer a powerful symbolic message. For example, the decision to abstain from wine may signal the dangers of addiction and the necessity of cultivating a clear mind. The command against cutting hair may teach that egocentric concern for how one looks and for fashion and exterior style do not replace inner substance and quality of character. The nazirite's prohibition against touching a dead body may imply not a rejection of the inevitability of death but an acceptance that the most holy or pure occupation is to work for every cause that preserves and promotes life.

Unraveling the meaning of the nazirite's vow raises serious questions, not only on abstinence and the enjoyment of life's gifts, but also on fundamental considerations for controlling our needs and shaping our desires to benefit ourselves and our community and to serve God.

QUESTIONS FOR STUDY AND DISCUSSION

1. How does Jewish tradition "protect" wives from the jealous abuse of husbands? What other safeguards can you add? What about the rights of husbands?

2. Is it responsible to "excuse" immoral behavior by citing "mental instability" as its cause? How can individuals and the justice system function "fairly" if the system takes into consideration "mental" causes for antisocial behavior?

3. Does the nazirite, who abstains from wine, the cutting of hair, and the touching of a corpse, achieve a greater sense of holiness? What does Jewish tradition teach about achieving a "spiritual" nearness to God? What divides Jewish commentators on this issue? What standards of behavior can one choose today to achieve Maimonides' ethical life of the "middle of the road," or moderation?

4. Rabbi Judah taught that, "in the spring when we see the beautiful trees swaying in the breeze, we should stop to recite a prayer. We

should say, 'Be praised, O God, for creating a world where nothing is lacking, a world filled with beauty to delight the human heart.' " (*Eruvin* 43b) Do you agree that a positive acknowledgment of the gifts of life is superior to abstinence and self-denial as a means of encouraging people to appreciate human existence and avoid self-destructive habits?

PARASHAT BEHA'ALOTECHA
Numbers 8:1–12:16

Parashat Beha'alotecha contains instructions for installing the *menorah* in the sanctuary and for consecrating the priests and Levites. It also describes the procedure to be followed by any Israelite who misses bringing the Pesach sacrifice, and it includes a description of the Israelites' journey through the desert. When the people complain about their diet of manna, Moses asks God, "Why have You laid the burden of all this people upon me?" He is counseled to appoint seventy experienced elders and officers to share leadership and the spirit of prophecy with him. Among the appointed are Eldad and Medad, who are filled with enthusiasm. Despite Joshua's complaint about them, Moses defends their right to act as prophets. Miriam and Aaron criticize Moses for his marriage to a Cushite woman. Miriam is punished with leprosy. Both Aaron and Moses plead on her behalf. After being excluded from the camp for seven days, she is cured.

OUR TARGUM

· 1 ·

The commandment to install the seven-branched *menorah,* or "candelabrum," is repeated here. (See Exodus 25:37; 27:21.)

· 2 ·

Moses calls the Levites to the sanctuary and consecrates them to help the priests with the sacrifices. They are selected from the Israelite community and take the place of the firstborn who would otherwise be designated for the sanctuary work. The career of the Levites extends from the age of twenty-five to fifty, when they retire.

· 3 ·

Moses tells the people what to do if they are defiled by touching a corpse, or if they are on a long journey at the time specified for the Pesach festival (the fourteenth day of Nisan at twilight). Since, in both situations, they are unable to offer the Pesach sacrifice, provision is made for them to bring the sacrifice to the sanctuary a month later. At that time they are to eat it with unleavened bread and bitter herbs, observing the event as if it were Pesach. Furthermore, Moses informs the people that strangers residing among the Israelites shall observe all the rituals and laws of Pesach without discrimination.

·4·

A cloud covers the sanctuary during the day, and a cloud of fire covers it at night. When the cloud lifts, the Israelites break camp and journey onward through the desert. God instructs Moses to create silver trumpets to be blown by Aaron's sons, the priests, on four occasions: (1) to signal the beginning of a journey; (2) to gather the people; (3) to call them to battle; and (4) to announce the celebration of a sacrifice, a festival, or a joyous occasion.

·5·

On the twentieth day of the second month in the second year after the Exodus from Egypt, Moses and the people begin their journey through the desert toward the Land of Israel. The tribes carry their individual banners as they march in order. Moses invites Hobab, son of his father-in-law, Jethro, to join the journey, but Hobab declines. With the ark in front of them, the people set out, and Moses declares: "Advance, O

Adonai!/May Your enemies be scattered,/And may Your foes flee before You!"

·6·

Traveling through the desert, the people complain to Moses about the lack of meat, and they complain about their mundane diet of manna. God warns them to stop their ungrateful griping, but they persist in protesting. Overwhelmed by their criticism, Moses asks God: "Why have You dealt ill with Your servant? Why have I not enjoyed Your favor? Why have You laid the burden of all this people upon me? Did I conceive all this people? Did I bear them, that You should say to me, 'Carry them in your bosom as a nurse carries an infant,' to the land that You have promised on oath to their fathers? . . . I cannot carry all this people by myself, for it is too much for me. . . ."

God instructs Moses, as Jethro had counseled him earlier (see Exodus 18:13–27), to appoint elders and officers with whom to share leadership. God provides food enough for the people

and places the spirit of prophecy upon the seventy appointed leaders. Two of these, Eldad and Medad, continue to speak in the spirit of prophecy, seeming to challenge the authority of Moses and Aaron. Joshua, Moses' trusted attendant, reports the matter to Moses, who refuses to restrain them. He tells Joshua, "Would that all *Adonai*'s people were prophets!"

·7·

Later Miriam and Aaron speak out publicly against Moses because of his marriage to a Cushite woman. They question their brother's integrity, saying, "Has God spoken only through Moses? Has not God spoken through us as well?"

God summons Miriam and Aaron and explains that, while *Adonai* speaks to other prophets through visions, *Adonai* speaks to Moses plainly, directly, and without riddles. For criticizing her brother, Miriam is punished with leprosy. When Moses and Aaron intervene on her behalf, God orders her excluded from the camp for seven days.

THEMES

Parashat Be-ha'alotecha contains two important themes:

1. Understanding and responding to complaints.
2. Understanding the motives of others before criticizing them.

PEREK ALEF: *Responding to Murmuring and Complaints*

Just after the people of Israel are liberated from Egyptian slavery, they approach Moses with complaints about conditions in the wilderness. (See Harvey J. Fields, *A Torah Commentary for Our Times,* Volume II, *Parashat Beshalach, "Perek Bet,"* UAHC Press, New York, 1991, pp. 36–39.) Moses responds by requesting God to provide them with water and food. They are given manna each day with a double portion on Fridays so that they will not have to work at collecting it on the Sabbath. Fresh water is also supplied in abundance.

Now, two years later, after receiving the com-

mandments at Mount Sinai and building their sanctuary, the Israelites once again raise their voices with bitter complaints. They protest about their living conditions in the desert. As a result of their behavior, God punishes them with fire throughout the camp. Seeing this, Moses intervenes, and the fire ceases.

The complaints, however, are just beginning. Joining with the non-Israelites who have accompanied them out of Egypt, the people wax nostalgic, deceiving themselves about the conditions under which they had lived in Egypt. "If only we had meat to eat! We remember the free fish we used to eat in Egypt, the cucumbers, the melons, the leeks, the onions, and the garlic. Now our stomachs are shriveled. There is nothing at all! Nothing but this manna to look to." (Numbers 11:4–6)

Interpreters of Torah ask two questions about the grievances and grumblings of the people: What caused them? What might have been an appropriate response by Moses?

Rashi

Rashi offers an excuse for the people. He suggests that they are exhausted from their first three-day journey. Upset, even angry, that Moses is pushing them along and not allowing them time to rest, they raise their voices in protest. Cranky and tired, they whine like children, recalling easier times when all their needs for food and comfort had been provided by others. (Commentary on Numbers 11:1)

Ramban (Nachmanides)

Nachmanides agrees with Rashi. He explains that the people have justifiable reasons for their complaints. Moses has taken them from the familiar surroundings of Mount Sinai, where they had camped for two years, to a desolate wilderness, where they are uncertain about the future. Frightening questions confront them: Are they safe from enemies? Will there be sufficient food and water? Who will provide it? Their anxiety is painful. It confuses them. All their murmurings, says Nachmanides, grow out of their mental anguish and self-pity. "They react like others under duress and compulsion." (Commentary on Numbers 11:1)

Nachmanides, however, does not offer his explanation as an excuse or justification for the people's reaction. Instead, he sees self-centered demands as a lack of faith. He condemns the Israelites for their refusal to trust in God. Rather than giving thanks for all they enjoy, they are ungrateful, even disloyal. Instead of trusting that they are in safe hands with Moses and God, they

gripe about food and offer false and exaggerated comparisons between their lives as slaves in Egypt and their existence as a free people. Fixed on nostalgic and erroneous perceptions of the past, they become mired in bitter criticisms, making them incapable of sharing a vision and strategy for their future. (Commentary on Numbers 11:4–6)

Hirsch

Rabbi Samson Raphael Hirsch offers a different viewpoint. The Israelites, he argues, suffer not from nostalgia but from boredom. All their needs are met. They enjoy a near perfect situation in the wilderness. Each day they are given manna and plenty of fresh water. Nothing is lacking. Nonetheless, comments Hirsch, they "feel themselves buried alive."

"The people," he continues, "were as if in mourning over themselves. They look on themselves as already dead." With all their needs met, their Torah given, their sanctuary complete, their lives "offer them no compensation, remain worthless and without meaning in their eyes." Frustrated at having no new goal, challenge, or mission, they begin murmuring against Moses and God.

Hirsch imagines them saying to Moses, "It is not nourishment that we lack . . . what we lack are the tasty, stimulating foods that excite the appetite. We miss the change of diet so necessary for health. The complete monotony, the unvarying sameness of our food makes it unbearable." The Israelites, Hirsch maintains, are desperately seeking a way out of boredom. They want excitement, stimulation, and variation of foods and experiences. Their complaints to Moses evolve from their need for new challenges, visions, and opportunities. (Commentary on Numbers 11:1–11)

They were confused . . .
The children of Israel witnessed the revelation at Sinai and had certainly become uplifted by

that event, but the inspiration soon wore off. After a while, instead of remaining transformed by that experience into a holy people, capable of becoming a light unto the nations, their memories are of Nile smorgasbords, big kiddushim, *and fancy bar mitzvahs with open bars and Viennese tables. At Sinai the vision was sharp and vivid, but the desert muted these visions and replaced them with an obsession for the materialistic. The Jews felt bereft and empty, and so they complained, not even certain themselves of what they really wanted. (Rabbi Shlomo Riskin,* Jerusalem Post, *May 27, 1990)*

Peli

Pinchas Peli echoes Hirsch's viewpoint but turns it critically upon the Israelites. "Bored with the affluent life, they are seeking ever new thrills and new cravings to titillate and stimulate them. Too demoralized to look towards the future, they turn to the past. . . . Their memory is very selective indeed. They do not remember the torture and humiliation of slavery. They do not remember the joys and excitement of liberation. All they remember is the fish they ate in Egypt."

Peli's point is clear. Like Hirsch he believes that the complaints of the Israelites rise out of their dissatisfaction with the near perfect status quo of the community. What remains unclear is whether Peli and Hirsch mean to suggest that human beings simply cannot tolerate perfection. (See *Jerusalem Post,* June 15, 1985.)

Why did they complain?
The cry of the rebels was for meat and variety, not for food as such, for there was no hunger among the people. . . . Satiety, boredom, lack of challenge, and the inconveniences of nomad existence were seeds of discontent as potent as want and poverty. (W. Gunther Plaut, The Torah: A Modern Commentary, *UAHC Press, New York, 1981, p. 1095)*

Bad will be the day . . .
Bad will be the day for human beings when they become absolutely content with the life that they are living, with the thoughts that they are thinking, with the deeds that they are doing; when there is not forever beating at the doors of their souls some great desire to do something larger, which they know they were meant and made to do because they are still, in spite of all, the children of God. (Philip Brooks)

In contrast to those who explain the grievances of the Israelites as expressions of their anxiety or boredom, Samuel, who was the head of the academy of learning in Nahardea, Babylonia, during the third century, hints at another reason. He calls attention to the words used by the Israelites in their complaint. What did they mean, he asks, when they cried out, "We remember the free fish we ate in Egypt"?

In response, Samuel speculates that by "free fish" the Torah is hinting at forbidden sexual relations. In other words, the real complaint of the Israelites derives neither from their recollection of delicious foods nor from their boredom with manna. What they resent, according to Samuel, is the Torah's curtailment of various behavioral norms (e.g., the Torah forbids sexual relations out of wedlock, especially with members of the family, including sexual intercourse with parents, siblings, aunts or uncles, grandparents, stepparents, or in-laws). This kind of regulation that would radically change their behavior, explains Samuel, is the reason the people stood at the door of their tents murmuring against Moses and God.

Samuel's students amplify his observation, maintaining that the people resent the manna because it identifies those who have indulged in forbidden sex! How so? The manna, they claim, fell before the tents according to the needs of each family. If a man commits adultery and a child is born, then an extra portion of manna falls in front of *his* tent. At that point everyone knows that he has fathered a child out of wedlock. For this reason, the people rise against Moses. The law and manna change their way of life, forcing upon them a new moral code. They bitterly resent being held accountable for their ethical actions. (*Yoma* 75a)

Rabbi Meir Simcha Ha-Cohen (1845–1926), author of the commentary *Meshekh Hochmah*, suggests that not only the moral laws of Torah cause the early Israelites to rebel. They also object to other restrictions, especially those that regulate what they may or may not eat. The laws of *kashrut* forbid the eating of pork and certain other meat products and define how animals are to be slaughtered. Ha-Cohen claims that the Israelites protest because they want to eat meat without restrictions as they did in Egypt. "Stop making matters difficult for us," they gripe to Moses. "Let us eat whatever we desire."

Rabbi Reuven P. Bulka agrees with Ha-Cohen's observation, pointing out that "one of the essential ingredients of the Torah's life-style is that it proposes self-control for fulfillment's sake. Judaism is a disciplined life-style in which the discipline itself is seen as the necessary ingredient for bringing fulfillment." Applying this view to our Torah portion, Bulka writes, "It is, perhaps, this element of control that was brought forth in the disciplined supply of food afforded by the manna. Rebellion against this became rebellion against the entire Jewish life-style. The rebels rejected control. Instead, they demanded a life of instant gratification." (*Torah Therapy: Reflections on the Weekly Sedra and Special Occasions,* Ktav, New York, 1983, pp. 83–84)

Rabbi Jacob Weinstein views the matter differently. He rejects finding fault with the complaining Israelites. Instead, he argues for compassion and an appreciation of their difficult situation. The people are desperate, fearful, and uncertain about their future. What we have here, says Weinstein, is an indication of "how present difficulties cast a retroactive glow of delight over the past and suffuse old woes and mute old indignities." To put it another way, our perspective of the past is influenced by our experience in the present. The Israelites did what many people in similar circumstances do. They idealized the past because they were so frightened about the uncertainties of the future. (*The Place of Understanding,* p. 103)

Rabbi Morris Adler strongly disagrees with Weinstein. He refuses to excuse the Israelites for their complaints. Instead, he believes that what we have in this Torah report is an example of how "memory can be a dangerous thing." Human beings distort and change history to suit their prejudices. The Israelites "did not remember the lashes . . . the brutal hand of the oppressor. . . . They remembered the food they used to eat, the security they used to have . . . their memories became an accusation against Moses . . . a source of their resentment, and they brought tragedy upon themselves. They became the generation of the wilderness, destined to wander forty years, but never to arrive, never to inherit because they lacked the spirit." (*The Voice Still Speaks,* p. 297)

Interpreters through the ages provide a number of explanations for the constant complaining of the Israelites. In doing so they expose some significant reasons for political and social protest in every age. The Torah text, however, also deals with the reaction of Moses to the protesting people. Hearing their complaints, Moses voices a few of his own. Feeling lonely, isolated, and besieged, he asks God: "Why have You dealt ill with Your servant, and why have I not enjoyed Your favor, that You have laid the burden of all this people upon me?" According to the Torah, God responds by telling him to appoint seventy elders and officers, people of experience, to share the burden of leadership with him.

Once before, Moses' father-in-law, Jethro, gave him similar advice. (See *A Torah Commentary for Our Times,* Volume II, *Parashat Yitro,* pp. 42–47.) Moses followed it and was helped in caring for the people. Now, perhaps, as rabbinic tradition suggests, those leaders are dead, having been put to death because of their involvement in the building of the golden calf. So Moses again bears the burden of leadership alone and discovers that it is too much for him. The complaints of the people make this clear. To lead them, he requires the wise counsel and assistance of those who can help him ease their anxieties and nurture their creative energies for the benefit of their community.

The Torah is suggesting a model for leadership. The most productive way to handle complaints is not to whine before God nor to grumble that "the task is too much for me." Such negativity leads to certain defeat. Instead, Moses is told to face his troubles with others, to shape the future by gathering around him those with whom he can share the burdens of leadership and a vision for the future.

Rabbi Judah identifies the moment of complaining as one of the ten trials of the Israelites in the desert. In each trial, the survival of the people is at stake, and a lesson is learned. In this case, the trial teaches the moral of "collaboration." Trials are best confronted and creatively solved when they are shared. (*Eruvin* 15b)

PEREK BET: *Why Do Miriam and Aaron Protest against Moses?*

After the appointment of the seventy leaders, the people journey from Kibroth-hatta'avah to Hazeroth in the Sinai desert. We are told that, while camping at Hazeroth, "Miriam and Aaron spoke against Moses because of the Cushite woman he had married." They said, "Has *Adonai* spoken only through Moses? Has God not spoken through us as well?" (Numbers 12:1–2)

What prompts Moses' sister and brother to protest against him? Why does it appear to be a public matter rather than a private, "in-the-family" discussion?

Some commentators express surprise at this story, claiming that there is no apparent explanation for Miriam's and Aaron's criticism of Moses. Others argue that the explanation is clearly offered in the text. Are we not told, they point out, that Moses' sister and brother condemn him for his marriage to a Cushite woman and for acting as if God speaks exclusively through him? Those maintaining that there is no apparent explanation for Miriam's and Aaron's criticism respond that, while the Torah text provides a hint of an explanation, it does not offer any evidence that Moses claimed to speak "exclusively" for God. Neither are we given an identity for the Cushite woman he married.

Given this justified difference of opinion, how do we make sense of this Torah story? Why do Miriam and Aaron speak against their brother? Why is Miriam more severely punished for doing so?

Seeking explanations for these complexities in this Torah story, the author of *Targum Onkelos* explains that Miriam and Aaron criticize Moses for having separated himself from his beautiful wife, Zipporah. Furthermore, since the Torah mentions Miriam before Aaron, this must mean that she took the lead and provoked Aaron against Moses. For that reason she deserves a more severe punishment.

Rashi agrees with this explanation but raises a question: Since there is no evidence in the text, how does Miriam know that Moses has separated from his wife, Zipporah?

Rashi answers his own question with a view expressed by Rabbi Nathan, a teacher who lived in Babylonia during the second century. Rabbi Nathan traces the roots of the confrontation involving Aaron, Miriam, and Moses to the story of Eldad and Medad. Miriam, he explains, happens to be standing next to Zipporah when she hears the report of the prophesying in the camp by Eldad and Medad. Because she is aware that Moses always separates himself from her when the word of God comes to him, Zipporah cries out, "Oh, their poor wives! Their husbands will abandon them just as Moses stays away from me."

Upon hearing Zipporah's remark, explains Rabbi Nathan, Miriam reports the matter to Aaron. Without investigating the truth of the accusation, Miriam and Aaron rush to judgment. They embarrass Moses, publicly confronting him with what they believe is the insensitive and unfair desertion of his wife.

Using Rabbi Nathan's creative addition to our Torah story, Rashi concludes that Miriam is punished for wrongfully accusing Moses of being insensitive to his wife and for speaking disrespectfully against her brother in public. (Commentary on Numbers 12:1)

Objecting strongly to these creative inventions and additions by Onkelos, Rabbi Nathan, and Rashi, interpreter Joseph ibn Kaspi charges them with subverting the meaning of the Torah text. "I am shocked," he says, "at these ancients, who are so much more perfect than I . . . and who explain a Torah text by the very opposite of its written meaning or substitute a word or add phrases that change its meaning."

Kaspi goes on to contend that this Torah text means only that Moses took another Cushite woman besides Zipporah as his wife. "He did so for reasons of his own, and it is not right for us to pry into his business or his motives. . . . It is [also] unacceptable to suggest, as do Onkelos, Rabbi Nathan, and Rashi, that Moses became a celibate. He was no Franciscan, Augustine, or Carmelite monk!"

Kimchi also registers strong objections to those who invent additions to the Torah text. How does he account for the public criticism of Moses by Miriam and Aaron?

Kimchi claims that the words of the Torah text mean that Miriam and Aaron object to Moses' marriage to *another* Cushite woman. Kimchi explains that Moses is already married to Zipporah, who is a Cushite. Without seeking to understand his motives for marrying an additional woman, Miriam and Aaron criticize him. They leap to conclusions. They mistakenly assume, insists Kimchi, that, as prophets, they are the equals of Moses; they, therefore, believe they comprehend his reasons for marrying again. In truth, says Kimchi, they criticize him without justification and out of ignorance. Consequently, they are punished. (Commentary on Numbers 12:1ff.)

Given Kimchi's explanation, one wonders if he is not as guilty as Onkelos, Rabbi Nathan, and Rashi of inventing additions to the Torah text to explain the protest of Miriam and Aaron against Moses.

In contrast to Kimchi, Jacob ben Isaac Ashkenazi, author of *Tze'enah u-Re'enah,* a commentary for women, suggests two possible reasons for Miriam's and Aaron's condemnation of Moses. Ashkenazi speculates that their criticism, "He married a Cushite woman!" stems from their conviction that Moses considers himself superior to his people. Miriam and Aaron, suggests Ash-

kenazi, are upset that, rather than finding a wife among the Israelites, Moses seeks out and marries a Cushite. Ashkenazi, perhaps worried about some intermarriages in his own community, claims that Miriam and Aaron ask Moses accusingly, "Are none of your own people's women good enough for you?"

> **They object to his marrying a Cushite woman . . .**
> *Philosopher Martin Buber holds that "the reason for the 'talk against Moses' is his wife." Miriam "takes the lead" because "this is a family affair. . . . What the brother and sister reproach Moses with is conditioned not by a general tendency to keep the blood pure but by the concept that continuation of the gift of prophecy . . . would be unfavorably affected by the alien element." (Moses, Harper and Row Publishers, Inc., New York, 1958, pp. 167–168)*

In addition, writes Ashkenazi, there may be another explanation for Miriam's and Aaron's complaint against Moses. Perhaps, Ashkenazi speculates, they are outraged over Moses' treatment of Zipporah, his wife. They may have overheard him tell her, "I am occupied with important work on behalf of the community and have no time for you." Consequently, they could conclude that Moses is neglecting her and even refusing to have sexual relations with her. The Torah's explanation, "because of the Cushite woman," might therefore be understood as an expression of concern for Zipporah's well-being. This also, argues Ashkenazi, may account for the reason Miriam and Aaron decide to speak out publicly against their brother. (*Tze'enah u-Re'enah* on Numbers 12:1)

> **They slandered Moses . . .**
> *One who slanders another in secret will not be forgiven. One who slanders a member of one's family will find no forgiveness. . . . We are told that Miriam and Aaron slandered Moses for marrying a Cushite woman. . . . Was she*

not Zipporah . . . different from all other women by her dark skin, her kind words, and her good deeds? . . . And were not the Israelites also called by God Cushites, as in the phrase, "Are you not like the Cushites to Me, O children of Israel?" (Pirke de-Rabbi Eliezer 53)

Leibowitz

After reviewing various explanations of the criticism of Moses by Miriam and Aaron, Nehama Leibowitz concludes that this Torah story is about the dangers of slander and gossip. She comments that "the desire to make the great person small, to blacken the reputation of the famous, to belittle the character of the good person, and minimize any symptom of human greatness is prevalent among the small-minded, those who prey on human weakness, those who themselves fail to achieve any heights of greatness or heroism."

Leibowitz suggests that this was precisely the human weakness of jealousy that filled Miriam and Aaron. It drove them to speak "against Moses." "Evidently," explains Leibowitz, "the Torah did not wish to prohibit merely explicit gossip about people in general and the spiritual leaders of our generation in particular. It wished to prohibit any kind of talk or gossip disparaging of others."

Citing Bachya ben Joseph ibn Pakuda, the author of the ethical text *Hovot ha-Levavot,* "Duties of the Heart," Leibowitz warns: "Should one of your friends be superior to you . . . in deeds . . . do not allow your evil inclination to say, 'Stir up the opinion of others against him. Find fault with him. Spread lies to diminish his good reputation.' Instead, say to your evil inclination, 'Remember what happened to Miriam and Aaron when they spoke against Moses.'" (*Studies in Bemidbar,* pp.132–133)

Because the story of Miriam and Aaron speaking against Moses does not clearly spell out their motives, Torah interpreters become inventive in suggesting their own. Little wonder that this ancient story continues to excite debate. Is it jealously or concern for Moses' role as a leader that leads his brother and sister to protest his marriage to the Cushite? No one can be sure. However, each of the differing explanations of our interpreters raises serious ethical questions about human behavior and the resolution of conflict. Once again, the Torah text invites controversy and focuses upon continuing moral issues.

QUESTIONS FOR STUDY AND DISCUSSION

1. Interpreters suggest several reasons for the Israelites' complaints about their situation. They fear the uncertainty of the future, are spoiled and resist change, are bored and lack challenge, are obsessed with materialistic desires and seek new thrills. They resent the restraints of ethical laws and idealize their bitter past. Which of these "reasons" provides the best explanation for their complaints to Moses and to God? How should human beings at various stages in their lives appropriately express such complaints? What is the most helpful way of dealing with such complaints? Why is it important for leaders to "share," as Moses did, the protestations of their constituents rather than bear the burden alone?

2. It is a serious matter to invent or read into the Torah text meanings that may have not been intended by the original author or authors. It is like lifting out of context what another person has said. Note how Joseph ibn Kaspi takes Onkelos, Rabbi Nathan, and Rashi to task for "subverting" the Torah text with additions and interpretations. Would you agree with him? Why? Which interpreter makes the most sense in explaining what led Miriam and Aaron to protest against Moses?

3. The author of Proverbs 10:18 claims that the person "who slanders another is a fool." Rabbinic tradition teaches that "a slanderer deserves to be stoned." (*Arakin* 15b) How would you define "slander"? Why do you think the rabbis find slandering another person a serious sin? Why do you think Jewish tradition considers slander a capital offense? (See *Tosefta Peah* 1, 2.)

PARASHAT SHELACH-LECHA
Numbers 13:1–15:41

Parashat Shelach-Lecha describes how the twelve spies, each representing a tribe of Israel, scout the Land of Israel. After forty days they return. Ten of them report that the land is fruitful, but its cities and countryside are filled with powerful warriors—giants. Two of the spies, Caleb and Joshua, disagree. They urge the people to conquer the land. Hearing the divided report, the people protest against Moses and Aaron, telling them, "Let us go back to Egypt." God threatens to abandon the people for their disloyalty and to create a new people for Moses to lead. Moses pleads with God to pardon the people, pointing out that God's reputation is at stake. He argues that, if the people are destroyed, it will appear that God freed them from Egypt to crush them in the desert. The people are told that, because of their lack of faith, they will die before entering the Land of Israel, and only after forty years of wandering in the desert will their children conquer the land. Offerings to be presented at the sanctuary are described, as is the treatment of the *ger,* or "stranger," who resides among the Israelites. The Israelites are warned that the penalty for gathering wood on the Sabbath is death by stoning. They are commanded to attach a blue cord or thread to the fringes at the corners of their garments as a reminder of their responsibility to fulfill all the commandments of Torah.

OUR TARGUM

·1·

God instructs Moses to send twelve spies, one from each tribe, to scout the Land of Israel. "See what kind of country it is," they are told. They are instructed to investigate its cities, people, soil, and forests and "bring back some of the fruit of the land."

The scouts spend forty days exploring the land. Before they return they stop in the valley of Eshkol near Hebron, where they cut a cluster of grapes and gather some pomegranates and figs. Upon their return, they show the fruits to the Israelites, proving that the land they scouted is indeed flowing "with milk and honey." However, ten of the spies frighten the Israelites. After displaying the fruit of the land, these ten tell stories of the powerful people, the large fortified cities, and the dangerous inhabitants.

The report terrifies the community. Caleb, however, seeking to assure the people, says, "Let us by all means go up [to the land], and we shall gain possession of it, for we shall surely overcome it."

Spreading even more fear, the ten spies claim that the country "is one that eats up its inhabitants. All the people we saw are giants," they say. "We looked like grasshoppers to ourselves, and so we must have looked to them."

The entire community of Israelites turns on Moses and Aaron, shouting at them, "Why is *Adonai* taking us to that land to fall by the sword? Our wives and children will be carried off! . . . Let us head back for Egypt."

At that point, Joshua and Caleb tell the community that the land is "exceedingly good" and that, with faith in God, the people will conquer it. Rejecting their counsel, the people threaten to pelt them with stones.

God tells Moses that, since the people have no faith, they will be destroyed. "I will provide you with a nation far more numerous than they!" Moses, like Abraham, responds by challenging God. "What will the Egyptians say when they see that God has freed the people only to kill them? What will the nations conclude about God's power when it becomes known that God is powerless to bring them into the Promised Land?" (For Abraham's challenge to God, see Genesis 18:16–33.)

Moses pleads with God to forgive the people for their lapse of faith. Agreeing, God declares, "*Adonai!* Slow to anger and abounding in kindness; forgiving iniquity and transgression . . ."

The people are told that for their lack of faith they will wander for forty years and that the entire generation of those who were freed from Egypt will die in the desert. Only their children, led by Caleb and Joshua, will go up to conquer the land.

Despite what they hear, the people declare that they have changed their minds and are now ready to conquer the land. Moses warns that they will not succeed. Defiantly, they attack and are shattered by the Amalekites and Canaanites at Hormah.

· 2 ·

Moses instructs the people about the offerings by fire that they are to bring to the sanctuary. The people are advised to seek forgiveness for sins committed unintentionally by bringing sacrifices. Those who deliberately sin, however, will be punished.

Moses also tells them that the *ger,* "stranger" or "convert," is to be treated like an Israelite: "The same ritual and the same rule shall apply to you and to the stranger who resides among you."

· 3 ·

Journeying through the wilderness, an Israelite is discovered gathering wood on the Sabbath. Because he has broken faith with the commandment to observe the Sabbath, he is put to death by stoning.

· 4 ·

Moses is told to instruct the Israelites to attach a cord of blue [a dye made from the blood of a rare mollusk] to the fringes at the corners of their garments. The fringes are to remind the people "to observe all the commandments and to be holy to God."

THEMES

Parashat Shelach-Lecha contains two important themes:

1. The sin of the spies in not separating fact from fiction and truth from falsehood.
2. The meaning of wearing *tzitzit,* or "fringes."

PEREK ALEF: *What Was the Sin of the Spies?*

The Torah provides us with two versions of the story of the spies sent to scout the Land of Israel. *Parashat Shelach-Lecha* (Numbers 13:1–14:45) contains a much more extensive account than does *Parashat Devarim* (Deuteronomy 1:19–45). Both versions, however, agree that twelve tribal leaders are sent to explore the land.

The spies return to the people in the wilderness after a forty-day journey and bring back ripe fruits. Ten of the twelve scouts report that it is "a land that flows with milk and honey," *but* it is also a land of the Anakites, or "giants." "We felt like grasshoppers in their sight," they say. They report that it is also the land of the Amalekites, enemies of the Israelites.

Joshua and Caleb disagree with the ten other scouts, urging the people to go up and conquer the land.

In panic, the people protest to Moses: "Let us go back to Egypt." Angered by the report of the spies and by the reaction of the people, God punishes them with forty years of wandering in the desert, a year for each of the forty days of the spies' journey. The people are told that not one of the generation liberated from Egypt will enter the Land of Israel. Only their children, led by Joshua and Caleb, will victoriously enter the land.

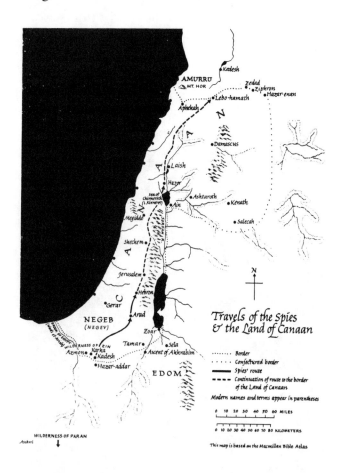

Travels of the Spies & the Land of Canaan

```
............  Border
· · · · · ·   Conjectured border
───────       Spies' route
- - - - -     Continuation of route to the border
              of the Land of Canaan
```
Modern names and terms appear in parentheses

0 10 20 30 40 50 60 MILES

0 10 20 30 40 50 60 70 80 KILOMETERS

This map is based on the Macmillan Bible Atlas

Clearly something drastic has happened! The people who suffered long years of Egyptian slavery are condemned to wander in the wilderness for forty years and to die there. What causes this catastrophe? What do the spies either say or do to bring on such severe punishment? What is their sin?

As we may imagine with so significant an event, there are a variety of views among Torah interpreters.

An author of an early rabbinic interpretation suggests that the spies, like Miriam, engage in the sin of slander. (See the discussion in *Parashat Beha'alotecha, "Perek Bet."*) Instead of remembering Miriam's punishment for publicly criticizing Moses, the spies return from their journey and, immediately and publicly, speak slanderously about the Land of Israel. They tell the people: "It is a land that eats up its inhabitants," meaning that the land is difficult to farm, its soil is of poor quality, and its air is polluted, bringing ill health. For their deliberate slander of the land, they and the generation accepting their report are punished. (*Numbers Rabbah* 16:2)

In his study *Moses as a Political Leader,* Aaron Wildavsky suggests that the sin of the spies is more serious than slander. The people have left Egypt with the promise of conquering the Land of Israel. This is their goal. The spies, says Wildavsky, return and take advantage of the people's anticipation of their report to "discredit the entire enterprise." That is their sin.

They conspire to convince the people that God is leading them not to a land of opportunity and plenty but to disaster. Reporting that the cities of the land are protected by high walls and guarded by powerful giants, they strike fear into the hearts of the people. They destroy their dreams and willingness to go forward to conquer the land. Because the spies kill the hopes of their people, they and their generation are condemned to wander and die in the wilderness. (University of Alabama Press, 1984, pp. 114–118)

Isaac Arama suggests that the sin of the spies was their rejection of the Land of Israel. "It is this rejection of the Land of Israel," argues Arama, a fifteenth-century commentator living in Spain during the reign of Ferdinand V and Isabella I, "that explains our tribulations and exile. . . . We shall never recover our spiritual and physical balance until we return to it." Since the spies

scorn and spurn the land and rally the people to tell Moses to take them back to Egypt, they are all condemned to die in the desert. Because of their disloyalty to the land, they are unworthy of reconquering it and rebuilding their nation.

Chasidic teacher Yitzhak Meir of Ger views the matter differently. He comments that the sin of the spies is not their plan to undermine the expectations of the people to settle the land but their actual carrying out of the plan after their scouting mission. Human beings, observes Rabbi Meir of Ger, are not held responsible for evil thoughts or for evil plans. They sin when they translate their evil plans into the reality of deeds. This is the sin of the spies. With their unfavorable report they turn a whole nation away from its goal of conquering their land. (A.Z. Friedman, *Wellsprings of Torah,* 2 vols., Judaica Press, New York, 1969, p. 306)

Other commentators also accuse the spies of misleading the people. For example, Sforno explains that, when they mention the Anakites, or "giants," they mean to suggest that the climate of the land is so polluted that only the strongest among them will survive. When they claim that they felt like "grasshoppers," the spies are deliberately exaggerating the physical size of their enemies to frighten the people.

Peli

By observing that "it is a land that eats up its people," modern commentator Pinchas Peli argues that the spies are conducting a "demoralizing campaign," deliberately deceiving the people with lies about the land they have just scouted. (*Torah Today,* B'nai B'rith Books, Washington, D.C., 1987, pp. 169–172)

Leibowitz

Ramban (Nachmanides)

"The spies," comments Nehama Leibowitz, "knew their job well. First they sing the praises of the Promised Land, aware that a lie to succeed must have a modicum of truth in it to give it an appearance of objectivity. They knew how to pass from an apparently objective report to a subjective expression of opinion." For instance, they tell the people, "We came to the land you sent us to; it does indeed flow with milk and honey, and this is its fruit." Then they say, "But we saw giants there." It is for the sin of inciting the people to fear about going up to conquer the land, for lying to them, for misleading them with deliberate exaggerations, and for not separating fact from fiction that the spies are punished. (See *Studies in Bemidbar*, pp. 135–146.)

Rabbi Menachem M. Schneerson agrees that the sin of the spies is in their deception of the people. However, he points out that they also mislead themselves. They are pious and good and worry about the spiritual life of their people. However, they fear, explains Schneerson, that the people will enter the Land of Israel and become so busy with materialistic concerns, with work, feeding their families, building their homes, creating entertainments for themselves, and caring for their communities that they will have "progressively less time and energy for the service of God."

That, explains Schneerson, is what they mean when they said, "It is a land that eats up its inhabitants." Their sin is in misleading the people and themselves with "their opinion . . . that spirituality flourishes best in seclusion and withdrawal." The spies, concludes Schneerson, "were wrong. The purpose of a life lived in Torah is not the elevation of the soul: It is the sanctification of the world . . . taking possession of the Land of Israel and making it a holy land." (*Torah Studies*, Lubavitch Foundation, London, 1986, pp. 241–242)

Nachmanides disagrees with most of these interpretations. The spies, he contends, do not present any false facts, nor do they exaggerate what they saw. They show the people the fruit of the land, and they tell the truth about it. Their fault, argues Nachmanides, is in misunderstanding the purpose of their mission and in their manner of reporting about it.

They are sent, Nachmanides points out, on a "reconnaissance mission" with the task of bringing back strategic details on how best to conquer the land. Since Moses is preparing for war, their assignment is to return with details about the land and its people, which will guarantee victory. The entire future of the people depends upon their report.

Their sin, says Nachmanides, is the tone in which they deliver their information. Upon their return they begin speaking in glowing, positive terms about the wonderful fruit of the land; then, however, they turn negative. Using the word *efes*, or "but," they declare, "But the people of the land are powerful." That evaluation, concludes Nachmanides, "signifies something negative, beyond human capability, something impossible to achieve under any circumstances." It produces fear. Quite obviously it is the negative presentation by the spies that panics the people and causes them to reject conquering the Land of Israel.

The positive versus the negative
Rabbi Abraham Chill notes that the spies were confronted with the negative dangers of conquering the land as opposed to the positive consequences victory would bring. They were faced with a positive versus a negative choice. "The tosafot *deal with this enigma," says Chill, "by reasoning that, if one is confronted by the necessity to make a choice, the preference should be for positive thinking. . . . The dynamics of*

positive thinking should supplant the debilita-tion of negative defense." (The Sidrot, *Geffen Publications, Jerusalem, 1983, p. 132*)

Nachmanides also accuses the spies of withholding valuable information. Moses asks them to determine whether their enemies are few or many. The scouts never furnish those crucial numbers. Furthermore, they compound their sin by seeking to undermine Moses' authority. Instead of delivering their report privately to him, they present it publicly to the people. Afterwards, adds Nachmanides, the ten spies go from tent to tent, spreading more of their "evil report." It is the withholding of information and the deliberate undermining of Moses' authority that result in their punishment. (Commentary on Numbers 13:1–14:2)

Contemporary interpreter Rabbi Morris Adler suggests another reading of the spies' behavior. Their sin is the "subversion" of the people by the deliberate misuse of their position and power. Adler reminds us that the spies are not ordinary Israelites. They are carefully chosen leaders, "whose words carried great weight." The people rely upon their judgment and trust them. When they lie about what they have seen, they destroy the people's confidence.

This story, says Adler, is a lesson of how "the prominent, the highly educated, the well-placed . . . undermined the morale of the people in a way that was just short of a brutal military assault. They breached the wall of the people's confidence; they brought panic and disillusionment as surely as if the enemy's legions had actually trampled upon the Israelites. This," explains Adler, "was the kind of subversion that these princes in Israel practiced, and the result was almost the annihilation of the entire people."

Why did the spies, these leaders of their people, engage in such subversion? Adler believes that they were pleased with the status quo of the desert. They opposed change. Everything was provided: food, water, shelter. Life was good enough for them. They did not want to take on the burden of conquering the Promised Land nor the risk of losing the power and security they already possessed. That was their sin, Adler concludes. They wanted to pull down the blinds on all the pain and sorrow of the world and live in the security of their own safe desert. They chose to subvert the dream of achieving the Promised Land, where justice, freedom, and peace would prevail for all. (*The Voice Still Speaks,* pp. 301–305)

Adler's view of the spies' intentions is supported by one of the earliest comments on their mission. Rabbi Simeon ben Yochai (second century C.E.) told his students that "the spies went up to the Land of Israel with evil thoughts and returned with evil thoughts." In other words, before they began their reconnaissance mission, they had already reached conclusions on what they would tell the people. What they would see or hear would not alter their opinions. On the contrary, they would use examples that supported their preconceived ideas, rejecting all others. That was their sin. They failed themselves and their people by closing their minds, by refusing to scout the land without prejudice or narrow-mindedness. (*Sotah* 35a; also Rashi on Numbers 13:26)

Why were they possessed with such preconceived notions? What might have caused the spies, these leaders of Israel, to bring back such a negative report? Why panic the people about conquering the land? A clue might be found in the last observation they share with the Israelites about the people of the land. In a moment of rare candor they say, "All the people that we saw in it are men of great size; we saw the Nephilim there—the Anakites are part of the Nephilim—*and we looked like grasshoppers to ourselves,* and so we must have looked to them."

The spies reveal their low self-esteem. "We looked like grasshoppers to ourselves," they say, indicating little respect for their capabilities. They see themselves as weaklings, powerless, without strength or imagination to overcome their enemies. Their lack of self-respect breeds self-contempt and fear of others.

Psychologist Erich Fromm observes that "the affirmation of one's own life, happiness, growth, and freedom is rooted in one's capacity to love."

We love productively only when we learn to love ourselves.

We can only conquer "Promised Lands" when we have regard for our talents and believe in our creative powers. The sin of the spies grows from their failure of self-love and self-respect. Perhaps that explains their punishment. Unable to appreciate themselves, they are condemned to wander and die in the desert. Only Joshua and Caleb, who refuse to see themselves as "grasshoppers," are worthy of entering the Promised Land.

PEREK BET: *The Meaning of Wearing Tzitzit, or "Fringes"*

The Torah tradition concerns itself with nearly every aspect of human existence, including clothing. For example, it forbids women from dressing as men, men from dressing as women, and either from wearing *sha'atnez*, a garment made of a mixture of wool and linen. (Deuteronomy 22:5, 11) Of particular importance is the commandment on wearing *tzitzit*, or "fringes." It is not only found in our Torah portion but also in Deuteronomy 22:12.

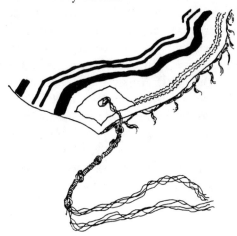

Moses instructs the Israelites to wear *tzitzit* on the corners of their garments "throughout the generations." Each fringe is to include a *petil techelet*, or "blue thread." As for the purpose of the *tzitzit*, Moses tells the people: "Look at it [the fringe] and recall all the commandments of God and observe them, so that you do not follow your heart and eyes in your lustful urge. Thus

you shall be reminded to observe all My commandments and to be holy to your God. I *Adonai* am your God, who brought you out of the land of Egypt to be your God: I, *Adonai* your God." (Numbers 15:39–41)

Throughout the centuries Jewish men have been placing *tzitzit* on the four corners of a garment known as a *talit katan*, a "small prayer shawl," worn either over or under a shirt, and upon the four corners of the *talit* worn at prayer. The mitzvah to wear *tzitzit* is considered so important by the rabbis who composed the first prayers of the synagogue that they included it as one of four paragraphs recited each morning and evening after the *Shema*, the declaration of God's unity.

The *petil techelet*, however, did cause problems. Apparently the blue dye from which it was made either became impossible to acquire or the secret of its manufacture was lost. Some scholars speculate that it was made from the blood of a rare mollusk called *chilazon*, living off the coast of the Land of Israel. When the mollusk could no longer be found, the rabbis did not abandon the making and wearing of *tzitzit*. Instead, they deliberately overlooked the prescription of Torah and decreed that the fringe could be made without the *petil techelet*.

Clearly, they believed that wearing *tzitzit*, even without the *petil techelet*, was of great significance. As a matter of fact, both Rabbi Simeon ben Yochai and Rabbi Meir teach that "carefully fulfilling the mitzvah of wearing *tzitzit* guarantees seeing the face of God!" Others claim that "the mitzvah of wearing *tzitzit* is equal in importance to all of the commandments." (*Menachot* 43a; also Jerusalem Talmud, *Berachot* 1:2; *Nedarim* 25a)

What prompts such an evaluation? Why does Jewish tradition attach such importance to wearing *tzitzit*?

Rashi

Commenting on the word *tzitzit*, Rashi notes that its numerical value is 600 (*tzadei* = 90, *yod* = 10, *tzadei* = 90, *yod* = 10, *tav* = 400) and that the fringe is tied with eight threads and five knots. Together the full numerical equivalent comes to 613, which is the number of commandments Rabbi Simlai, in the fourth century, found in the Torah.

Later Jewish tradition refers to these 613 commandments by the acronym *TaRYaG Mitzvot* (*tav* = 400, *resh* = 200, *yod* = 10, *gimel* = 3). Together they total 613 and are understood to be divided between 165 positive commandments and 365 negative commandments. Rashi maintains that wearing the *tzitzit* and "looking upon it [the fringe]" remind one of the obligation to fulfill all 613 commandments of Torah. (Commentary on Numbers 15:37ff.; also *Makot* 23b)

Rashi's observation is drawn from a view expressed by earlier rabbinic commentators. They hold that, when Jews look upon the *tzitzit,* they are reminded of the commandments, and "looking leads to remembering them, and remembering them leads to doing them." Since the performance of every mitzvah is important, the *tzitzit* function as a powerful symbol stimulating Jewish behavior. When worn and seen, they are a sign pointing to the carrying out of the commandments. (*Numbers Rabbah* 7:5)

In some communities Jews, while putting on the *talit* with its fringes, recite the following mystical prayer, capturing the symbolic meaning of the *tzitzit:* "For the purpose of unifying God's name . . . and in the name of all Israel, I wrap myself in this *talit* and *tzitzit.* So let my soul and my 248 limbs and 365 veins [which is 613] be wrapped in the light of the *tzitzit.* . . . Through the fulfillment of this commandment may my soul, spirit, holy spark, and prayer be saved from all distractions. . . . And may the doing of this commandment be considered by God as important and fulfilling as all the particulars, details, and intentions of the 613 commandments that depend upon it."

Noting that the Torah commandment for wearing *tzitzit* includes the instruction to "look at it [the fringe] . . . so that you do not follow your heart and eyes in your lustful urge," the rabbis comment that the meaning of the *tzitzit* is more than a symbolic reminder to observe the commandments. It functions, as well, to preserve ethical and, particularly, sexual purity. "The heart and eyes tend to mislead the body." Our senses require direction and discipline, say the rabbis. That is the purpose of the *tzitzit.* They save those who wear them from evil temptations. (*Numbers Rabbah* 7:6)

The *tzitzit,* however, do not have magical powers. Pinchas Peli explains that the *tzitzit* "are not a talisman, an amulet to guard the person who wears them from demons and evil spirits." Instead the fringes represent "the inner conscience of the religious person."

Peli tells the talmudic story of the man who once hired a prostitute. She prepared a tempting room with seven beautiful beds in it. Lying naked on the bed, she invited him to join her. As he took off his clothing, his *tzitzit* struck him in the face, and he fell to the floor. When she inquired what was wrong, he told her that in seeing the *tzitzit* he had been reminded of his ethical duty. "They testify that I am doing something wrong!" he told her. Upon seeing how his faith functioned in his life, the woman decided to study and become a convert to Judaism. ("Torah Today" in the *Jerusalem Post,* June 18, 1986; *Menachot* 44a)

People, comments Peli, are absentminded, careless, forgetful of their obligations, and easily tempted into dangerous behavior. They often follow their eyes and hearts without calculating the consequences of what they are doing to themselves and others. The commandment to wear fringes is given to counter such tendencies, to alert us to our ethical and religious obligations.

In his discussion of the *tzitzit,* Professor Yeshayahu Leibowitz, brother of Torah commentator Nehama Leibowitz, draws a distinction between "ethical" and "religious" obligations. In an ethical decision, Leibowitz argues, a person relates to another as a human being and relates to treating that person as a human being with no criteria other than that it feels right or wrong. One might say, "I will do unto others as I would like them to do unto me," or one might ask, "If everyone did what I am about to do, would the world be a just, kind, and peaceful place?"

On the other hand, religious decisions, explains Leibowitz, place a person before God and require that one live in accordance with the commandments because that is what God demands. Rather than asking, "Does it feel right or wrong?" or "Is this what I would want others to do?" the only question one asks is: "What does God require of me?" *Tzitzit*, concludes Leibowitz, remind us not to go astray by following the whim of our heart or eyes. They are a powerful reminder of a Jew's religious obligations to God. (*Weekly Parashah,* Shmuel Himelstein, translator, Chemed Books, Brooklyn, New York, 1990, pp. 138–141)

Leibowitz's view that the *tzitzit* remind the people of Israel's obligations to God agrees with an early rabbinic observation that the fringes are an insignia of the people's liberation and relationship to God. Before the Exodus, say the rabbis, the people were forced to wear badges of slavery, emblems indicating that they were the property of Pharaoh. The badges were a form of humiliation. Like the "yellow star" forced upon Jews by the Nazis, they identified the people as objects of scorn and targets for hatred and brutality.

Once liberated, the people are commanded to wear *tzitzit*. The fringes are a badge of freedom. They symbolize the liberation of the Jews: Jews will never again be slaves to other human beings and will serve only God. (*Menachot* 43; also *Shabbat* 57a)

David Wolfson, an early Zionist leader, provides another meaning for *tzitzit*. When Theodor Herzl asked him to make the preparations for the First Zionist Congress in Basle, Switzerland, in 1897, Wolfson sought colors and a flag that would unite delegates from all over the world. He was faced with the problem of choosing a flag to decorate the congress hall. Wolfson relates: "Then it flashed upon my mind; but we do have a flag indeed! It's white and blue: the *talit* in which we wrap ourselves during prayer. This *talit* (with its *tzitzit*) is our coat of arms, our emblem. Let us take out the *talit* and unfurl it before the eyes of Israel, before the eyes of all nations." (See B.S. Jacobson, *Meditations on the Torah,* p. 223.)

Today, *tzitzit* continue to be prized by Jews as a symbol of their historic covenant with God and as a badge of freedom and national existence. Looking at the fringes recalls ethical and ritual responsibilities. They are a reminder that the Jew, as a servant of God, must confront temptation and confusion between right and wrong behavior in light of what the 613 mitzvot of Jewish tradition demand. *Tzitzit* remain a proud badge of Jewish identity and commitment.

QUESTIONS FOR STUDY AND DISCUSSION

1. Most commentators seek an answer to the question: "What was the sin of the ten spies who returned from the Land of Israel?" Of all the different responses, which makes the most sense to you? Why?

2. Isaac Arama claims that the sin of the spies was their rejection of the Land of Israel. One of the first ministers of religion in the new State of Israel, J.L. Maimon, declared in 1951 that "anyone who spreads an evil report about the Land of Israel—even if it is true—is a spy." Is it wrong to criticize one's nation? Is it a sign of disloyalty? Is it disloyal for a Jew to "spread an evil report" about the State of Israel?

3. Modern philosopher Rabbi Abraham Joshua Heschel comments: "*A real symbol* is a visible object that represents something invisible; something present representing something absent. . . . The purpose of ritual art objects in Judaism is not to inspire love of God but to enhance our love of doing a mitzvah. . . ." How does the wearing of *tzitzit*, or "fringes," fulfill Heschel's definition of a Jewish religious symbol? How do the Shabbat candles, the *Havdalah* spice box, the *matzah* eaten at Pesach, the *mezuzah*, or the *lulav* and *etrog* waved during Sukot services "enhance our love of doing a mitzvah"?

PARASHAT KORAH
Numbers 16:1–18:32

Parashat Korah tells of the rebellion of Korah, Dathan, Abiram, and On against the leadership of Moses and Aaron. With 250 respected leaders of the community, they accuse Moses and Aaron of acting "holier" than the other Israelites. Hearing their complaint, Moses instructs them to bring offerings to the sanctuary on the next day and tells them that God will demonstrate who is to be trusted as leader of the community. The next morning the leaders of the rebellion and their followers are punished. Some are swallowed when the earth opens; others are killed by fire or plague. The community then accuses Moses and Aaron of bringing death upon the people. God threatens to destroy the entire people, but Moses orders Aaron to place an offering on the altar, which is meant to save the people from harm. Moses then organizes the priesthood to be headed by Aaron and his descendants. They, along with the tribe of Levi, are to be responsible for managing all gifts donated to the sanctuary. Unlike other tribes of Israel, Levites are not given any territory. They are given offerings as payment for their work in the sanctuary.

OUR TARGUM

·1·

Korah, the great grandson of Levi, along with Dathan, Abiram, and On, descendants of Reuben, and 250 elected leaders of the community organize a rebellion against Moses and Aaron. "All the people are holy," they complain. "Why then do you raise yourselves above God's congregation?"

Stunned by their accusation, Moses challenges Korah and his followers to bring fire pans and incense with them to the sanctuary the next morning. "God will make known who is holy and who is not," he says.

Turning to Korah, Moses questions his motives. "You have been given special duties in the sanctuary and opportunities for leadership. Why do you now seek the priesthood that God has given to Aaron?"

When Moses asks Dathan and Abiram to meet with him, they refuse. "For what reason should we meet with you?" they say. "You have brought us out of a land flowing with milk and honey to die in this wilderness. Do you now also need to demonstrate your power over us? We will not come." Stunned, Moses prays to God, "Pay no regard to their words. I have never taken anything from them nor wronged them."

·2·

The next morning Moses and Aaron meet with Korah and his followers in front of the sanctuary. Each is carrying a fire pan with red hot coals and incense on it. By that time Korah has organized the entire community against Moses and Aaron.

God speaks to Moses and Aaron, telling them to withdraw from Korah and the community because they are about to be destroyed. Moses and Aaron plead to God on behalf of the people, asking, "If one person sins, will You be angry with the whole community?"

God tells Moses to order the people to withdraw from the area around the tents of Korah,

Dathan, and Abiram. Then, as the people look on, Moses announces, "If these people die by a natural death, it will mean that I have not been designated by God to lead you. If they are swallowed by the earth opening up, that will be a sign that God has sent me to lead you." At that point, the earth opens and swallows Korah, Dathan, Abiram, and their families, as well as their 250 followers.

·3·

Moses orders Aaron's son, Eleazar, to collect all the fire pans and beat them into sheets to be used as plating for the altar. The bright plating is to remind all Israelites that only Aaron's descendants may serve as priests.

·4·

The day after Korah's rebellion, the Israelites bitterly accuse Moses and Aaron of bringing death upon their community. Hearing the accusation, God tells Moses and Aaron, "Remove yourselves from this community that I may annihilate them in an instant." Seeing that a plague is breaking out among the people, Moses tells Aaron to place a fire pan on the altar to gain forgiveness for the people. When the plague ends, 14,700 are dead.

·5·

Moses asks the chief of each of the twelve tribes to deposit a staff inside the sanctuary. Each chief is to write his name on his own staff. Aaron's name is to be inscribed on the staff of Levi. The next day, upon entering the sanctuary, Moses notices that Aaron's staff has sprouted blossoms and almonds. After the staffs are returned to the tribal chiefs, Moses returns Aaron's staff to the sanctuary as a warning to those who might in the future rebel against God.

·6·

Aaron and his sons are commissioned as *kohanim,* or "priests," to oversee all rituals of the sanctuary. The Levites are to help them, but the Levites are to have no contact with the altar or other sacred objects. All offerings are to be given to the priests for their use, and tithes (a tenth of the products harvested) are to be designated for the Levites as payment for their service to the sanctuary.

Neither the *kohanim* nor the Levites are to be given land holdings.

THEMES

Parashat Korah contains two important themes:

1. The difference between just and unjust disputes.
2. Magic and miracles in Jewish tradition.

PEREK ALEF: *Korah's Rebellion: A Deadly Dispute*

Appearances can at times deceive us into believing we understand what we see or read. This seems to be the case with the data we are given about the rebellion led by Korah, Dathan, Abiram, and On against Moses and Aaron. At first, this appears to be a single story about a protest organized by these leaders and 250 followers. However, as most modern biblical scholars point out, the truth may be that the Torah report is an edited version of at least two different stories.

Untangled, there is first the report of Korah, the son of Izar, son of Kohath, who was the son of Levi. Korah protests the appointment of Aaron and his family as priests, suggesting that Moses is unjustly singling out his brother for privileges that belong equally to other descendants of Levi, including Korah himself. Mocking Moses, Korah publicly denounces him with the accusation: "You have gone too far! For all the community are holy, all of them, and *Adonai* is in their midst. Why then do you raise yourselves above God's congregation?"

Clearly, Korah's intent is to undercut Moses' authority and gain the priesthood for himself and his family. In response, Moses asks Korah, "Is it not enough for you that the God of Israel has set you apart from the community of Israel and given you access . . . to perform the duties of God's Tabernacle . . . ? Yet you seek the priesthood too!"

Woven into this battle over the priesthood is a second protest led by Dathan, Abiram, and On against Moses. They accuse him of promising the people a land flowing with milk and honey but instead exposing them to death in the desert.

Like Korah, they seem intent on stirring up a rebellion against Moses' leadership.

In both stories, Korah, Dathan, Abiram, and On are joined by 250 chieftains, "respected leaders." These chieftains are not identified by name, nor are we given any reasons for their rebellion against Moses and Aaron. As participants in the protests, however, they are put to death by fire at the same time that Dathan, Abiram, and Korah are swallowed up by the earth.

Several questions remain unanswered about the protests led by Korah, Dathan, and Abiram. What were these protests really about? For example, the author of Psalm 106, after making the observation that "those who act justly and who do right at all times are happy" (Psalms 106:3), then offers a judgment about Dathan's and Abiram's rebellion against Moses and Aaron: "There was envy of Moses in the camp, and of Aaron, the holy one of God./The earth opened up and swallowed Dathan, closed over the party of Abiram./A fire blazed among their party, a flame that consumed the wicked." (Psalms 106:16–18) Is the Psalmist correct? Was it "envy" that fueled the dispute or were there other more significant motives among the ancient Israelites?

Unfortunately, the Torah text leaves us guessing as to the real causes of the rebellions led by Korah, Dathan, and Abiram. That absence of information, however, does not inhibit later commentators from developing their own theories. As we have seen previously in our studies of Torah, the absence of details and descriptive facts is often an invitation to imaginative speculation and invention. Faced here with the need to explain the dramatic punishments and the deaths of Korah, Dathan, and Abiram, commentators offer us a rich variety of explanations.

Early rabbinic interpreters suggest that Korah draws support from the 250 tribal chiefs by using "persuasive words." He is a clever and effective public speaker, arguing his cause in a compelling way. People are moved by his soothing tone of voice and the convincing ways in which he presents his claims and arguments. His style, inflections, and rich vocabulary sway the people into believing that his claims against Moses and Aaron are just.

Other rabbinic commentators add that Korah's attack on Moses and Aaron grows out of frustrated ambition and the claim that he has been robbed of privileges guaranteed by family position. How is this so? Interpreters point out that Amram, father of Moses and Aaron, was the brother of Izhar, Hebron, and Uzziel. Korah was the eldest son of Izhar. Yet, when leadership appointments over the people of Israel are made, Korah sees Moses and Aaron receiving high appointments as sons of his eldest uncle. He also watches Elizaphan, the eldest son of Uzziel (the youngest brother of Amram) elevated to prince of the Kohathites. Angered that, as the firstborn of Izhar (the second eldest brother after Amram), he is being bypassed by Moses' appointment of Elizaphan, Korah raises an angry voice of public protest. "I am the next in age!" he claims. "The appointment is rightfully mine. Moses is acting unjustly. Should the son of the youngest of my father's brothers be superior to me?"

Korah misleads the people
To foment his rebellion, Korah spends all night going from tribe to tribe accusing Moses and Aaron of wrongdoing. He carefully crafts his speech for each audience, but his message always makes the same point: "I am not like Moses and Aaron, who want to attain fame and power for themselves. I want all of us to enjoy life." He wins the support of the people by misleading them. (Numbers Rabbah 18:10)

Many commentators sympathize with Korah's argument. They maintain that in bypassing Korah, the eldest son of the second eldest brother of Amram, and elevating Elizaphan, the eldest

son of the youngest brother of Amram, Moses breaks with the tradition of appointing the eldest before the youngest, setting off a deeply emotional family dispute. Korah's pride is hurt; his expectations are shattered. Feeling cheated of his rightful inheritance, he is justified in leading a rebellion against Moses and Aaron.

Other interpreters disagree, pointing out that, while Korah's disappointment may be understandable, his public repudiation of Moses and Aaron is irresponsible. For his behavior he deserves the punishment he receives. On the basis of the Torah's claim that Korah publicly impugns the authority of Moses, these interpreters offer some creatively inventive examples. They claim that, to embarrass Moses, Korah waves his finger at him and asks, "Since the Torah claims that *tzitzit* must be made with a blue thread, does it mean that a person wearing a shirt made of blue threads need not wear *tzitzit*?" On another occasion, Korah asks, "If a house is filled with Torah scrolls that contain all the words inside a *mezuzah,* does the house require a *mezuzah* on the door?" By raising apparent contradictions within the Torah, Korah seeks to ridicule Moses and Aaron. Korah's ultimate target, say these interpreters, is the Torah itself. In mocking Moses over inconsistencies within the Torah, Korah derides not only the Torah but God, the source of Torah. (*Numbers Rabbah 18:1–4*)

Other commentators claim that Korah goes further than scorning the Torah. He actually distorts its meanings. Walking among the Israelites, he points out that the Torah laws are difficult, suggesting that they are even unjust. Seeking to stir the emotions of the people against Moses and Aaron, Korah tells them about a poor widow and her daughter who have been harassed constantly by Moses and Aaron with one legal claim after another. She is about to plow, and they tell her, "According to the Torah you cannot plow. . . ." When she is ready to cut the wool of her animals, Aaron claims that the Torah gives him the right to collect his priestly tax on the first of the wool. Smiling cynically, Korah concludes, "You see they are exploiting our poor and needy." (*Midrash Shocher Tov* on Psalms 1:1)

These imaginative interpretations by rabbinic commentators seek to explain why Korah was punished with death for his rebellion. But what of Dathan, Abiram, and the 250 leaders of the community? How do we account for their being swallowed alive by the earth?

Some of the early rabbinic interpreters argue that it was a matter of association with the wrong neighbor. Dathan and Abiram happen to pitch their tents near Korah and his family. They hear Korah's constant criticism of Moses and Aaron and are convinced that Korah's cause is just. As a result of their friendship they join his rebellion and, in the end, are punished along with Korah. From the experience of Dathan and Abiram we are taught, "Woe to wicked people, and woe to their neighbors."

Other commentators argue that they are punished for much more than simply "associating with bad neighbors." Dathan and Abiram "invite punishment with their mouths" and with their "stubbornness." When Moses asks them to join him for a discussion about their differences, they refuse. As he approaches their tents, hoping that his show of humility will convince them to change their minds, they rebuke him and seek to humiliate him. In doing so, they foment rebellion among the people. For their "insolence" and "contentiousness" they are destroyed along with Korah. (*Numbers Rabbah* 18:4,5,12; also *Midrash Tanchuma* on *Korah*)

Unlike the early rabbinic interpreters who invented a background of events to explain why Korah, Dathan, and Abiram deserve their punishment, other commentators seek the reasons for their deaths within the Torah account itself.

Ibn Ezra

Abraham ibn Ezra explains that the whole episode is an ugly political dispute over the changes Moses initiates concerning the rights of firstborn males. Moses alters those rights when he appoints the Levites, in place of the firstborn, to care for the sanctuary sacrifices. Many of the people, argues ibn Ezra, believe that he introduces this change to benefit his own clan. Afterwards, explains ibn Ezra, Moses appoints his

brother, Aaron, and Aaron's sons to preside over the Levites. This upsets the Levites who had assumed they would control the sanctuary, without taking orders from others.

Ibn Ezra explains that Dathan and Abiram join the rebellion because they feel that Moses is taking privileges away from their tribe (Reuben) and giving more power to the tribe of Joseph. Korah, who is also firstborn, organizes all this discontent into the rebellion against Moses and Aaron, telling them: ". . . all the community are holy, all of them. . . . Why then do you raise yourselves above God's congregation?" This rebellion, ibn Ezra concludes, is fueled by the anger of the firstborn. Korah accuses Moses of discrimination and of robbing the rights of the firstborn in order to take those rights and privileges for himself and his family.

Ramban (Nachmanides)

Many commentators disagree with ibn Ezra's conclusions. Nachmanides, for instance, notes that Korah's mutiny does not occur at the time when Moses appoints the Levites or confers special responsibilities upon Aaron and his family for service in the sanctuary.

Rather, says Nachmanides, Korah organizes his protest when the spies return from the Land of Israel with their troubling and divided reports and after the people bitterly complain about the difficult conditions of life in the desert. "Korah," Nachmanides points out, "finds the opportune moment to pick his quarrel with Moses and his policy. He assumes that the people will side with him because of their frustration and discomfort."

According to Nachmanides, this emphasis on the psychological readiness of the people to attack Moses and Aaron also explains the defiant behavior and accusations of Dathan and Abiram. They not only refuse to meet with Moses for a discussion of their grievances, but they distort historical fact to inflame the people against him. Lies become stepping stones to personal advantage. Publicly Dathan and Abiram ask Moses, "Is it not enough that you brought us from a land flowing with milk and honey to have us die in the wilderness. . . ?"

Cleverly they distort the past. Suddenly Egypt, which is associated with oppression, slavery, and starvation, is glorified as "a land flowing with milk and honey." Because they take advantage of the confusion and fears of the people, perverting the truth and misleading them, Dathan and Abiram are punished. (Commentary on Numbers 16)

Two different views on "holiness"
Philosopher Martin Buber suggests that "both Moses and Korah desired the people to be . . . the holy people. But for Moses this was the goal. In order to reach it, generation after generation had to choose again and again . . . between the way of God and the wrong paths of their own hearts; between life and death. . . . For Korah, the people . . . were already holy . . . so why should there be further need for choice? Their dispute was between two approaches to faith and to life." (Moses: The Revelation and the Covenant, *Harper and Row Publishers, Inc., New York, 1958, pp. 189–190)*

Leibowitz

On the basis of the discussion in *Pirke Avot* 5:17, Nehama Leibowitz reaches still another conclusion about why Korah, Dathan, Abiram, and the company of 250 leaders are punished so severely for their rebellion. *Pirke Avot* states that there are two kinds of disputes: one that is pursued for a "heavenly" or good cause and one that is pursued for selfish reasons. As an example of the first, the rabbis cite the arguments between the great teachers Hillel and Shammai, which were always over matters of ethical or ritual principle. On the other hand, the chief example of "selfish" and unworthy controversy is that of Korah and his followers.

Leibowitz writes that Korah and his followers "were simply a band of malcontents, each harboring [individual] personal grievances against authority, animated by individual pride and ambition, united to overthrow Moses and Aaron, hoping thereby to attain their individual desires." Eventually, "they would quarrel among themselves, as each one strove to attain selfish ambitions. . . ." They deserve their punishment, argues Leibowitz, because all their motives were self-serving, meant to splinter and divide the Jewish people. (See *Studies in Bemidbar*, pp. 181–185.)

Rabbi M. Miller agrees with Leibowitz's views on Korah and the 250 leaders. However, citing a sixteenth-century commentary of Rabbi Judah Loew ben Bezalel, known as the Maharal from Prague, Miller maintains that Dathan and Abiram had no justifiable, legitimate grievances for joining Korah's rebellion. Rather, they "split the people out of sheer delight in mischief." They enjoyed "degrading the great, in denying value to any other human being. . . ." What drove them was "a love of evil for its own sake . . . the unadulterated joy of hearing the denigration of others." (*Sabbath Shiurim*, Feldheim, New York, 1979, pp. 245–252)

The importance of law
Rabbi Shlomo Riskin suggests that "the conflict between Moses and Korah reflects a tug of war within the human spirit. . . . Korah denies the importance of the laws. He says, 'Who needs this system of do's and don'ts, you shalls and you shall nots? We're holy already.' Certainly this perspective was attractive to every Israelite who wanted to be left alone. Who wants to be told what to do and what not to do? If I want to commit adultery, who are you to tell me I shouldn't?" (Jerusalem Post, *July 1, 1989)*

One other interpretation of Korah's rebellion and God's destruction of all its participants ought to be considered. Korah, Dathan, Abiram, and the other leaders make the claim that "all the people are holy." In doing so, they call into question the authority of Moses and Aaron to make communal decisions. While they advocate the holiness of each person, they do not take the next step. They do not call for a vote of each person or anything resembling democracy. Their dispute is over *who* will lead and who will make decisions for the community and is meant to put those powers into their hands.

Their mutiny raises a significant tension that is both political and religious. When Korah attacks Moses and Aaron with the claim "all the people are holy" and with the question "Why do you raise yourselves above God's congregation?" he is focusing on the common confusion between individual freedom and the limits to individual freedom that living in society imposes. As an individual, I would like to be free to walk anywhere I wish; as a member of society, I must restrict my wanderings at the fence of my neighbor's property. But living within a community demands that I must often sacrifice personal liberty, comforts, pleasures, and possessions for the well-being of others.

This dispute between Korah, Dathan, Abiram, and the 250 leaders on one side and Moses and Aaron on the other is about who will decide what is right for the community and who will define the accepted law and practice of society. Will it be left to the designated interpreters of Torah (Moses and Aaron) or to the whim of rabble-rousers (Korah and his followers)? Will it be a community ruled by the loudest voice with the most might or by the laws of Torah, publicly open to all?

It seems apparent from the punishment of Korah and all the followers of his rebellion that the Torah tradition promotes a rule of law even when it curbs the absolute freedom of the individual to pursue self-interest. Korah's rebellion is condemned, not only because it was self-serving, but also because it perpetuated a false and dangerous notion that society can exist without any limitations on individual liberty. For society to function, the rights of individuals must be limited, and leaders must be given special powers and responsibilities within the context of law.

Rav Huna, a leader of Babylonian Jewry for forty years during the third century, underscores this bias when he comments that, if one listens to the earth at the place where Korah and his followers were swallowed, one hears them saying over and over again, "Moses and his Torah represent the truth. We are liars." Individual rights are guaranteed and protected by law. They crumble when society lapses into a tyranny of individuals claiming, as Korah did, "I am holy, so I have the right to do whatever I wish." (See *Baba Batra* 74a.)

Jewish commentators are critical of Korah, Dathan, Abiram, and their followers. All agree that their rebellion grew out of evil, self-centered motives and that they deserved the punishment they received. For modern readers, the ancient tale and its interpretations remain a valuable source of lessons about the differences between a just and an unjust dispute and about the definition of a just and free society.

PEREK BET: *Magic and Miracles in Jewish Tradition*

After Korah, Dathan, Abiram, and their followers publicly question and criticize the leadership of Moses and Aaron, Moses challenges them to bring pans of fire and incense to the sanctuary. Moses commands the people to separate themselves from the rebels. He declares that God will make known who has the authority to lead the people. "By what happens in the morning," Moses says, "you will know that it was *Adonai* who sent me to do all these things."

The next morning the people assemble. According to the Torah, they watch as the earth miraculously opens, swallowing Korah, Dathan, Abiram, and their families, households, and possessions. All is lost inside the smoldering earth. Soon a fire blazes forth killing all 250 of Korah's followers. The entire community witnesses this gruesome scene.

Later in our *parashah,* Moses commands each of the twelve tribal chieftains to bring a staff for deposit in the sanctuary. The next day he discovers that Aaron's staff has miraculously sprouted, producing blossoms and almonds! Despite the wonder, however, the people of Israel continue to complain about their conditions.

Miraculous events are reported in many different places within the Torah. Ten plagues are sent to punish the stubborn Pharaoh. The Red Sea aparts before the fleeing Israelites and drowns the pursuing Egyptians. Manna is sent to feed the wandering Israelites on their journey through the desert. Water flows from a rock when Moses strikes it. In *Parashat Balak* a donkey speaks to her master.

How are we to understand such incidents that defy the known laws of nature? Are Jews expected to accept such wonders on faith? If one rejects as "impossible" or questions the reliability of such miracles, are the authority of Torah and its meaning diminished? If the Torah contains miracle stories like the earth opening and swallowing up Korah, Dathan, and Abiram, can we conclude that it is more a work of fiction than of profound religious truth?

It should not surprise us that Torah interpreters have struggled with such questions for many centuries. Early rabbinic commentators accept the descriptions of miracles within the Torah as a matter of faith. They take for granted that, if the Torah reports them and they were witnessed by others, such incidents are credible.

Yet, how can events like manna falling from heaven, an animal speaking, a sea opening, the earth swallowing Dathan and Abiram possibly be *rationalized* within the scheme of the laws of nature? How can one account for such miracles?

Facing that question, early Jewish interpreters suggest that such miracles were planned by God at the very creation of the heavens and earth. These events described in the Torah are not interruptions of natural law. Rather, they are *programmed* into creation to occur at precisely the historic moment when they are necessary. We can understand miracles, therefore, as preprogrammed "natural" events. (*Avot* 5:6)

However, the rabbinic acceptance of this theory about miracles is combined with blunt skepticism. "Miracles cannot be cited as proof for any argument," say the rabbis. "In danger, one must not rely on a miracle." Similarly, Yannai warns that one should "never depend on a miracle." Nachman ben Jacob teaches, "Miracles occur, but food is rarely provided by them." (*Yevamot* 121b; *Kiddushin* 39b; *Shabbat* 32a,52b)

Rambam (Maimonides)

Philosopher and commentator Moses Maimonides actually bases his proof of God's governing power over all nature on the reality of miracles. Taking the Torah as a reliable source of information about the world, Maimonides argues: "We might be asked, 'Why has God inspired a certain person and not another?' 'Why has God revealed Torah to one people and not another?' 'Why has God's power been revealed through one prophet and not another?' We answer all such questions," explains Maimonides, "by saying: 'That is God's will. That is God's wisdom . . . and we do not understand why God's will or wisdom determined any of these things.' " In essence, Maimonides contends that, while the miracles reported in Torah raise questions, they also demonstrate God's mysterious and wonderful power over all nature. (*Guide for the Perplexed*, pp. 199–200)

Nachmanides suggests that great miracles like the parting of the Red Sea teach human beings to appreciate "the hidden miracles" around them. He explains that "everything that happens in our affairs, private or public, is miraculous." Life itself is a wonder-filled gift! (See comments on *Balak*.)

Seventeenth-century Jewish philosopher and interpreter Baruch Spinoza offers a very different view on biblical miracles. Believing that nothing can violate the laws of nature, Spinoza rejects miracles as ignorant "prejudices of an ancient people," who believe that God intervenes in nature for their benefit. This accounts for the way in which stories like the punishment of Korah, Dathan, and Abiram are presented. They are distorted, says Spinoza, by the innocent but false assumptions and opinions of events that the early Hebrews could not understand or explain. (*Theological-Political Treatise*, R.H. Elwes, translator, Dover Publications, New York, 1955, pp. 82–93)

Spinoza's rejection of miracles is disputed by

modern philosopher and commentator Martin Buber. He writes that "the concept of miracle" described within the Torah "can be defined at its starting point as an abiding astonishment." Such "astonishment" is a natural occurrence. Furthermore, says Buber, "the great turning points in religious history are based on the fact that again and ever again an individual and a group attached to [that individual] wonder and keep on wondering at a natural—or historical event—at something that intervenes fatefully in the life of this individual and this group." The point of "astonishment" comes in the realization that one grasps the "cause" of the miraculous event and is permitted "a glimpse of the sphere in which a sole power, not restricted by any other, is at work."

Placed in the context of our Torah portion, the earth opening up to swallow Korah, Dathan, and Abiram is an astonishing miracle in which one sees the "power" of God "at work." Experiencing the miracle, one knows the certainty of God's existence and "power." The miracle is a window into God's presence. (See *Moses*, pp. 74–78.)

Belief in miracles

Every miracle can be explained—after the event. . . . Every miracle is possible, even the most absurd, even that an ax floats. . . . In fact nothing is miraculous about a miracle except that it comes when it does. The east wind has probably swept bare the ford in the Red Sea hundreds of times and will do so again. . . . But that it did this at a moment when the people in their distress set foot in the sea—that is the miracle. (Franz Rosenzweig, The Star of Redemption, *William H. Hallo, translator, Beacon Press, Boston, 1972, pp. 93–94)*

Rabbi Mordecai M. Kaplan, the philosopher who inspired the creation of the twentieth-century American movement of Reconstructionist Judaism, disagrees with Buber and also rejects most traditional explanations of biblical miracles. "In our day, when humanity has achieved marvels of control over nature by a technology that assumes the uniformities of natural law, belief in miracles that contravene natural law is a psychological impossibility for most people." Kaplan dismisses the arguments of those who point out that the miracles of the Torah did not occur privately but were witnessed by many people. Today's science challenges "the credibility of miracles," he writes, repudiating them as factually inaccurate. (*Questions Jews Ask: Reconstructionist Answers,* Reconstructionist Press, New York, 1956, pp. 155–156)

 Peli

Pinchas Peli does not argue for the "credibility of miracles" but maintains that each one mentioned within the Torah contains an important lesson. "Korah's spectacular downfall," for example, "was to serve as a warning. It was meant to call our attention to the differences between authentic, responsible leadership and illusory, appealing rhetoric." The report of the miraculous process of growth of the blossoms and almonds on Aaron's staff is meant "to teach us that true leadership is not necessarily demonstrated by the ability to produce immediate results . . . with instant cures to all problems. Even the leader chosen by God in a miraculous act cannot skip the several stages in the growth of an almond. The orderly sequence must be followed. First sprouts, then blossoms, and only then the finished product." ("Torah Today" in the *Jerusalem Post,* June 29, 1985)

It is apparent that Jewish interpreters approach the subject of miracles from varying points of view. Some are skeptical; others find profound symbolic and spiritual meanings; still others dismiss miracles as figments of primitive imagination, unworthy of contemporary consideration. "Miracles," Nehama Leibowitz comments, "cannot change human minds and hearts. They can always be explained away." (*Studies in Bemidbar,* p. 231)

There can be no doubt, however, that the Torah's miracle stories are intriguing. The mystery they embody seems to attract our attention and underscore their importance. We read them with fascination, wondering about their meaning and sensing that they contain secrets we should try to fathom. It is, after all, nearly always the extraordinary, not the ordinary, that captures our attention, challenging us to unravel its hidden, illusive code and message. Could this explain the miracles mentioned in the Torah? Are they meant as powerful invitations—bait for tempting, bending, and stretching the human mind, imagination, and heart—into new realms of reasoning and faith?

QUESTIONS FOR STUDY AND DISCUSSION

1. Is there a difference between the rebellion of Korah and that of Dathan and Abiram? Are there modern parallels to their protests? What did they do, according to our interpreters, to justify such serious punishment?

2. Korah claims that Moses and Aaron are acting as if they were more "holy" than others among the Israelites. How do the various interpreters explain this accusation? What do individuals and societies learn today from their points of view?

3. David Ben-Gurion, the first prime minister of Israel, once said: "In Israel, to be a realist, you must believe in miracles." What did he mean? How does such an observation apply to some of the stories about miracles in the Torah?

PARASHAT CHUKAT
Numbers 19:1–22:1

Parashat Chukat begins by describing the ritual slaughter and sacrifice of the *parah adumah*, or "red cow," by Eleazar the priest, and the ritual cleansing for those who touch a corpse. Miriam, the sister of Moses and Aaron, dies at Kadesh. Again the people complain that they have no water to drink. God tells Moses to take his rod and order a rock to bring forth water. Angry at the complaining people, whom he calls "rebels," Moses strikes the rock with his rod. Water pours out. The people drink and water their animals. God informs Moses that because of his anger he will not be allowed to lead his people into the Land of Israel. Moses asks the king of Edom for permission to pass through his land. The king refuses, and the Israelites take another route. When they reach Hor, Aaron dies, and his priestly authority is passed on to his son, Eleazar. The people mourn Aaron for thirty days. Afterwards they are attacked by the Canaanites, whom they conquer with God's help. However, the people continue to complain to Moses: "Why did you make us leave Egypt to die in the wilderness?" God sends snakes among the people to bite them for their disloyalty. Moses begs forgiveness for them when they admit their wrongdoing. God tells Moses to place a *seraph* figure—a snake made of copper—on his staff. When the people see it, they will be healed. The Israelites are later attacked by the Amorites and the people of Bashan and Og. In each battle the Israelites emerge victorious, conquering towns and acquiring large territories.

OUR TARGUM

·1·

Moses and Aaron are told that the ritual for preparing and cleansing water to remove the sins of the people is to begin with the slaughter and sacrifice of a *parah adumah,* or "red cow." The animal must have no defect and must never have worn a yoke. After its slaughter, Eleazar the priest is to sprinkle its blood seven times in front of the sanctuary and then burn all its flesh. Ashes from the red cow are to be kept and added to water used to purify the Israelites.

·2·

Those who touch a corpse are unclean for seven days. On the third and seventh day they may purify themselves with the water from the ritual of the red cow.

·3·

After the Israelites arrive at Kadesh in the wilderness of Zin, Miriam, the sister of Moses and Aaron, dies and is buried there.

·4·

The community is without water and complains to Moses and Aaron asking, "Why did you make us leave Egypt to bring us here to die in this desolate desert?" Angry at the people's ingratitude, Moses and Aaron pray to God, who tells them to gather the people together before a rock from which water will flow. When the people, whom Moses calls "rebels," gather in front of the rock, Moses takes his rod and strikes the rock. Water pours out. There is enough to satisfy not only the people but their flocks as well. However, Moses and Aaron are told that because of their anger they will not be allowed to enter the Land of Israel. The place of this incident is named Meribah, which means "quarrel."

·5·

Seeking friendship, Moses sends messengers to the king of Edom to ask permission for the Israelites to pass through his land on their way to the Land of Israel. He promises the king that the Israelites will not take food or drink as they cross his territory. The king refuses, threatening to launch a war against the Israelites if they enter his land.

·6·

Moses is told by God to bring Aaron and his son, Eleazar, to the top of Mount Hor. There Moses removes and gives Aaron's priestly garments to Eleazar. Aaron dies on the mountain, and the Israelites mourn for thirty days.

·7·

Moving through the Negev, the Israelites are attacked by the Canaanites. With God's help, the Israelites defeat their enemies.

·8·

Near the Sea of Reeds the people complain again to Moses about their lack of bread and water. They question his taking them out of Egypt. God punishes their rebellious behavior by sending snakes to bite and kill them. Realizing what they have done, they plead for Moses to intervene. God tells Moses to fashion a *seraph*—a copper snake—and place it on his staff. When the people see the staff, they are healed.

·9·

The Israelites, attacked by the Amorites and the people of Basham and Og, are victorious, conquering towns and acquiring large territories.

THEMES

Parashat Chukat contains two important themes:

1. The mystery and meaning of rituals.
2. The reason Moses and Aaron are not allowed to enter the Land of Israel.

PEREK ALEF: *The Parah Adumah: What Is the Meaning of This Strange Ritual?*

The ceremony of the *parah adumah,* or "red cow," must have been an intriguing and important ritual to the early Israelites. According to the Torah, and later reports in the Talmud, the priests are to search for a cow with a perfect red coat—a perfect cow that has never worn a yoke or been used for work. Upon finding such a cow, the priest slaughters it outside the sanctuary, sprinkles some of its blood seven times in the direction of the sanctuary, and then builds a fire. He throws the cow's remains into the fire along with a piece of cedar wood and hyssop tied together with a red string. After the cow has completely burned, its ashes are divided into three parts: one for use in purifying those who have touched a corpse; one to be kept outside the sanctuary for safekeeping; and one for use in the future to be mixed with the ashes of another red cow. Some reports indicate that, from the time of Moses until the Temple is destroyed by the Romans in 70 C.E., only nine such red cows were used for this special ceremony.

And how did the purification ceremony using the ashes of the red cow work?

A ritually pure person would mix together a jar of fresh spring water with some ashes from the red cow. The water would then be sprinkled on a ritually impure person during the third or seventh day of impurity. At the setting of the sun on the seventh day, the person would become pure again. (*Yoma* 2a, 14a, 42b–43b; *Sotah* 46a; *Niddah* 9a; *Nazir* 61b; *Megillah* 20a; *Kiddushin* 25a, 31a, 62a; see also Abraham Chill, *The Mitzvot: The Commandments and Their Ra-*

tionale, Bloch Publishing Co., New York, 1974, pp. 348–349)

This strange ceremony has puzzled many interpreters. Why, they have asked, do the ashes of a red cow contain the power to purify those who touch a corpse? Why is this ceremony so important? What is its meaning and power?

Apparently, non-Jews also were baffled by this ceremony of the red cow. The famed Rabbi Yochanan ben Zakkai, head of the Sanhedrin at the time of the destruction of the Temple, was once asked by a non-Jew to explain the ritual. "Do you really believe that some ashes from a red cow purify a person who has touched a corpse? Are you not practicing magic?" he challenged.

Rabbi Yochanan answered the man by comparing the ritual of the red cow to the commonly practiced ritual among non-Jews for curing an insane person. "Don't you expose the mad person to the smoke of roots and sprinkle water upon him in order to cure him? Are not both ceremonies similar?" asked the rabbi.

Later, Rabbi Yochanan's students, who had overheard the conversation, said to him, "Appealing to common sense, you provided the non-Jew with a simple answer. Now share with us the real meaning of the ritual of the red cow."

Rabbi Yochanan responded by telling them that there is no explanation. The ritual is commanded by God. It is set out within the Torah law. That is what justifies its observance, not some rational interpretation. (*Pesikta de-Rav Kahana* 4:7)

Rabbi Isaac, possibly a student of Rabbi Yochanan, agrees, claiming that even wise King Solomon could not fathom the reasons for the ritual of the red cow. This view is shared by Rabbi Joshua of Siknin, who explains that the ritual of the red cow is one of four "laws of Torah" for which there is no rational explanation. (*Yalkut Shimoni* 759; *Numbers Rabbah* 19:5)

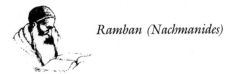

Ramban (Nachmanides)

In contrast, Nachmanides criticizes those who are satisfied with saying "there is no explanation

of this ritual" and offers an explanation of his own. Pointing out that most human beings, like Adam, make mistakes and are sinful, Nachmanides holds that their corpses are impure, and those who touch them become impure. In order to remove this impurity, water mixed with the ashes of the red cow must be sprinkled upon them. The ritual purifies them by removing from them the association with sin. (Commentary on Numbers 19:2)

Rabbi Joseph Becor Shor provides another interpretation for the ritual of the *parah adumah.* He explains that the ritual is meant to prevent Jews from sinning by contact with corpses. It is a natural tendency to cling to loved ones who have died and, occasionally, to want to caress and embrace their dead bodies, if only for a final time. Shor holds that, to warn Jews against this tendency or against the practice in some societies of worshiping the dead or wearing garments made from their skin or bones, the Torah declares contact with a dead body defiling.

Leibowitz

A sprinkling by waters mixed with ashes from the red cow is the only rite for purification from such sin. The ritual possesses both educational and purifying powers. It not only purifies from sin, but it also functions as a dramatic reminder that Jews are forbidden to touch or venerate the bodies of their dead. (See Nehama Leibowitz, *Studies in Bemidbar,* pp. 233–235.)

Purifying polluted water
Analyzing the ritual of the red cow, research chemist Dr. Robert Kunin writes that "our biblical ancestors were well aware of water pollution and were also aware of technology capable of treating such polluted water. . . . A chemist analyzing this ritual carefully soon realizes that the mixture of ashes is a mixture of granular and powdered activated carbon and bone char—a mixture of virgin carbonaceous adsorbents capable of removing practically all known toxins, viruses, and pollutants, in-

cluding radioactivity. It should be noted that the components of the ash and the basic method of treating water as described in Numbers is essentially the only method currently approved by the United States government. ("The Mystery of the Red Heifer," Dor le Dor, Spring 1985, pp. 267–269)

Obadiah Sforno offers a symbolic explanation. He points out that the priest takes cedar wood, identified with pride because the cedar tree stands tall, and hyssop, identified with humility because it is a fragrant low-growing plant, along with a red scarlet thread, identified with sinfulness, and throws all three into the fire consuming the red cow. The ashes, which combine *pride, humility,* and *sinfulness,* are then mixed with water for the purification ritual.

For Sforno, the power associated with the red cow ritual pulls the sinner back from the evil of pride toward the ideal of humility. The mixture of ashes and water provides a method for repentance. Specifically, if arrogance pushes one to neglect the laws of Torah by touching a corpse, that one then requires purification. The ritual for this purpose is composed of symbolic messages. By being sprinkled with the mixture of ashes from the red cow, cedar wood, hyssop, and a scarlet thread, the sinner who has allowed pride to rule is purified and reminded to pursue humility and more moderate paths of behavior. (Commentary on Numbers 19:1–10)

Hirsch

Rabbi Samson Raphael Hirsch also maintains that the meaning of the ritual of the *parah adumah* is symbolic. Yet his interpretation differs significantly from that of Sforno. For Hirsch, the ritual represents "the proclamation of the public conviction of the possibility of freedom from sin,

the ability of mastering all physical temptations and allurements, proclaiming the fact of the moral power of the human will. . . ." In other words, human beings can correct their wrongdoing; there is a way out of the harm and hurt they do.

How does Hirsch reach such a conclusion?

He begins by pointing out that the red cow exemplifies the "animal nature" of human beings— all of the unmastered, uncontrolled powers each person possesses. Such powers, Hirsch argues, are expressed in behavior that is self-destructive and often abusive of others. For example, driven by uncontrolled anger, a person will lash out at loved ones, hurting them and damaging future relationships.

In slaughtering a red cow that has never worn a yoke, symbolizing our unrestrained powers, Hirsch explains, we achieve "full mastery over the animal." Uncontrolled inclinations and ambitions are put to the service of free will. In offering the red cow that has never worn a yoke outside the sanctuary, the ancient Israelites celebrate taking control of their "animal side" and freely choosing to direct the expression of its powers. They demonstrate that they are free to shape the moral decisions that affect their lives and society.

Yet, continues Hirsch, free-choosing human beings are subject to the same physical laws of disintegration and death as "the rest of the physical-organic world." Human beings are born and die. They "touch" death constantly, and doing so makes them impure. Hirsch states that it contaminates them and sets limitations on them— the limitations of the human animal.

The ritual of the *parah adumah* enables human beings to overcome such contamination and go beyond the boundaries of life and death. That is its meaning and power. Hirsch maintains that mixing the "ash" of the slaughtered red cow, which symbolizes the triumph over the animal within us, with the "living water" demonstrates that each human being is endowed with a "never dying immortal spiritual being. . . ." By controlling and guiding human powers for creativity, justice, and love, the human being defies death and achieves immortality. The ceremony of the red heifer celebrates our power to live beyond the mysterious doors of death. (Commentary on Numbers 19:1–10)

No person, however sinful, is lost
I believe that this ritual of the red heifer,
strange though it may seem, preserving within
it seemingly primitive elements, dramatizes ef-
fectively and vividly how the Jew and Judaism
look upon human beings. Here is an instru-
ment for cleansing the impure, for no person is
hopeless . . . there is no person who has fallen
so low, who has so completely expelled from
[within] the image of God. . . . No person,
therefore, has to stagger through life crushed
and oppressed by the burden of guilt, to be
perpetually and eternally doomed by one error
or by a series of mistakes. There is an opportu-
nity through religious belief to start anew.
(Morris Adler, The Voice Still Speaks, *p. 333)*

In contrast to Hirsch's inventive symbolic inter-pretation of the ritual of the *parah adumah*, modern biblical scholar Jacob Milgrom maintains that this ancient ritual is meant to purge the individual and sanctuary of wrongdoing. It is a ceremony of ethical cleansing.

Ancient Jews, explains Milgrom, believed that acts of immorality affected more than just those involved in them. There are consequences of wrongdoing that infect and pollute the entire community. Milgrom describes three categories of such sins: individual wrongdoings committed inadvertently, communal sins committed inad-vertently, and deliberate wrongdoings commit-ted with design. In all cases, these sins have a contaminating effect, not only upon the guilty individuals, but also upon the community and sanctuary. Asking forgiveness through sacrifices and prayers, even repairing the wrong through apology or restitution, is not enough to purify what is soiled by wrongdoing.

For the ancients, says Milgrom, the ritual of the *parah adumah* alone has the power to remove or exorcise such sinfulness. "By daubing the altar with blood or by bringing it inside the sanctuary, the priest purges the most sacred objects and areas of the sanctuary on behalf of the person who caused their contamination by physical im-purity or inadvertent offense." In other words, the person and the community corrupted by wrongdoing are restored to a state of purity and can then go on without the burden of guilt. (Jacob Milgrom, editor, *JPS Torah Commentary: Numbers,* Jewish Publication Society, Philadel-phia, 1989, pp. 438–447)

As we have seen, Torah interpreters do not agree on the meaning of the *parah adumah* ritual. The significance of the selection and sacrifice of a pure red cow that has never worn a yoke and the unique mixture of ashes, combining cedar wood, hyssop, and the red thread with water, remains a mystery. Contemporary scholar David I. Kertzer seeks a solution by pointing out that purification rituals often "separate members from the rest of the world." They make them feel unique by unifying them "as a solidarity unit." (*Ritual, Politics, and Power,* Yale University Press, New Haven, 1988, pp. 17–18)

Does the ritual of the red cow signify com-munal bonding, like induction ceremonies where one drinks or eats special foods or circumcision as a sign of the covenant? Such rituals can pro-vide participants with a unique identity, distin-guishing them from "the rest of the world."

Clearly, the ritual of the red cow functions as a means of reentry into the sacred community for one who has broken the taboo of touching a corpse. Separation from the community and the sanctuary is a serious matter. Wrongdoers, those who break the law or transgress appropriate prac-tices of the group, feel banished; they require a way back into the comfort of community soli-darity. A ritual like the *parah adumah* guarantees their return, their acceptance back into full-group membership and participation.

The original meanings of each element of the *parah adumah* ceremony elude understanding. One matter, however, is clear: All interpreters agree that the ritual sprinkling of the mixture of ash and water removes the sinner's contamina-tion and allows reentry into the sanctuary of the people. In this way, this ceremony, like ritual circumcision and the laws of *kashrut,* preserves the "solidarity" and "sanctity" of the Jewish peo-ple. The ritual serves Jewish survival.

PEREK BET: *Decoding the Sin and Punishment of Moses and Aaron*

As the mysterious ritual of the *parah adumah* challenges commentators, so, too, does the harsh punishment of Moses and Aaron described in this *parashah*.

The people arrive at Kadesh in the wilderness of Zin. Miriam, the sister of Aaron and Moses, dies and is buried there. Again the people "join against" Moses and Aaron, blaming the two brothers for bringing them to die in the desert. "Why did you make us leave Egypt to bring us to this wretched place? . . . There is not even water to drink!"

Moses and Aaron turn to God and are instructed: "You and your brother Aaron take the rod and assemble the community, and before their very eyes order the rock to yield its water. Thus you shall produce water for them from the rock and provide drink for the congregation and their beasts."

The two leaders assemble the people in front of the rock, and Moses speaks to them: "Listen, you rebels, shall we get water for you out of this rock?" Then he raises his hand and strikes the rock twice with the rod. Water flows out for the entire community. The people drink and water their animals.

God, however, is not finished with Moses and Aaron. They are told: "Because you did not trust Me enough to affirm My sanctity in the sight of the Israelite people, therefore, you shall not lead this congregation into the land that I have given them." God gives the complaining Israelites water while publicly humiliating Moses and Aaron.

What have they done to deserve such severe punishment? How can these two devoted leaders of their people for nearly forty years now be sentenced to die in the desert, without ever seeing the Promised Land? And, if Moses, who held the staff and spoke to the Israelites, did something wrong, why is Aaron also punished?

These questions bother Jewish interpreters. How can a God of justice inflict such a sentence upon loyal leaders?

Some commentators are sympathetic to Moses. Early rabbinic interpreters see some justification for Moses' actions. Not only do the people rally against Moses, they also taunt him as he stands before the rock. "You claim to be a miracle worker," they tell him. "We know your tricks. You are standing before a rock that you have prepared for a magic display of your powers. If you want to prove yourself, move to that rock over there, to the one chosen by us, not by you!" Furious at their insults, Moses loses his temper. He calls them *hamorim*, which means "rebels," or "fools." He strikes the rock, but only a trickle of water comes forth. The people laugh at him. Making fun of him, they say, "Moses, is this all you can do? Is this your big miracle? This is not even enough water for a few babies, and we need enough for thousands." Embarrassment and anger swell within him. He pauses, then he strikes the rock again, producing a powerful gush of water.

These rabbinic interpreters reconstruct the situation: The people exasperate Moses. Embarrassed and ashamed, he loses patience. He becomes justifiably angry. However, the Israelites are also at fault, not just Moses. His punishment is only partially warranted. This also seems to be the conclusion of the Psalmist who, reflecting on this incident, writes: "They [the people of Israel] provoked anger at the waters of Meribah/and Moses suffered on their account,/because they rebelled against God/and he spoke rashly." (*Numbers Rabbah* 19:9; also Psalms 106:32–33)

Other early rabbinic commentators disagree with this explanation. They point out that both Moses and Aaron are guilty of arrogance. Their instruction is to *speak* to the rock, not *strike* it. Instead, Moses publicly strikes it not once, *but twice!* In doing so, Moses implies a lack of faith in God to bring forth water. For this reason he is told, "Because you did not trust Me enough to affirm My sanctity in the sight of the Israelite people, therefore, you shall not lead this congregation into the land that I have given them." (*Numbers Rabbah* 19:10)

Rambam (Maimonides)

Moses Maimonides claims that God punishes Moses because of his exasperation with the complaints and quarreling of the Israelites. Extreme anger is his downfall; intelligence and impatience condemn him. Instead of remaining even-tempered, Moses flies into a rage. He insults the people by calling them "rebels." In doing so, he fails as a leader and as a model for their own behavior. Maimonides argues that Moses should have exercised moderation by being more understanding of the Israelites' frustrations and more accepting of their criticism, including their baseless accusations. Instead, he allows anger to control him, insults the people, flies into a rage, calls them names, and forcefully shatters the rock. Such an extreme response, says Maimonides, deserves punishment. (*Shemonah Perakim* 4)

The sin was raising the rod
Rabbi Samson Raphael Hirsch explains that the sin of Moses grew out of his deep disappointment with the people. He is stunned that after forty years he still must carry his staff to prove his credibility. For that reason he speaks "in words of deep reproach . . . and in passionate agitation struck the rock." It was, Hirsch insists, "the impulsive vehement raising of the rod . . . in which the wrong consisted." (See commentary on Numbers 20:10–12 in The Pentateuch, *L. Honig and Sons Ltd., London, 1959, pp. 368–370.)*

On anger
Anger kills the foolish person. (Job 5:2)

Loss of temper leads to hell. (Jonathan ben Eleazar in Nedarim 22a)

Anger deprives a wise person of wisdom, and a prophet of vision. (Simeon ben Lakish in Pesachim 66b)

Anger begins in madness and ends in regret. (Abraham Hasdai, Ben ha-Melek ve-ha-Nazir 30: 1230)

Peli

Aaron does nothing
Pinchas Peli writes that Aaron is condemned because he watches silently while his brother flares out of control. He does nothing to pacify him, nor does he speak out to defend the Israelites. "Aaron could have pointed out to Moses

---

his error and requested him to stop. . . . Through not protesting, he became an accomplice and was penalized accordingly. (Torah Today, pp. 177–179)

Nachmanides takes issue with Maimonides' explanation. Accusing Maimonides of adding "nonsense to nonsense," Nachmanides points out that nowhere in the Torah text does it say that either Moses or Aaron is angry with the people. Quite the opposite, says Nachmanides. It is the people who are angry. Over and over again they complain about their situation, demonstrating a lack of faith in God.

As for Moses and Aaron, Nachmanides maintains that their sin lies in misleading the Israelites. They speak carelessly to the people. Gathering them before the rock, they declare, "Listen, you rebels, shall *we* get water for you out of this rock?" rather than "shall *God* get water for you out of this rock?" Their words imply that it is their power, not God's, that will cause water to gush forth.

This deliberate deception of the people, argues Nachmanides, is the serious wrongdoing of Moses and Aaron. They seduce the people, and perhaps themselves, into thinking that the water pours from the rock at their command or by their skill. Nachmanides concludes that Moses and Aaron deserve criticism and condemnation for two reasons: They take matters into their own hands, giving the impression that they have little confidence in God, and, by calling attention to themselves, they fail to "sanctify" God's power before the people. For these reasons they are not permitted to lead the people into the Promised Land. (Commentary on Numbers 20:1–13)

Rabbi Levi Isaac of Berdichev, a famed chasidic teacher of the seventeenth century, extends Nachmanides' assessment. Always supportive of the people of Israel, he maintains that the two leaders are punished for *how* they express their criticism.

Levi Isaac explains: "There are two types of criticism. One makes use of kind, understanding words, uplifting others by reminding them that they are created in God's image and that their good deeds bring God much pleasure. . . . When criticism is then given, it does not tear a person down but strengthens the will of the person to accept and fulfill the commandments of Torah." The second kind of criticism, says Levi Isaac, "is harsh. It demeans people, makes them feel bad about themselves, and means to shame them into fulfilling the commandments of Torah."

Moses and Aaron are punished because as leaders of their people they criticize with needlessly harsh words. They shame them by calling them *hamorim*, or "rebels." Instead of building up their pride, reminding them that they are made in the image of God, they rebuke them with a nasty slur and insult. Their lack of understanding and support for their people brings about their punishment. (See David Blumenthal, *God at the Center*, Harper and Row, San Francisco, 1987, pp. 118–119.)

Lack of humility leads to violence

In all the sins of Moses, whether we consider the murder of the Egyptian, the breaking of the commandments, or the striking of the rock, there are the common elements of anger and violence, of unbridled self-will, and of temporarily ignoring God. The sin of Moses at Meribah is thus characteristic of the man, one of a series, and serious. Why serious? Serious because civilization depends on humility. Without a sense of limits that flows from the awareness of a moral law and an ethical God, every brutality, every corruption, every atrocity becomes possible. (Rabbi Norman D. Hirsch, "The Sin of Moses," CCAR Journal, October 1965)

Modern commentator Aaron Wildavsky sees Moses' failure differently. "At Meribah," he writes, "Moses substitutes force for faith. In his hands, the rod reduces a divinely ordered act to a trickster's shenanigans. But the import runs deeper. If Moses' strongest leadership quality has been his ability to identify with the people, then the lack of faith at Meribah is a double one. Moses not only distances himself from God by doubting the adequacy of God's work but also distances himself from the people by assuming power that was God's."

It is ironic, says Wildavsky, that Moses, who

in this instant "rebels" against God's command, calls the people "rebels." In fact, "Moses was guilty of the worst form of idolatry—self-worship." When he says to the people, "Listen, you rebels, shall *we* get water for you out of this rock?" and then strikes the rock, he leaves the impression that he, not God, is responsible for the miracle of producing water. In doing so, Moses rebels against God. He assumes the role of God by suggesting through his behavior that the power to perform miracles is in his hands and in the rod. "Spiritually," concludes Wildavsky, "he has gone back to slavery, as if to replace Pharaoh." It is, then, for the sin of *idolatry*—self-worship—that Moses is punished. (*Moses as a Political Leader*, pp. 155–158)

As we have seen, there are a number of views about why Moses and Aaron deserve the punishment they receive. The Torah text seems to leave the matter unclear. For that reason commentators from every age have sought to solve the riddle. In all their explanations, however, they may have missed an obvious clue. Modern interpreter Rabbi Morris Adler suggests that the Torah text is deliberately vague because it means "to teach us by indirection, as it so often does, the great truth that the sins of leaders are not necessarily overt, blatant, obvious; that the important failings of great leaders could be subtle yet deep, unclear yet destructive."

Adler's thesis is a significant one. Few leaders, he points out, are corrupt criminals. Instead, they fall prey to "more invisible temptation." They seek the approval of the people by bending the truth, by blurring principle, by compromising their independent decision-making for financial support. They make judgments not on the basis of what is true but on how it will be received. Placing themselves on pedestals, they ask, "What are the newspapers saying about me?" and not "What is the right policy to support?"

"So," says Adler, "the Torah does not spell out the sins of the leader . . . but is purposely vague and uncertain. Maybe there was a moment of pride . . . of anger . . . a careless word. . . . Maybe he failed to apply the wisdom of his mind to today and was satisfied with repetitions of insight taken from remote yesterdays."

Perhaps the message of this Torah portion is

that, just as we are unclear about what sin brought about the punishment of Moses and Aaron, so it is with most leaders—most people. It is not the gross and obvious sins that spell defeat but rather "the subtle and intangible and impalpable corrosions" that prevent them from entering the Promised Land. (*The Voice Still Speaks,* pp. 341–345)

QUESTIONS FOR STUDY AND DISCUSSION

1. Some commentators argue that ritual and religion are matters of faith and should not be subject to reason. "Some matters," they say, "must be accepted on blind faith." How does such an argument relate to the ritual of the *parah adumah*? How does this argument relate to other Jewish rituals? Is a certain amount of "blind faith" justifiable or dangerous? Is "blind faith" necessary for religion (and science) to flourish?

2. Several interpreters suggest symbolic meanings for the ritual of the red cow. Which makes the most sense? Which carries the most meaning? How do other rituals like circumcision, the Pesach seder, going to the *mikveh,* and wearing a *talit* convey powerful messages for modern Jews?

3. Biblical interpreter Samuel David Luzzatto observes that "Moses committed one sin, but the commentators charge him with thirteen and more . . . everyone invents a new offense for him." Which of the many "sins" suggested by the commentators make the most sense? Why?

4. Rabbi Shlomo Riskin writes: "That Moses could not enter the Holy Land was not so much a result of his own failure as it was a result of the nation's shortcomings." How would you assess the pressure of the Israelites on Moses? Is Riskin correct in his assessment, or was Moses solely to blame for his wrongdoing? Would you blame society or the environment for the failings of individuals?

PARASHAT BALAK
Numbers 22:2–25:9

Parashat Balak takes its title from Balak son of Zippor, king of Moab. Afraid that the Israelites will attack his nation, Balak sends messengers to invite Bala'am ben Beor, a well-known pagan prophet, to come and curse the people of Israel. At first, God forbids Bala'am to grant Balak's request. Then the seer is sent but told that he must say only what God commands. On the way, Bala'am's donkey sees an angel standing before her and refuses to go forward. Bala'am beats her. After the donkey protests that she is being mistreated, Bala'am himself sees the angel. Fearful, he asks if he should return home, but the angel tells him to continue, warning once again that he is to say only what God commands. On three occasions King Balak asks Bala'am to curse the Israelites, but each time the seer blesses them. Furious, Balak tells Bala'am to return home. In parting, the seer predicts that Israel will soon "smash the brow of Moab." Later, when the Israelites camp in Shittim, they have sexual relations with Moabite women and offer sacrifices to the Moabites' god. As a result they are punished with a plague. When Pinchas, son of Eleazar the priest, witnesses an Israelite entering a tent with a Moabite woman, he takes a spear and kills both of them. His action ends the plague after 24,000 Israelites have died.

OUR TARGUM

·1·

Fearing that the Israelites will attack his country, Balak son of Zippor, king of Moab, sends messengers to Bala'am son of Beor in Pethor, a town located on the Euphrates River in ancient Mesopotamia. Bala'am is known as a pagan prophet with special powers to bless and curse. Balak promises to pay him richly for cursing the people of Israel. When Balak's messengers tell Bala'am what their king wants, Bala'am asks them to stay the night while he considers the offer.

During the night, God tells Bala'am, "Do not go with them. You must not curse that people, for they are blessed." The next morning, Bala'am tells the messengers that he cannot accept Balak's offer. When these messengers report Bala'am's response, Balak sends other messengers who, as Balak instructs them, promise Bala'am anything he wishes. Bala'am listens to the offer and declares: "Though Balak were to give me his house full of silver and gold, I could not do anything . . . against the command of God."

Later that night, God tells Bala'am to go with the messengers but to say only what God commands.

· 2 ·

Bala'am sets out for Moab on his donkey. Along the way, an angel holding a sword appears in front of the donkey, blocking her way. The donkey swerves off the road. In anger, Bala'am beats her. Again the angel appears before the donkey. The donkey presses against a fence, hurting Bala'am's foot. Bala'am beats her with a stick. When the angel appears for a third time, the donkey sits down, refusing to move. Bala'am beats her again.

Finally, the donkey speaks, complaining to Bala'am, "Why are you beating me? Am I not the donkey you have been riding for many years? Have I behaved this way before?"

At that moment, the angel, with the sword drawn, appears to Bala'am and reveals that, had the donkey not turned aside, he would have killed Bala'am. Fearing the angel, Bala'am tells him, "I will turn back if that is what you wish." The angel answers, "Go with Balak's servants, but say only what I tell you."

·3·

When Bala'am arrives, Balak asks why he refused to come the first time he was invited. Bala'am answers, "I can say only the word that God puts into my mouth."

Bala'am orders Balak to build several altars and prepare sacrifices for them. Standing next to the sacrifices, Bala'am praises the Israelites, declaring, "How can I damn whom God has not damned? . . . May my fate be like theirs."

Hearing this praise, Balak cries, "What have you done to me?" He then takes Bala'am to Pisgah, a high place where he builds seven altars. But, again, instead of cursing the Israelites, Bala'am blesses them, predicting, "No harm is in sight for Jacob, . . . *Adonai* their God is with them."

Furious, Balak takes Bala'am to the peak of Peor. On seeing the Israelites camping below, the pagan prophet declares: "How fair [beauti-ful] are your tents, O Jacob,/Your dwellings, Israel!/. . . Blessed are they who bless you,/Cursed are those who curse you!"

Exasperated with Bala'am, Balak once again seeks to bribe him into cursing the Israelites. Bala'am responds, claiming he can say only what God has commanded. He then speaks a final blessing, promising that the Israelites will triumph over all their enemies, including the people of Moab.

·4·

While camping at Shittim, the Israelites have sexual relations with the women of Moab and begin worshiping their idols. God punishes them with a plague. As an Israelite is taking a Moabite woman into his tent, Pinchas, son of Eleazar the priest, attacks them with a spear and kills them. The plague ends after 24,000 Israelites are dead.

THEMES

Parashat Balak contains two important themes:

1. God's mysterious and wonderful presence in history.
2. Encountering the unknown future.

PEREK ALEF: *Bala'am and His Strange Book*

The Talmud justifiably calls this Torah portion the "Book of Bala'am." Bala'am, identified as the son of Beor from Pethor, a town along the Euphrates River in what is now Syria, is the main character of the drama. The Torah, how-ever, provides no background information about him. We are told only where he comes from and that Balak, the king of Moab, says of him: "He whom you bless is blessed indeed, and he whom you curse falls under the curse." (*Baba Batra* 15a)

This "Book of Bala'am" raises several impor-tant questions: Who is Bala'am? What are his powers? Is he an enemy or a friend of the Jewish people? Does God really speak to him and appear to his donkey? How significant are these events in which Moses is not even mentioned and in which the main characters are non-Jews?

The first interpretations of Bala'am's powers and intentions are found in the Hebrew Bible. In Numbers 31:8 we find that, after their victory over the Midianites, the Israelites, without expla-nation, "put Bala'am son of Beor to the sword."

A reason for the punishment may be found in Deuteronomy 23:4–6, where we are informed that "no Ammonite or Moabite shall be admitted into the congregation of *Adonai*; none of their descendants, even in the tenth generation . . . because they did not meet you with food and water on your journey after you left Egypt, and because they hired Bala'am son of Beor, from Pethor of Aram-naharaim, to curse you.—But *Adonai* your God refused to heed Bala'am; in-stead, *Adonai* your God turned the curse into a blessing for you, for *Adonai* your God loves you.—" This view of Bala'am as a Moabite, a hired diviner who intends to curse and harm Israel but whose scheming is reversed by God, is repeated in Joshua 13:22, 24:9–10; Micah 6:5; and Nehemiah 13:2.

Early rabbinic interpreters also share this negative view of Bala'am. In discussing him, Rabbi Eliezer and Rabbi Yochanan agree that the blessings he speaks about Israel are not his but those that God puts into his mouth. Eliezer argues that an "angel" places them there; Yochanan disagrees. They are extracted, he says, with a "hook." Bala'am speaks the blessings against his will. Even God must force them out of his mouth. (*Sanhedrin* 105b)

Rabbi Abba ben Kahana agrees with Yochanan, declaring that Bala'am was one of three people pronounced "despicable" by God. The others are Cain, who murders his brother Abel, and Hezekiah, whose self-centered boasting leads to Israel's destruction by Babylonia. Rabbi Abba ben Kahana says that Bala'am is the "vilest of sinners" because he intends to curse and injure the people of Israel. Other rabbinic interpreters label him a "money changer" because he sells his advice, including curses and blessings, to leaders of nations.

Some rabbinic interpreters speculate that Bala'am is directed by Satan and that he hates the Israelites more than Balak because they never seek his advice. He also doubts God's promise to protect them. Summing up the early rabbinic view of Bala'am, one commentator says, "He possesses three qualities: an evil eye, a haughty spirit, and a greedy soul." (*Numbers Rabbah* 20:6–11)

Peli

Bala'am perverts his gifts
Claiming that Bala'am is responsible for helping to lure the Israelites into whoring with the Moabites, modern interpreter Pinchas Peli comments: "God grants human beings various degrees of talent in different areas of creativity; it is they themselves who are responsible, however, for putting this latent gift to the right use. Many waste their gifts; others pervert their use. Bala'am was among the latter. . . . After uttering some of the most lofty songs in praise

of Israel, Bala'am proceeds to offer their enemies some of the most sinister pieces of advice on how to go about destroying Israel and its 'goodly tents'; behind their backs, he plots their annihilation through the lure of fertility goddesses." (Jerusalem Post, *July 19, 1986, p. 22*)

Ibn Ezra

Following early rabbinic tradition, ibn Ezra claims that Bala'am is a deceptive schemer, a dangerous man. He substantiates his accusation by pointing out that Bala'am never tells Balak's messengers that God will not permit him to curse the Israelites. He allows them to believe that he is willing to damn the king's enemies. Moreover, Bala'am orders Balak to build altars and make sacrifices without telling Balak that God will permit him only to bless the Israelites. Bala'am withholds information and distorts the truth. He seeks to take advantage of the king's fears for his own financial gain.

Ramban (Nachmanides)

Nachmanides agrees with ibn Ezra's observation but sees in it something much more sinister than "financial gain." He claims that "it was God's original desire that Bala'am go with the messengers and bless the Israelites . . . for God wanted Israel blessed by a prophet of the nations." In failing to make clear his intentions to the messengers, Bala'am creates the false impression "that God has given permission to curse the people. . . ." Consequently, "when they see that God does not curse the Israelites," they may assume "that God has had a change of mind and is fickle. . . ." For Nachmanides, Bala'am is a dangerous person because he not only fails to tell Balak's messengers that he can only bless Israel, but he has no scruples in misleading others about God's true intentions. (Commentary on Numbers 22:20)

Hirsch

Rabbi Samson Raphael Hirsch offers a very different view from that of Nachmanides. For Hirsch, Bala'am's faith in God evolves, as does his willingness to do God's will. When Bala'am first agrees to go with Balak's messengers, "his mind is still obscured by the obsession that he would be able to achieve the purpose desired by Balak and himself." That purpose is to curse Israel. However, after he sees that "God cannot be influenced by means of sorcery," his intentions shift.

Realizing that he cannot damn the people, Bala'am "becomes a vehicle for the will of God." With experience, his faith in God becomes more profound. He becomes more open to hearing and doing God's will. At that point, Hirsch concludes, "It is not a question of God putting a word into his mouth against his will, *in spite of himself,* as heretofore, but of the spirit of unconstrained prophecy informing his utterances." (Commentary on Numbers 22:22, 24:1–2)

Leibowitz

Nehama Leibowitz shares Hirsch's view that Bala'am may have begun with sinister intentions toward Israel, but he evolves into a person whose faith in God increases with experience and proximity. She points out that Bala'am ascends from a "common sorcerer to a prophet 'who hears the words of God.'" First, explains Leibowitz, Bala'am asks Balak to build altars and offer sacrifices. His purpose is to invoke "divine aid through magical means, striving to accommodate the divine will to his interests rather than to achieve closer communion" with God. Finally, after two experiences of blessing Israel "against his will," Bala'am "leaves

all his schemes and wholeheartedly gives himself up to the divine prophetic urge."

Bala'am was a convert
Modern biblical scholar and archeologist W.F. Albright concludes that "Bala'am was really a North-Syrian diviner from the Euphrates Valley, that he became a convert to Yahwism [Israel's faith], and that he later abandoned Israel and joined the Midianites in fighting against the Yahwists." (W. Gunther Plaut, The Torah: A Modern Commentary, *pp. 1184–1185)*

Unlike some earlier commentators, Leibowitz boldly claims that Bala'am is a "prophet," not a diviner, sorcerer, or magician for hire. Like Hirsch, she applauds Bala'am's spiritual growth and evolution from a man who sees less than his donkey to a person who achieves "pure prophecy." To those who question whether "prophecy" is a power given to non-Jews as well as Jews, Leibowitz quotes modern Israeli scholar Ephraim E. Urbach. He concludes that in Jewish tradition "prophecy is not the exclusive gift of Israel. . . . On the contrary, prophecy . . . was given at the outset to all human creatures." (*Studies in Bemidbar,* pp. 282–327)

Philosopher Martin Buber takes issue with Nehama Leibowitz. Bala'am, he argues, never reaches "pure prophecy." A prophet, explains Buber, never foretells "a fixed, unchangeable future." Prophets do not predict what will happen tomorrow. Instead, "they announce a present that requires human choice and decision." It is a present "in which the future is being prepared" but whose outcome depends upon the work and decisions of human beings.

Bala'am, Buber explains, is not "commissioned," not "sent" by God. He fails to make decisions on his own. Rather, "God makes use of him." Bala'am may have the potential to be a prophet and take initiative, but he never fulfills that potential. He remains detached and aloof from others. He never engages others. Instead, he announces God's words, exercising no will of his own. He speaks about tomorrow but does not participate in making the choices and decisions that will shape the future. Consequently, he remains a common magician. (*Moses,* pp. 170–171)

Modern biblical and literary critic Robert Alter extends Buber's view of Bala'am. Pointing out that the "Book of Bala'am" contains "high comedy," Alter observes that Bala'am, a seer who cannot see, is cast ironically into a story about seeing! For comic relief the author treats us to the sideshow of a donkey with better vision than that of her owner. Bala'am, the most renowned of all magicians, is exposed as a pagan professional. He claims he has the power to manipulate God but ends up being controlled and maneuvered by God.

This entire story, Alter argues, is meant to demonstrate the flaws of paganism. "Paganism, with its notion that divine powers can be manipulated by a caste of professionals through a set of carefully prescribed procedures, is trapped in the reflexes of a mechanistic worldview while, from the biblical perspective, reality is in fact controlled by the will of an omnipotent God beyond all human manipulation." For the pagan, knowledge of the world and how to dominate it are consigned to expert magicians or seers like Bala'am. That explains why Balak is willing to pay him such a high price to curse Israel. By contrast, the Torah puts forth the view that no human being can truly comprehend, and certainly not manipulate, God's will. God's will is beyond understanding, too awesome to be grasped. (*The Art of Biblical Narrative,* Basic Books, New York, 1981, pp. 104–107)

The "Book of Bala'am" is more than an example of the Torah's art. It reveals early Jewish views about sorcery and magic and contains a critique on professional prophets who made their living either cursing or blessing the enemies or allies of their rulers. In this ancient story about a seer who cannot see and whose donkey understands more of God's will than he does, pagan notions about manipulating God are ridiculed and condemned. The tale seems to make the point that human history and Israel's history are in the power of an unfathomable God. No person can fully understand God's intentions. Often what is perceived as a curse turns into a blessing, and what seems to be a benefit sours into a disappointment.

PEREK BET: *Decoding Bala'am's Poetry and Blessings*

The "Book of Bala'am" contains not only a moving narrative about a pagan prophet summoned to curse the people of Israel but also some very beautiful poetry. Balak, the king of Moab, fears that the Israelites will "lick clean" his land and fortunes. Bala'am, he hopes, will predict their destruction. Yet each time Bala'am prepares to curse Israel, his words become blessings. His pronouncements rise with poetic rhythm and power to praise the very people Balak wants him to curse.

Modern biblical commentators differ on the time Bala'am's poetry was composed. Some believe that the poetic sections reflect a time different from that of the Torah narrative. They speculate that these "poetic descriptions date from the time of Saul and of David" and echo national aspirations meant to demonstrate Israel's superiority over surrounding pagan peoples.

Other interpreters disagree, arguing that the narrative and poetry of the story of Bala'am "form an organic unity." Still others point out that the narrative portion and the poetic portions may have been independent of each other at one point but were later fused "by a single editorial hand," thus producing "a new artistic creation." (See Julius A. Bewer, *The Literature of the Old Testament,* Columbia University Press, New York, 1962, pp. 13–14; Yehezkel Kaufmann, *The Religion of Israel,* Schocken Books, New York, 1972, pp. 84–91; and Jacob Milgrom, *JPS Torah Commentary: Numbers,* pp. 467–468.)

This disagreement on the time and authorship of Bala'am's poetry may never be settled. Unfortunately, there are no existing documents that can move the discussion beyond speculation. That, however, does not remove the challenge of interpreting the meaning of Bala'am's poetry about the people of Israel. Each of the three poems contains puzzling and enchanting expressions.

In the first, Bala'am says of the Israelites:

As I see them from the mountain tops,
Gaze on them from the heights,
There is a people that dwells apart,
Not reckoned among the nations.

(Numbers 23:9)

What does this verse mean?

Rashi

Rashi, working with the literal translation of the original Hebrew, suggests that Bala'am is predicting a secure future for the people of Israel. He means to say: "I look at your origins [mountain tops] and see that you are strongly rooted in your ancestors [heights]. You are distinguished [dwell apart] by your Torah traditions, and because of them you will not suffer the fate [be reckoned] of extinction but will survive and prosper."

Hertz

Rabbi Joseph H. Hertz agrees with Rashi, interpreting the phrase "a people that dwells apart" to mean that "Israel has always been a people isolated and distinguished from other peoples by its religious and moral laws and by the fact that it has been chosen as the instrument of a divine purpose." His understanding of the meaning of "not reckoned among the nations," however, differs from that of Rashi. Hertz quotes the work of Marcus Jastro, a modern student of Hebrew and other ancient Middle East languages, who notes that *yitchashav*, or "reckon," may be better translated as "conspire." Thus the verse means that "Israel is a people that dwells alone; *it does not conspire against the nations.*" (*The Pentateuch and Haftorahs,* Soncino Press, London, p. 674)

Hertz's interpretation may reflect the mood of late nineteenth- and early twentieth-century England rather than the accurate intention of the Torah text. He seems to be saying that, while Jewish tradition differs from other religious expressions, it is not hostile toward other peoples or cultures. Worried about anti-Semites, who claim that Jews believe themselves to be "superior" to other religious and cultural groups, Hertz seizes the words of Bala'am to prove that such claims are false.

Rabbi Samson Raphael Hirsch also seems uncomfortable with Bala'am's statement, ". . . I see them from the mountain tops . . . a people that dwells apart." Hirsch maintains this statement means that Bala'am has a "panoramic view" of the Jewish people "in a future time." That view, says Hirsch, means Israel "will live in an insulated land without much intercourse with other nations." It will sustain "its 'internal' national mission as a national social body and will not seek its greatness as a nation among nations." In other words, the people of Israel does not seek "control of the world," as anti-Semites claim. Rather, Jews seek only a peaceful, cooperative coexistence with other peoples and nations. (Commentary on Numbers 23:9)

Each of the above interpretations finds the Torah's description of Israel as "a people that dwells apart,/Not reckoned among the nations" perplexing and disturbing. It raises fundamental questions about the definition and nature of Jewish existence. Are Jews a nation like other nations, or are they a religious group without national aspirations? Within Bala'am's poetic praise, Jewish commentators locate some of their painful ambivalence and their serious concerns about the harmful misunderstandings of Jews and their tradition promulgated by anti-Semites.

These views, however, seem imposed upon the poetic words of Bala'am. The question remains: Can we uncover what Bala'am, or the author of these poems ascribed to him originally, had in mind?

Perhaps in the simplest terms they mean that the people of Israel "dwells apart" in a sacred covenant relationship with God, and, because of that covenant, it is judged differently by itself and by others. When Bala'am looks upon the people, he sees in their traditions and values a uniqueness worthy of blessing.

Bala'am's second poem of blessing includes the following verses:

No harm is in sight for Jacob,
No woe in view for Israel.
Adonai their God is with them . . .

Lo, a people that rises like a lion,
Leaps up like the king of beasts,
Rests not till it has feasted on prey
And drunk the blood of the slain.

(Numbers 23:21, 24)

Nachmanides offers a different reading of the Torah text. He believes: "No harm is in sight for Jacob,/No woe in view for Israel" is not an accurate translation of the original Hebrew. He insists that the Hebrew word *aven,* translated above as "harm," means "wrongdoing," and the Hebrew word *amal,* translated as "woe," denotes "deception." Thus, argues Nachmanides, the phrase should read "No wrongdoing [among the people of] Jacob,/No deception [among the people of] Israel."

Nachmanides perceives that Bala'am is not predicting the future but making a judgment about the character of the Israelites. Because they do not engage in falsehood, cheating, or deliberate harm to others, God is with them. Therefore, they merit protection from their enemies and, like the lion, the "king of beasts," will be victorious over all who attack them. (Commentary on Numbers 23:21,24)

Early rabbinic tradition provides a different interpretation of the phrase "a people that rises like a lion,/Leaps up like the king of beasts." This phrase, say the rabbis, captures the unique and surprising quality of the Jewish people. "One moment they are asleep, neglecting the Torah and its mitzvot; the next moment they awake and rise 'like a lion.' They read the words, 'Hear, O Israel; *Adonai* our God, *Adonai* is One,' and set out to apply the ethics of their Torah tradition to every aspect of their business dealings and relationships with others." They are animated by their faith and commitment to God. As a result of such behavior, explain the rabbis, Bala'am understood that he and the five kings of Midian, Evi, Rekem, Zur, Hur, and Reba, (Numbers

31:8) would be defeated. Inspired by their moral way of life, the people of Israel would rise up like a lion and not rest until its enemies were crushed. (*Numbers Rabbah* 20:20)

Bala'am's third poem of praise for the Israelites includes the following phrases:

How fair are your tents, O Jacob,
Your dwellings, O Israel!
Like palm groves that stretch out,
Like gardens beside a river,
Like aloes planted by *Adonai,*
Like cedars beside the water;
Their boughs drip with moisture,
Their roots have abundant water. . . .

God who freed them from Egypt
Is for them like the horns of the wild ox.
They shall devour enemy nations,
Crush their bones,
And smash their arrows.

(Numbers 24:5–7, 8)

Rashi interprets the verse "How fair [beautiful] are your tents, O Jacob" with an imaginative speculation about what Bala'am sees as he gazes down at the Israelite tents. Rashi supposes that Bala'am "notices that their tents are not directly facing one another." From this, Rashi suggests that the Israelites are following a unique moral principle that guarantees privacy for each home. They situate their dwellings so that one cannot look into the private space of another. Each home is guaranteed its seclusion and solitude.

Elaborating on Rashi's explanation, Nehama Leibowitz comments that "Bala'am, who had been reared among the idolatrous and immoral practices of his home country, is here praising the purity and chastity characteristic of the Jewish people." The term *tovu,* or "fair," says Leibowitz, means "perfection in all respects—beauty and charm, simplicity and purity." What Bala'am sees, Leibowitz concludes, is a remarkably "perfect" people—pure in every way. (*Studies in Bemidbar,* pp. 290–296)

Rabbi Joseph H. Hertz elaborates on this idealization of the Israelites. He argues that Bala'am "is swept away in rapt admiration of the Israelite encampments and homes arrayed harmoniously and peacefully, a picture of idyllic happiness and prosperity." Citing what some rabbinic interpreters have made of Bala'am's poetic words, Hertz explains that "the 'tents' are the 'tents of Torah,' and the 'dwellings' (literally, 'homes') are the synagogues." He concludes by declaring, "There loomed up before Bala'am's mental vision the schoolhouses and synagogues that have ever been the source and secret of Israel's spiritual strength." (*The Pentateuch and Haftorahs,* p. 678)

To suggest that Bala'am somehow sees the future institutions of Jewish life, its schools and synagogues, is a rather farfetched idealization. Yet his poetic words, "How fair are your tents, O Jacob,/Your dwellings, O Israel!" are found inscribed on many synagogue walls and, as the first words of the *Pesukei de-Zimra,* or "Verses of Praise," begin the Jewish worship service. While Bala'am may have meant them as praise for the people of Israel, they have come to embody the enthusiasm of Jews for their synagogues, schools, and homes.

Modern interpreter Jacob Milgrom views the phrases of Bala'am's poetry not as praise for Jewish institutions but as a prediction of Israel's future. The poet, says Milgrom, suggests that their tents will be set out in a lush garden environment "beside the water," recalling the Garden of Eden. The garden will be filled with sweet-smelling aloe trees, tall cedars with boughs that drip moisture, and roots fed by "abundant water." The people will enjoy victory over their enemies. "God who freed them from Egypt" will crush their foes and "smash their arrows." This prediction for a people living in an arid land, fearful of enemies all about them, is reassuring. It provides hope for the future.

One common thread unites Bala'am's three poems: anxiety about the future, the fear of unknown dangers ahead. Bala'am's poems deal directly with the apprehensions of a people whose history has been uncertain and filled with anxiety. The first poem defines the Israelites as unique among the nations, protected when they fulfill their covenant with God. The second promises triumph over those plotting Israel's destruction. The third poem transforms Israel into a people enjoying an ideal existence of safety and abundance in the Garden of Eden.

In our times, concern for security and dreams of prosperity continue as central themes not only for Jews but for all human beings. Peace with justice remains elusive. Greed and hostility still endanger our human family. Politicians, fortune-tellers, fanatics, and religious frauds still promise more than they can deliver. Perhaps that explains why Bala'am's ancient poetic art retains its power and captures our imagination.

QUESTIONS FOR STUDY AND DISCUSSION

1. What accounts for the negative view of Bala'am by so many commentators?

2. Philosopher Martin Buber argues that Bala'am never reaches "pure prophecy." What does he mean? What is the significance of the distinction he makes? What does critic Robert Alter add to Buber's conclusions about Bala'am?

3. Rabbi W. Gunther Plaut writes: "At its worst, the setting apart of the Jew has meant ghettoization, disenfranchisement, anti-Semitism, and, finally, the Holocaust. At its best, it has signified the attempt to render an entire people holy. . . ." How do those who interpret Bala'am's poetic phrase "There is a people that dwells apart" define its meaning?

4. In Bala'am's third poem, water is a recurring theme. How is it used? Why? Compare its use in Bala'am's poem with its use in Genesis 2:8–10; Psalms 1:3; Jeremiah 17:8, 31:11; and Isaiah 58:11.

PARASHAT PINCHAS
Numbers 25:10–30:1

Parashat Pinchas elaborates on the incident at the end of *Parashat Balak:* Pinchas, son of Eleazar, kills Zimri son of Salu and Cozbi daughter of Zur, a Midianite, who have entered a tent to have sex. Pinchas's zealousness saves the Israelites from a plague. God rewards him with a covenant of peace and his descendants with the office of the priesthood for all time. Moses tells the people to crush the Midianites for their "trickery" in seducing the Israelites into idolatry and whoring with their women. After the plague, Moses and Aaron take a census of the entire Israelite community. The total number of Israelites is 601,730. Moses also announces the division of the land, providing larger tribes with greater holdings and smaller tribes with lesser ones. Each person is assigned a lot of equal size, except for the Levites who are not given land but are compensated monetarily for their work in the sanctuary. During the taking of the census the case of the daughters of Zelophehad—Mahlah, Noah, Hoglah, Milcah, and Tirzah—arises. They claim that, because their father has died and left no sons, they should have the right to inherit his holdings. God confirms their claim and instructs Moses to announce that, if a man dies without leaving a son, a daughter will inherit his property. Moses is told to climb to the top of Mount Abarim to see the Land of Israel, and he is informed that he will die there. When Moses requests that his successor be chosen, God tells Moses to appoint Joshua. Moses is to instruct Joshua to present himself to Eleazar the priest, who will consult the Urim for important decisions and instructions regarding the community. The *parashah* concludes with a description of the offerings to be presented daily, on the Sabbath, on new moons, for Pesach, Shavuot, Rosh Hashanah, Yom Kippur, and for each of the days of Sukot, including the eighth day, or Shemini Atzeret.

OUR TARGUM

·1·

Elaborating on the final incident in *Parashat Balak,* the Torah informs us that Pinchas, son of Eleazar the priest, zealously kills Zimri son of Salu and Cozbi daughter of Zur, a Midianite, for entering a tent to have sexual relations. According to the Torah, Midianite women are leading the Israelites into whoring and idolatry. Pinchas rushes forward to punish Zimri and Cozbi for their sin. Because Pinchas has displayed such zeal, God rewards him with a covenant of peace and bestows upon his descendants the office of the priesthood for all time.

Moses is told to attack and defeat the Midianites because, through prostitution, they have sought to lure the Israelites into worshiping their idol-god, Ba'al-peor, and have caused a severe plague upon the people.

·2·

After the plague, Moses and Aaron take a census of the Israelites above the age of twenty-seven who are able to bear arms. They total 601,730.

·3·

God gives Moses directions for dividing the Land of Israel among the tribes. The tribes are to receive land proportional to their size, and the individuals are to receive lots of equal size. The Levites, who number 23,000, are not to receive land since they are to receive monetary compensation for their service to the sanctuary.

·4·

The daughters of Zelophehad—Mahlah, Noah, Hoglah, Milcah, and Tirzah—approach Moses with the claim that they deserve to inherit their father's land since their father has died without leaving a male heir. God informs Moses that

their cause is just and that he must transfer their father's share to them. Furthermore, the right of all daughters to inherit land when there is no male heir is established as a law of Torah.

·5·

God tells Moses to climb the heights of Abarim. From there he will see the Land of Israel, but he, like Aaron, will not be permitted to lead his people there because he disobeyed God's command at the Waters of Meribath-kadesh.

Moses requests that God appoint a successor so the "community may not be like sheep that have no shepherd." God tells Moses to choose Joshua son of Nun and to commission Joshua before all the people. Moses is also to instruct Joshua to consult with Eleazar the priest on all matters concerning the community. Joshua is to follow the instruction Eleazar receives when he seeks direction from the Urim (these "lights" attached to the breastplate of the High Priest, a jewel for each of the tribes, were believed to be a sacred means of divination).

·6·

Moses describes the offerings to be brought to the sanctuary and to be presented daily, on Sabbaths, new moons, Pesach, Shavuot, the "day when the horn is sounded" (Rosh Hashanah), Yom Kippur, and each day of Sukot, including the eighth day (Shemini Atzeret).

THEMES

Parashat Pinchas contains two important themes:

1. The dangers of fanaticism.
2. Concern for the rights of women.

PEREK ALEF: *Pinchas: Dangerous Fanatic or Hero of Faith?*

The incident of Pinchas's spearing and killing of Zimri son of Salu, of the tribe of Simon, and Cozbi daughter of Zur, a tribal head of the Midianites, raises serious moral questions.

As the Torah states, the Israelites are whoring with Midianite women, who are also enticing them into the worship of their idol, Ba'al-peor. God commands Moses to put to death all the ringleaders who have led the people into wrongdoing. At that moment, Zimri and Cozbi publicly parade past Moses and enter a tent with the intention of having sexual relations. Pinchas, son of Eleazar son of Aaron, is furious. He takes his spear, rushes into the tent, and stabs both of them. The incident concludes with God rewarding Pinchas with a *berit shalom*, "a covenant of peace," and his descendants with the priesthood for all time.

Did Pinchas do the right thing? Should he be praised or condemned for his zeal, rewarded or punished for killing Zimri and Cozbi? Since Pinchas seems to benefit from breaking the commandment "You shall not murder," how do we explain the apparent contradiction?

Early rabbinic tradition is divided on whether or not Pinchas's act is justified. Some commentators point out that Moses, who is present in the camp, sees Zimri and Cozbi walk past him into the tent but does not signal others to punish them. Without speaking up or suggesting a hearing or trial, Pinchas rushes to execute Zimri and Cozbi. Pinchas does not consult with Moses, who is the highest authority of law within the community, but takes the law and power of prosecution into his own hands.

Rav, head of the Sura Academy, and Samuel, head of the Nahardea Academy in Babylonia, differ strongly in their assessment of Pinchas's actions. Rav condemns him. He holds that Pinchas sees what Zimri and Cozbi are doing and says to Moses, "Did you not teach our people when you came down from Mount Sinai that any Israelite who has sex with a non-Israelite may be put to death by zealots?" Moses, says Rav, listens to Pinchas and responds, "Let God who gave the advice execute the advice!"

Clearly Rav finds fault with Pinchas for his

fanaticism. "Why are you making the judgment and carrying it out?" he asks, criticizing him for failing to follow Moses' instruction. Rav argues that, although Pinchas may have acted within the law, he should have allowed God "to execute" its provisions rather than doing it himself.

On the other hand, Samuel, who often disagrees with Rav, praises Pinchas for his zeal. Samuel claims that this is a case where God's law is being publicly desecrated, and, therefore, Pinchas is correct, even heroic, for his decisive action. Furthermore, says Samuel, it is permissible in this case for Pinchas to ignore Moses' warning or authorization since the action taken by Pinchas is clearly meant to support the law that prohibits such prostitution and idolatry.

The demands of God

Pinchas "saw in Zimri's act an open breach of the covenant, a flagrant return to the practices that the compact at Sinai had forsworn. There was no precedent in the brief history of the people to determine how to deal with such a religious and moral emergency. . . . Pinchas's impulsive deed was not merely a kind of battlefield execution but reflected his apprehension that the demands of God needed human realization and required a memorable and dramatic example against permissiveness in the religious realm. (W. Gunther Plaut, The Torah: A Modern Commentary, *p. 1195)*

Rabbi Barpazzi raises the possibility that Moses and others in the camp were upset with Pinchas's fanatical behavior and were ready to punish him by excluding him from the community. They were bothered by his circumvention of Moses' authority, by his self-righteous assumption that he did not need the permission of the community, or of the courts, for his zealous behavior. However, just as they were ready to punish Pinchas with excommunication, says Rabbi Barpazzi, God intervened and announced that the actions of Pinchas were praiseworthy and would be rewarded with "a covenant of peace" and that the priesthood would be given to his decendants. With that, his critics fell silent.

Rabbi Barpazzi seems to be suggesting the possibility that, while Pinchas did the right thing by taking the law into his own hands, he erred in the way in which he acted. He should have consulted with Moses and, perhaps, others. His actions would have been more just had he gained the community's consent rather than acting alone. (Jerusalem Talmud, *Sanhedrin* 9:7, 11, 82a)

Still other interpreters claim that Pinchas acted only when he saw that Moses was neglecting his duty by not carrying out the laws of the Torah. Perhaps, these commentators claim, Moses was weak from long years of stressful leadership or so old that he forgot the laws forbidding sexual relations between Israelites and non-Israelites. Given the situation, and the danger of punishment by God to the entire people for Moses' neglect, Pinchas took matters into his own hands, saving the people from catastrophe. For that reason, these interpreters maintain that Pinchas was entirely justified and was rewarded by God. These teachers conclude that Pinchas's decisive actions teach one to be "fierce as a leopard, swift as an eagle, fast as a hart, and strong as a lion in doing God's will." (*Numbers Rabbah* 20:24; *Avot* 5:23)

Rambam (Maimonides)

Moses Maimonides agrees with this view and includes it in his *Mishneh Torah*. He writes that "a Jew may be put to death by zealots if he is found having sexual intercourse with a non-Jewish woman or prostitute." He points to the example of Pinchas, stating that "zealots are justified in killing such a person only if they catch him during the act itself. Should they kill him afterwards, however, they are to be charged with murder." ("Illicit Relations," 124–125)

Kanaim pogeim bo

Translated literally, kanaim pogeim bo *means that zealots may take justice into their own hands and may execute a transgressor on the spot. There are, to be sure, many halachic "legal" fences that serve to limit implementa-tion of this principle. First, punishment may be meted out only while the act is actually in the course of being performed. According to some authorities, the usual* hatra'ah, *or "warning," must be administered. More significantly, the rule that applies is:* halachah ve-ein morin ken; *while the punishment is justified, no one may be instructed to carry it out. Nevertheless, a person who acts in accordance with this prin-ciple acts in accordance with* halachah. *(J. David Bleich,* Contemporary Halachic Prob-lems, *Volume II, Ktav, New York, 1983, pp. 273–274)*

Differing from Maimonides, Turkish-born (16th century) commentator Rabbi Moshe ben Chaim Alshekh suggests that Pinchas's zeal may not have originated in the pure motive of defending the ethical laws of Torah. Rather, his stabbing of Zimri and Cozbi is a deliberate act meant to prove he is worthy of the priesthood and of passing on that privilege to his descendants.

According to Alshekh, Pinchas realizes his claim to the priesthood is flawed. His father, Eleazer son of Aaron, is not yet a priest at the time of his birth. Technically, Pinchas is not automati-cally in line to inherit his father's office. "He therefore decides to risk his life and, armed with the mitzvah of killing Zimri, hopes to wipe out what appears to him a stain on his character, namely, not being a priest though his father was a priest."

Alshekh believes Pinchas has an ulterior motive for his demonstration of zeal. He rushes forward to punish Zimri and Cozbi, not out of a sense of outrage at their public insult to God and Torah, but because he wishes to attract Moses' attention and secure the office of the priesthood for himself and his offspring. His act, therefore, must be denounced. (Commentary to Numbers 25:1)

Hirsch

Commentator Rabbi Samson Raphael Hirsch disagrees with Alshekh's argument. He justifies

and praises Pinchas's act as "not merely an exter-nal forward rush but the result of his deep inner feeling that made a betrayal of God's affairs feel like a treachery against one's own self." Zimri, he explains, is not an ordinary Israelite. He ranks as a "prince, as one who should set the example as a pattern of noble moral purity" for his people. His public act of entering a tent with the inten-tion of having sexual intercourse with a Midi-anite woman "derided God . . . Torah and Is-rael." It debased the Jewish people and faith.

In the face of Zimri's outrageous public be-havior, argues Hirsch, someone is needed to restore the people's faith in God and to demon-strate Israel's commitment to God's command-ments. Pinchas understands this and believes that, unless he acts, the people will forfeit their rela-tionship with God and "thereby their own future existence." Pinchas's conviction and "honest brave act," Hirsch concludes, save "the soul of his nation for faithfulness to God and to God's Torah." For this reason God rewards him with a covenant of peace and his descendants are designated as priests for all time. (Commentary on Numbers 25:6–15)

The danger of the true believer
The fanatic is perpetually incomplete and in-secure. He cannot generate self-assurance out of his individual resources—out of his rejected self—but finds it only by clinging passionately to whatever support he happens to embrace . . . he easily sees himself as the supporter and de-fender of the holy cause to which he clings. And he is ready to sacrifice his life to demonstrate to himself and others that such indeed is his role. He sacrifices his life to prove his worth. . . . Passionate hatred can give meaning and pur-pose to an empty life. Thus people haunted by the purposelessness of their lives try to find a new content not only by dedicating themselves to a holy cause but also by nursing a fanatical grievance. (Eric Hoffer, The True Believer, *Harper and Row, New York, 1966, pp. 80, 92)*

Hirsch's contemporary Rabbi Naphtali Zvi Ju-dah Berlin, author of the Torah commentary *Ha-*

Emek Davar, suggests that, while Pinchas's zeal may reflect deep conviction, it also reveals sinister and disturbing motives. People who are ready to murder, terrorize others, and destroy for a cause are often filled with hatred, bitter suspicions, and the poison of prejudice. As a result, their acts of vengeance against others are often followed by self-destructive acts. Feelings of guilt and regret lead them to target themselves or those close to them for punishment.

Berlin imagines that Pinchas, despite his courageous act of leadership and his demonstration of commitment to God's Torah, is deeply disturbed by his zealous, impulsive behavior. Despite the fact that his motives are pure, he remains agitated for taking the law into his own hands without consulting Moses and for not taking Zimri before the judges and courts of his day.

This, Berlin comments, explains why God gives him "a covenant of peace." It is not a reward for his impulsive behavior but a cure for it. This "covenant" is meant to calm him, "that he should not be quick-tempered or angry. Since the nature of his act, killing with his own hands, tended to leave his heart filled with intense emotional unrest, God provides a means to soothe him so that he can cope with his situation and find peace and tranquility of soul." Clearly, Berlin is troubled by Pinchas's zeal, finding in it signs of psychological disturbance that require the "healing" of God's "covenant of peace." (Discussion of Numbers 25:11–12)

Reviewing the variety of interpretations of Pinchas's behavior reveals deep differences of opinion about his execution of Zimri and Cozbi. Some applaud his action; others deplore it, leaving modern readers of the Torah with the continuing challenge of answering the question: Was Pinchas a dangerous fanatic or a genuine hero of faith?

PEREK BET: *Women's Rights: What Does the Torah Say?*

In preparing the people to enter the Land of Israel, Moses assigns portions of land to each family according to the listing of their tribes. The inheritance of property is to pass through fathers and sons from one generation to the next.

Hearing this, the five daughters of Zelophehad, whose tribe is Manasseh, one of Joseph's sons, rise in protest before Moses. Standing in front of the *mishkan,* where all official meetings of the community are held, they tell Moses and the leaders of the community that the law of inheritance from father to sons is unjust. "Our father was not one of Korah's disloyal faction, but he died in the wilderness, and he has left no sons. We ask that his name not be lost but that his portion be given to us, his daughters."

Moses consults with God and is told that their plea is justified. He announces to the community: "If a man dies without leaving a son, his property is to be transferred to his daughter." Obviously, the daughters of Zelophehad win a significant victory for women's rights.

But do they?

In the final chapter of Numbers (36:1–13), the tribal leaders of Manasseh issue a counterprotest. Approaching Moses, they accuse him of cheating them of their tribal lands. Since each tribe will receive a portion of land according to its size and that land will be passed from father to son, the area of the tribal land will remain the same. However, if the daughters of Zelophehad are given their father's land and marry out of the tribe of Manasseh, that land will pass from father to son into another tribe. "Our allotted portion will be diminished," the tribal heads tell Moses.

According to the Torah, God informs Moses that the leaders of the counterprotest have a just cause. To solve the dilemma, the daughters of Zelophehad are told they can marry only within their tribe, and the people of Israel are informed that "no inheritance of the Israelites may pass over from one tribe to another . . . every daughter . . . who inherits a share must marry someone from a clan of her father's tribe. . . ." (Numbers 36:7–8) While women win the right to inherit, it is clearly subservient to the higher principle of preserving the size and borders of tribal lands.

Interpreters of Torah raise several questions about this incident concerning the daughters of Zelophehad: Why were these women given such deferential treatment? What was the motivation for their treatment? Why did Moses turn to God for a decision rather than make it immediately on his own? Did the women really win a "victory"? What roles are considered appropriate for women within the Jewish community and within society?

Modern commentator Jacob Milgrom contrasts ancient Israelite practices of inheritance with those of their neighbors. He finds that the right of daughters to inherit property from their fathers is upheld in Sumerian law a thousand years before the Torah is written. The practice is common throughout Mesopotamia, in communities along the Mediterranean coast, and in the laws of ancient Egypt well before the liberation of the Israelites. Later Greek law also stipulates the right of daughters to inherit equally with sons.

In the face of such "equality" of treatment, Milgrom asks, "How then are we to explain the fact that the Bible gives women no inheritance rights except in the case where there are no sons?" In other words, why does the Torah appear to discriminate against women, especially a woman's right to inherit the land and property of her parents?

Milgrom suggests that, in contrast to ancient Israel's neighbors in Mesopotamia and Egypt where "centralized urban societies" already existed, the early Torah laws of the Israelites reflect a nomadic-clan structure. In such a society "the foremost goal of its legal system was the preservation of the clan." Equity between members of the tribe or family preserves peaceful relationships and strengthens cooperation between all persons.

This explains why the pleas of both Zelophehad's daughters and the leaders of the tribe of Manasseh are considered just. Both uphold the principle of preserving the clan. Zelophehad's daughters argue that, if they are not given the right to inherit, their father's name will be lost—his properties absorbed without identity. The leaders counter that, if the daughters marry outside the tribe, the clan will lose its rightful land holdings. The Torah's solution solves both problems. The daughters will inherit their father's property, thereby preserving his name; tribal lands will not be diminished because the daughters must marry within their tribe.

This solution, however, does not give daughters equality with sons in the area of inheritance.

Both the Torah and the Talmud make it clear that under normal circumstances, where there are sons and daughters, inheritance of property is from father to sons. Women share the lot of their husbands; they do not inherit from their fathers. (*JPS Torah Commentary: Numbers,* pp. 482–484)

Milgrom's sociological explanation of the nomadic and tribal laws of inheritance in ancient Israel and their comparison to such laws in other ancient societies clearly aid in understanding the reasons behind the Torah's laws of inheritance. What about the place of women in the rest of the Torah tradition? How do the interpreters of Torah view the protesting daughters of Zelophehad and their demand for equal rights within society?

Peli

Contemporary interpreter Pinchas Peli writes that these women "are not presented as private individuals but as genuine representatives and spokeswomen of all members of their sex. The case they pleaded is not regarded as a personal claim for land appropriation but rather as an outcry of women against discrimination and second-class citizenship." Citing insights from early rabbinic commentaries, Peli praises the five daughters of Zelophehad for their wisdom and approach to the problem facing them.

The rabbis, for instance, point out that, when the daughters hear Moses announce the laws of inheritance, they realize they are not included. Instead of immediately rushing forward and loudly challenging him, the Torah says that "they drew near." In other words, they demonstrate patience. They organize themselves, discuss the matter, formulate an approach, and then calmly "draw near" to Moses with their concerns.

According to Simeon ben Lakish, founder of a third-century academy for Torah study in Tiberias, they do not take their case directly to Moses. Instead, they discuss the matter with the tribal chiefs of tens, of fifties, hundreds, and thousands. Showing honor to each of them, the daughters ask that the officers consider the matter before they take it to their superiors. Finally, having patiently pursued their claim within the judicial process, "they draw near" to Moses.

Other rabbinic interpreters also claim that the five daughters chose their tactics and words of protest with great care. While they believe that the Torah law is unfair to them and to others, they demonstrate constant loyalty to Moses, to their people, and to the Torah. They draw the contrast between their father who had remained loyal to Moses and other Israelites who had followed Korah. Furthermore, they deliberately use words that clarify the distinction between them and those who had said to Moses: "Give us a captain, and we shall return to Egypt." Echoing that statement, they tell Moses, "Give us an inheritance in the land." In this way, say the rabbis, the daughters demonstrate their superior commitment to their people and to the Land of Israel. Instead of abandoning the Promised Land, they merely demand their just inheritance within it. (*Numbers Rabbah* 16:10–12)

Peli concludes from his review of early rabbinic commentaries that the daughters of Zelophehad "in their superb wisdom . . . chose a suitable place, a proper time, and the proper approach" to lobby Moses regarding the law of inheritance. He writes: "In their arguments in favor of women's rights . . . they made Moses see what he had overlooked before. In truth, says the Talmud, Moses was supposed to have written that daughters get their rights along with sons. It was, however, a special privilege granted to the daughters of Zelophehad that this should be written into the Torah as a result of their painful and powerful protest." (*Baba Batra* 119a; "Torah Today," *Jerusalem Post*, July 20, 1985)

Women more pious than men
The women of Israel were always more pious than the men: We see that they did not want to give their earrings for the golden calf. Also, when the spies came, the women did not agree with them. Thus, all the men died in the desert and never reached the Land of Israel, but the wives did. (See Numbers 26:64; Tze'enah u-Re'enah on Numbers 27:1.)

Rabbi Samson Raphael Hirsch sees much more than the issue of land inheritance in the incident between Moses and the five daughters of Zelophehad. Hirsch contends that the heart of the matter in question is the loss of the family name. He points out that the daughters do not only say, "Give us an inheritance of land," but rather they offer an explanation for their request. They plead with Moses, "Let not our father's name be lost. . . ."

The perpetuation of the family name is their just cause, says Hirsch. It is the reason why the Torah determines that "the daughter has a right of inheritance only if there is no son or descendant of one." For, in such a case, the family name would disappear. To safeguard against such a danger, "If there is no son and no descendant of a son, then the daughter or her descendant is the heiress." (Commentary on Numbers 27:1–4)

Hertz

Caring for daughters
The rabbis, while denying the daughters a share in the inheritance where there are sons, still make ample provision for their maintenance and support, as long as they remain unmarried. The cost and provision of such maintenance constitute the first charge upon the estate of the deceased. In case the estate was small, the principle was laid down: "The daughters must be supported, even if the sons are reduced to beggary." (J. H. Hertz, The Pentateuch and Haftorahs, p. 692)

Modern commentator Rabbi W. Gunther Plaut cites the daughters of Zelophehad as an example of the treatment of women during the biblical period. He observes: "While the Torah records a number of laws in which men and women are treated equally (for instance, as regards reverence for parents; punishment in cases of incest; and dietary observances), it is on the whole male-oriented. The male has rights the female does not enjoy. She is to be wife and mother, invested with inherent dignity, to be sure, but by law and social order relegated to a second-class status comparable to that of minors." Regarding the case of Zelophehad's daughters, Plaut concludes that they "are accorded special treatment—but only so long as they fulfill the primary purpose of preserving the integrity of tribe and land (Numbers 36:6), reflecting the fact that men always remained members of their tribe, while women might in effect join another tribe by marriage." (*The Torah: A Modern Commentary*, pp. 1218–1219)

As Plaut points out, the traditional Jewish view of women places them in a "second-class status." While some early rabbinic authorities hold that women are gossips, envious, gluttonous, lazy, quarrelsome, and weak-willed, others argue that they are more pious than men, more merciful, hospitable, sensitive to the needs of others, and wiser. Yet all are agreed that women may not act as witnesses; nor as judges; nor be counted as a part of the *minyan*, the "ten men required for worship"; nor sit with men during worship. Furthermore, every married woman, according to Moses Maimonides, is obligated "to wash the face, hands, and feet of her husband; mix for him his cup of wine; prepare his bed; and stand and serve him. . . ." Regarding the doing of mitzvot, women are exempt from all commandments that must be fulfilled within certain boundaries of time, such as the putting on of *tefilin* or worshiping three times daily. (See *Genesis Rabbah* 18; 45; *Avot* 2:8; *Shabbat* 33b; *Kiddushin* 30b; *Megillah* 14b; *Berachot* 6b; *Niddah* 45b; *Yad ha-Hazakah, Ishut* 21:3.)

While such a degraded view of women undoubtedly reflects the era and sensibilities of the premodern period, it is precisely this view that early Reform Jews in the nineteenth century rejected. In 1837, Abraham Geiger spoke out for the equality of the sexes proclaiming, "Let there be from now on no distinction between duties for men and women . . . no assumption of the spiritual inferiority of women . . . no institution of the public service, either in form or content, that shuts the doors of the temple in the face of women; no degradation of women. . . ."

Nine years later at the Breslau Rabbinical Con-

ference, a paper presented called for the equality of women in all religious duties, declaring that both sexes share equal responsibilities toward rearing children and that women are as obligated as men to pursue Jewish education. While it would be over one hundred years until the first women were ordained as rabbis or cantors, women played significant roles of leadership within the Reform Jewish community. (W. Gunther Plaut, *The Rise of Reform Judaism: A Sourcebook of Its European Origins*, UAHC, New York, 1963, pp. 252–255)

Contemporary traditional Jews have also responded to changing attitudes about women. Few Orthodox Jews demand of their wives the service defined by Moses Maimonides. Indeed, Rabbi Eliezer Berkovits, a leading Orthodox scholar, goes so far as to declare that such practice "is incompatible with the status that the woman had in the ethos of Judaism . . . our self-respect would not allow us to accept this kind of service from our wives, or even from any other human being." Referring to the case of Zelophehad's daughters, Berkovits comments that "notwithstanding the biblical law of inheritance, today in Orthodox Jewish families, wives do inherit their husband's property and daughters inherit together with sons." However, Berkovits makes it clear that women within traditional Judaism still suffer disabilities and inequalities and that these must be solved by seeking legally "valid possibilities" within the structure and interpretation of Jewish law. He warns that it is not only the status of women that is at stake but also the capacity of traditional Judaism to meet the requirements of the modern era. (From *Contemporary Jewish Ethics*, Menachem Marc Kellner, editor, Sanhedrin Press, New York, 1978, pp. 355–373)

Today women are assuming roles of leadership in every area of social, political, religious, business, and professional life. Equal numbers of men and women are working in information services as managers, administrators, and financial experts. As many women as men are starting new businesses, entering scientific professions, and attending liberal Christian and Jewish seminaries.

In such an age, women will also play an equal role in defining Jewish tradition and practice.

During biblical times it was the daughters of Zelophehad who challenged and altered an unjust law of Torah. Standing up for their rights, they extended fair treatment for others. Today, as both men and women struggle to define their rights and responsibilities, they will undoubtedly strengthen and revitalize some of the most significant ethical values and practices of Jewish tradition.

QUESTIONS FOR STUDY AND DISCUSSION

1. Two great teachers of Jewish tradition, Rav and Samuel, disagree on the justification of Pinchas in killing Zimri and Cozbi. What is the moral basis for their arguments? How do other commentators divide on this moral issue?

2. How would you apply the ancient talmudic principle *kanaim pogeim bo* to the incident of Pinchas's killing of Zimri and Cozbi? Does it protect against fanatics taking the law into their own hands? Could such a principle be applied on an international basis between hostile nations and peoples?

3. The Torah labels both the claim of the daughters of Zelophehad and the counterprotest of the tribal leaders of Manasseh as "just." Is the solution offered by the Torah a fair one?

4. Professor Paula E. Hyman comments: "Within the framework of traditional Judaism, women are not independent legal entities. Like the minor, the deaf-mute, and the idiot, they cannot serve as witnesses in Jewish courts. . . . They do not inherit equally with male heirs; they play only a passive role in the Jewish marriage ceremony; and they cannot initiate divorce proceedings. . . . What Jewish feminists are seeking . . . is not more apologetics but change, based on acknowledgment of the ways in which Jewish tradition has excluded women from entire spheres of Jewish experience and has considered them intellectually and spiritually inferior to men." (From "The Other Half: Women in the Jewish Tradition," in *Conservative Judaism*, Summer 1972) How are the modern movements within Jewish life dealing with what "Jewish feminists are seeking"?

PARASHAT MATOT-MAS'EY
Numbers 30:2–36:13

Parashat Matot-Mas'ey is one of seven designated Torah portions that, depending upon the number of Sabbaths in a year, is either read as two separate portions or combined to assure the reading of the entire Torah. While this volume will combine them, it will present an interpretation on each of their most important themes.

Parashat Matot reports the laws, given to the Israelites, for making vows. It also contains a description of the Israelites' war against the Midianites, including the distribution of the booty. The Torah portion concludes with Moses resolving a request by the Gadites and Reubenites for the lands of Jazer and Gilead.

Parashat Mas'ey recounts forty years of *mas'ey,* or "journeys," by the Israelites from Egypt to the Land of Israel. Moses provides instructions for conquering the land, defining its borders, and dividing it among the tribes. He also defines provisions for setting up six cities of refuge where those accused of manslaughter may go for safety and a fair trial. The Book of Numbers concludes with a counterprotest regarding the daughters of Zelophehad (see the discussion in *Parashat Pinchas*) and a further clarification of the Torah's laws of inheritance.

OUR TARGUM

·1·

Moses presents God's laws regulating vows. All vows must be fulfilled. However, when a woman makes a vow as a minor or as a wife, her promise is good only if her father or husband offers no objection to it. By contrast, the vow of a widow or divorced woman is binding upon her.

·2·

Moses commands the Israelites to organize war against the Midianites, who, with the Moabites, had lured the people into prostitution and the worship of Ba'al-peor, when they were camped at Shittim. (Numbers 25:1–9) The Israelites destroy the Midianite towns, capturing booty and many female captives and their children. Moses is furious with the chieftains, reminding them of their battle orders to slay every male. He commands them to carry out the order and to destroy every male among the children and every Midianite woman who has had sexual relations.

Warriors who have killed a person or touched a corpse are told to stay out of camp for seven days and cleanse themselves and their booty through rituals of water and fire. The priests and family heads inventory the booty, dividing it between the warriors and sanctuary.

· 3 ·

The Reubenites and Gadites, who own great numbers of cattle, approach Moses with the request to settle the lands of Jazer and Gilead on the east side of the Jordan River. They claim that these lands are better suited for cattle than the lands allotted to them inside the borders of Israel. While these lands have been conquered by the Israelites, they have not been designated as part of their inheritance.

Moses strongly objects. He accuses them of abandoning their people just when they are poised to enter their land, comparing their actions with the disloyalty shown by their fathers who had scouted the Land of Israel and returned with false reports. The Reubenites and Gadites pledge to act as shock-troops and lead the battle for conquering the Land of Israel and to keep their hereditary holding in the land. Convinced of their integrity, Moses assigns them the lands of Jazer and Gilead.

· 4 ·

Parashat Mas'ey records the names and locations of Israelite camps and journeys from the Exodus through forty years in the desert to the steppes of Moab at the Jordan River near Jericho. The Exodus begins on the fifteenth day of the first month, *Nisan*. Forty years later on Mount Hur, Aaron dies at the age of 123. When the people reach the steppes of Moab, near the Jordan River and the city of Jericho, Moses tells them to enter

the Land of Israel, overwhelm its inhabitants, destroy their idols, and demolish their cult sanctuaries. Afterwards, they are to divide the land by tribal lots.

The Way North

Moses informs the Israelites that the southern border of their land is from the southern tip of the Dead Sea to Kadesh-barnea in the middle of the Negev desert and to the Mediterranean Sea just south of what today is Gaza. The western boundary is the coast line of the Mediterranean Sea. The northern boundary is to run eastward from what today is near the Israel-Lebanon border to near Mount Hermon close to Damascus, Syria. The eastern border is to stretch south from near Damascus to the Sea of Galilee and from there along the Jordan River and Dead Sea.

Moses informs the people that the land inside these borders is to be divided between nine and one-half tribes, reminding them that the tribes of Reuben, Gad, and the half-tribe of Manasseh have been given their portion in land east of the Jordan River.

·5·

The people are also told to assign special towns and lands to the Levites and to choose six cities where one person who unintentionally murders another may flee, finding safety and a fair trial.

·6·

The family heads of the clans of Manasseh and Joseph complain to Moses about his allotment to the daughters of Zelophehad. They point out that, if these daughters marry men from another tribe, the tribal lands will pass into that tribe and not remain within the allotment given to Manasseh and Joseph. God informs Moses that their claim is just. To solve the problem of allowing daughters to inherit from their fathers, Moses decrees that every daughter who inherits a share of land must marry someone from a clan of her father's tribe. In this way the tribal portions will remain the same. Following this law, the daughters of Zelophehad marry men within their clans.

THEMES

Parashat Matot-Mas'ey contains two important themes:

1. Caring for yourself or others.
2. Justice for one who accidently harms another.

PEREK ALEF: *"Are Your Brothers to Go to War While You Stay Here?"*

Parashat Matot raises significant moral questions concerning the petition of the Reubenites and Gadites to settle the conquered lands of Jazer and Gilead on the eastern side of the Jordan River. The tribal leaders approach the aging Moses, Eleazar the priest, and the other heads of the community during the crucial months preceding the battle for the Land of Israel. They explain that the area of Jazer and Gilead is cattle country, and they are ranchers with many cattle. "Favor us," they say, "by giving us this land; do not move us across the Jordan."

Moses is infuriated by their request. Sensing betrayal, he angrily tells them: "Are your brothers to go to war while you stay here? Why will you turn the minds of the Israelites from crossing into the land that *Adonai* has given them?" Pausing, he continues by accusing them of the same sort of treason practiced by their ancestors. "That is what your fathers did when I sent them from Kadesh-barnea to survey the land. After going up to the valley of Eshkol and surveying the land, they turned the minds of the Israelites from invading the land that *Adonai* had given them. . . . And now you, a breed of sinful men, have replaced your fathers."

It is a stinging denunciation, but the Reubenites and Gadites hold their ground. Responding to Moses' charge, they request only enough time to build sheepfolds for their flocks and towns for their children. Afterwards, they are willing to serve in the vanguard of the Israelites' battle for the land and remain until "everyone of the Israelites is in possession of his portion." They also assure Moses that they will make no claim on any land west of the Jordan River.

Moses accepts their promise, warns them against breaking it, and tells them: "Build towns for your children and sheepfolds for your flocks, but do what you have promised."

Criticizing the request of the Gadites and Reubenites, the early rabbis comment on their explicit greed and link them to Korah, Goliath, and Bala'am, who acted unscrupulously to accumulate their wealth only to lose it. They argue that the petition brought before Moses by the Gadites and Reubenites is self-serving. It is the work of people "who love their money" and are willing to sacrifice the welfare of their people to protect their own narrow interests. In fact, say the rabbis, "they separate themselves from their people because of their concern for possessions."

In drawing the parallel between the Gadites and Reubenites to Bala'am, Goliath, and Korah, rabbinic interpreters suggest that they all suffer defeat for the same reason. They "snatch their wealth" by using strength, power, manipulation, and devious means. They are out for themselves, are inconsiderate of others, and will use any means to increase their riches. Their wealth is temporary, say the rabbis. It goes as quickly as it comes because it is not the "gift of God." Because of their greed, they lose it all within two centuries when they are exiled by the invading troops of Assyria.

The rabbis' charge, however, goes even further. They point out that the Gadites and Reubenites prove how foolish they were by their priorities. When Moses criticizes them for seeking land on the east side of the Jordan River before they have helped conquer the Land of Israel, they answer, "We will build here sheepfolds for our flocks and towns for our children."

Their response, claim the rabbis, reveals their priorities. Rather than speaking first about towns for their children and families, they emphasize building sheepfolds for their flocks. They show greater concern for their cattle than for human beings, more attention to their possessions than to their own flesh and blood. Moses, they conclude, is fully justified in denouncing them. (*Numbers Rabbah* 12:7–9)

Jewish historian Josephus Flavius, who lived during the first century (37 C.E. to 100 C.E.), agrees with this harsh rabbinic assessment of the Gadites and Reubenites. Moses, he writes, understands that they are seeking a strategy for securing their wealth on the east side of the Jordan River, not participating in the Jewish people's conquest of their land. For that reason he is justified, argues Josephus, in labeling them "arrogant cowards" because "they had a mind to live in luxury and ease while all the rest were laboring with great pains to obtain the land they were desirous to have." Josephus condemns them for pursing self-interest and neglecting responsibility to the common good of their people. (*Antiquities of the Jews,* IV, 5, A.L. Burt Co., New York, n.d.)

Peli

Modern commentator Pinchas Peli agrees, claiming that the Gadites and Reubenites represent a serious "separatist" threat to the Jewish people. "Moses' concern," Peli writes, "was . . . with the ethical implications of the seceding of the two tribes from a war that should be fought by all of Israel. The conquest of *Eretz Yisrael* was not incumbent only on those people who planned to live on the land. It was, in the eyes of Moses, the culmination of the drama of redemption that should be acted out in full by all the tribes that came out of Egypt."

According to Peli, however, Moses also worries about "the effect that the step taken by Reuben and Gad might have on the morale of the people." He scolds them with sharp language, calling them "a brood of sinful men," and linking them to the "slanderous spies" whose reports were designed to frighten an earlier generation from going up to conquer the Land of Israel. Their request to remain on the east side of the Jordan River undermines the unity of the people and threatens to deplete their strength just when it is most required. Moses, says Peli, understands that a divided people will not be victorious over its enemies. Their request is nothing less than treason. For that reason he severely reprimands them. (*Torah Today*, pp. 189–193)

Ramban (Nachmanides)

Nachmanides sympathizes with Moses' suspicion of the Gadites and Reubenites but maintains that their true intentions are misunderstood. Moses, he writes, is guilty of overreaction. Rather than patiently hearing them out, he rushes to condemn them. He "suspects that they are only suggesting that they stay on the east side of the Jordan because they are afraid of the people in the land of Canaan."

That explains, says Nachmanides, why Moses accuses them of a failure of nerve and of acting like their ancestors who, out of fear, spread lies that the people inhabiting the land are "giants" and would overwhelm the Israelites in battle. Nachmanides is critical of Moses and points out that the intention of the Gadites and Reubenites was never to abandon the effort to conquer the land but to enlarge the inheritance of the tribes by settling in desirable lands east of the Jordan River. Justifying his observation, Nachmanides quotes them as telling Moses: "We will hasten as shock-troops in the van of the Israelites until we have established them in their home. . . . Nor will we claim any share with them on the other side of the Jordan and beyond, having received our share on the east side of the Jordan." (Numbers 32:17–19)

Nachmanides' argument is that the Gadites and Reubenites came before Moses "with a request, not a confrontation." They were seeking, not only what was best for them, but also what they believed would be best for all Israelites. Their plan would give their people more, not less, land. Had Moses taken the time to hear them out instead of instantly condemning them, their real intentions would have been clear.

Moses is criticized
Our sages declare that Moses offends God by describing the Israelites as "a band of sinners" and was punished accordingly . . . in that one of his descendants became a priest to heathen worship. . . . It teaches us . . . if someone has a quarrel with another person, he should not in anger insult the ancestors of that person . . . there even exists an ancient ban against speaking ill of those already sleeping in the ground, even when there are justified reasons for doing so. (Yitzhak Magriso, Me'am Lo'ez on Numbers 32:14–15)

Abravanel

Abravanel agrees with Nachmanides and probes for an explanation of Moses' confusion and indignant response. What accounts, he asks, for Moses' immediate and angry answer to the Gadites' and Reubenites' request to settle their families and cattle east of the Jordan River? He discovers an explanation in the first words they speak to the aging leader. They say to him: "It would be a favor to us if this land were given to your servants as a holding; do not move us across the Jordan." (Numbers 32:5)

Their mistake, says Abravanel, is in putting the matter of their crossing the Jordan in negative terms. In doing so, they confuse Moses, leading him to assume that they fear the battle ahead and are seeking a way to avoid helping conquer the Land of Israel. Had they simply said: "We are ready to join in conquering the land and will be satisfied if you allow us to inherit this land east of the Jordan," Moses would not have misunderstood their motive. Their fault was in the carelessness of their presentation, in the thoughtlessness of their words. (Commentary on Numbers 32:5)

Abravanel's contemporary Isaac Arama believes that Moses should have apologized for his hasty, false assumptions about the Gadites and Reubenites. However, he argues that their motives were deeply divided and thus confused Moses. On the one hand, they were ready to fight alongside the Israelites; on the other hand, they would have been pleased to be excluded and allowed to remain east of the Jordan with their families. They alternated with ambivalence between loyalty to the people and a willingness to forgo their tribal inheritance in the Land of Israel. They knew that their people's destination for forty years was to inherit and live in the Land of Israel, but they also "wished to stay abroad because they had found territory that suited their cattle, as if they had come to this destination to accommodate their animals with choice pasture."

This serious confusion about their motives

accounts for the ambivalence Moses senses in their request, leading him to accuse them of treason. Their own lack of clarity about their goals and their destination leaves them incapable of articulating a direction. They become prisoners of their own ambivalence, unable to determine what they want because they do not know what they want. Little wonder that Moses did not comprehend their true intention. The Reubenites and Gadites hardly understood it themselves. (See *Akedat Yitzhak* on Numbers 32:1–27.)

The controversy continues

According to Rabbi Simcha Zissel of Kelm, the petition of these two and a half tribes not to cross the Jordan because of cattle boils down to a desire for money. Now it doesn't take a great flight of the imagination to relate the cattle and grazing lands of those days to the cattle and grazing lands of today. Why do Jews continue to live outside Israel—on the other side of the Jordan or the other side of the Atlantic? Because they've found good grazing lands for their cattle, and it's a shame to give it up. But even if the descendants of Gad and Manasseh petitioned someone today about their choices, we could very well assume that Moses would say today what he said then: "Why should your brothers go out and fight while you stay here?" (Comment on Numbers 32:6 by Rabbi Shlomo Riskin, Jerusalem Post, *July 21, 1990)*

In contrast to the explanations of Abravanel and Isaac Arama, Rabbi Moshe ben Chaim Alshekh excuses the Gadites' and Reubenites' request, arguing that it was motivated by generosity and realism, not by confusion. He points out that Gad and Reuben "seek to convince the tribal leaders that by their choice everybody will wind up having more land." "The reason they stress that they would *first* build enclosures for their cattle and then provide for their children is to convince Moses that the safety of their children is not their primary concern." Their first priority is to benefit their people.

Supporting his argument, Alshekh writes: "When Moses realizes that the intention of these tribes has been sound, that they have only erred in their semantics, having been imprecise in the use of language, he instructs Eleazar and Joshua that they should not be harassed for their decision to ultimately reside east of the Jordan River." As with Abravanel, Alshekh identifies the problem as one of "semantics." However, rather than blaming the Gadites and Reubenites for carelessness and confusion of goals, he dismisses the matter, saying that, once Moses understands the true intention of their request, "he accepts the fairmindedness of the Reubenites and Gadites and that his suspicions had not been based on fact." (Commentary on Numbers 32:20)

The differing views over the motives of the Gadites and Reubenites in asking to inherit lands east of the Jordan River and to remain in them until they build enclosures for their cattle and cities for their children raise significant moral questions about the division between responsibility to oneself and family and responsibility to one's community. The clash of Moses with the Gadites and Reubenites over interests and intentions is a common and continuing one.

Zugot

Hillel captures the dilemma with three hard questions: "If I am not for myself, who will be for me? But, if I am only for myself, what am I? And, if not now, when?" (*Avot* 1:14)

PEREK BET: *Cities of Refuge: Justice for Unintentional Homicide*

Parashat Mas'ey presents a revolutionary approach to providing justice for those who have committed involuntary manslaughter, meaning that they have unintentionally murdered another person. It suggests that in such accidents guilty parties may escape avenging relatives by going immediately to one of six *arei miklat*, or "cities of asylum." Within those cities, three of which are located in the Land of Israel (Hebron, Shechem, and Kedesh) and three east of the Jordan River (Bezer, Ramoth, and Golan), those who have committed involuntary manslaughter are to find safety and justice from those seeking to avenge the death of their loved ones.

How did these *arei miklat,* or "cities of asylum," function?

The Torah and rabbinic law provide us with some answers. During the biblical period, relatives of murder victims, whether premeditated or unintentional, had the right to find and execute those who were guilty of killing their loved ones. Those whose crime was committed by accident, however, had the right to save themselves from the revenge of families by going immediately to one of the six cities of asylum. All roads leading to these cities had to be clearly marked with signs pointing the way. In addition, roads were to be straight, level, and in good condition. No obstacle was to stand in the way of those seeking asylum.

Upon arrival at the city gate, unintentional murderers presented themselves to elders who offered hospitality. Once rested, they were taken to a court where it was determined whether they were guilty of premeditated murder or involuntary manslaughter. If judged guilty of premeditated murder, they were put to death; if guilty of unintentional homicide, they were allowed to live rent- and tax-free in the refuge city during the lifetime of the incumbent High Priest. After the death of the High Priest, they could return to their home cities, without fearing harm from avengers. (Numbers 35:9–34; Deuteronomy 4:43, 19:8–10; Joshua 20:7; *Makot* 10a–b, 13a)

Modern commentator Rabbi W. Gunther Plaut speculates that the "institutionalization of such asylum may be the earliest of its kind . . ." and points out that "the distinguishing features of the biblical provisions are the restriction of asylum to the unintentional slayer and the connection of the institution with the death of the High Priest." Plaut claims that the notion of the cities of asylum arose out of the need to end family feuds by taking the process of law out of the hands of private individuals and emphasizing the role of "public law enforcement."

For Plaut, the *arei miklat* serve three different

purposes. They are meant to protect unintentional murderers from the passion of avengers, to punish them, and "to contain and isolate the sin that had been committed." He suggests that the isolation of sin is the most important, explaining that "the killing of a human being, though it occurred without evil intent, was a moral injury to the total community" because the people of Israel have "a special God-relationship that was founded on zealous regard for the sanctity of every life." (*The Torah: A Modern Commentary,* pp. 1249–1250)

Rabbi Jacob ben Isaac Ashkenazi of Yanof, author of *Tze'enah u-Re'enah,* supports Plaut's view, maintaining that the *arei miklat* are a means of containing the sin of murder. He writes that each murder, intentional or unintentional, banishes God's Presence from the world because each human being is made in the image of God. When that image is destroyed, God's Presence is sent into exile. By contrast, the High Priest through his saintly function in the sanctuary brings God's Presence into the world. This is why, explains Rabbi Jacob, the unintentional killer is confined to the city of asylum until the High Priest dies. Those who diminish God's Presence "should not go into the world," should not contaminate it with their sin while the High Priest who labors to bring God's Presence into the world is alive. (Commentary on Numbers 35:25)

Hirsch

Rabbi Samson Raphael Hirsch amplifies the point made by Rabbis Plaut and Jacob concerning the sacredness of life by emphasizing the special relationship between the people, the Land of Israel, and God. He writes that "the land is only given on the condition of every human life being respected and being unassailably sacred to the Torah. One drop of innocent blood shed and no notice taken of it drops a stitch in the bond that connects the land with the nation and both with God."

Rambam (Maimonides)

Regulations for the arei miklat
The city of asylum should not be large or small, but average; it is to be established only at a place that affords marketing possibilities and water resources; if there is no water, it has to be installed; it has to be established as a place that attracts settlement in its environment. (Moses Maimonides, Mishneh Torah, *"On Homicide," 8:8)*

Unlike Plaut and Jacob, Hirsch does not look upon the asylum cities as places for the containment of those who "contaminate" the world through their sin of unintentional homicide. Instead, he sees them as providing opportunities offering forgiveness and rebirth. Hirsch argues that, just as when we are born, we are "set in the world as a permanent surrounding"; "consigning the unintentional murderer to a *miklat*-city is similarly a second confining birth. The *miklat*-city is henceforth the whole world to the one who is relegated to it."

According to Hirsch this "rebirth" within the *miklat*-city is not a form of punishment but a chance to find "a life there." For that reason, says Hirsch, the town "should be of medium size . . . not enclosed by a wall, provided with water and food markets . . . all national classes must be settled there." It must have teachers, students, people of science, of spiritual and intellectual quality. According to Jewish tradition, students must be allowed to follow their teacher if he is guilty of unintentional murder, and a teacher must be given the freedom to follow a student.

Quoting from the description of the *arei miklat* in Deuteronomy 19:5, Hirsch emphasizes that unintentional murderers are to "flee to one of these cities *and live.*" For that reason, the *arei miklat* are to be environments for "rebirth," nurturing places where human beings can enjoy the company of others, pursue their talents, and grow

both spiritually and intellectually. Despite the fact that the manslayer is confined to such cities until the death of the High Priest, they are not *prisons.* They "must form," concludes Hirsch, "a complete world on a small scale." (Commentary on Numbers 35:6–12)

Medieval commentator Aharon Halevi does not agree with Hirsch's point of view, stressing that asylum cities are meant as punishment places for those who cause the death of others. "Their crime is great because it corrupts the entire world. Our teachers say that a person who commits a premeditated murder will not be saved from death even though he may have observed all the other commandments of Torah. . . . Therefore, a person who has unintentionally caused the death of another deserves the punishment of exile because he has been the agent for a terrible accident. The punishment of exile is comparable to death in a social sense because he is separated from his loved ones and home. He is sent to live among strangers." (*Sefer ha-Hinuch,* 410)

Halevi's view reflects the opinion of some early rabbis who compare the "exile" of Adam from the Garden of Eden to the "exile" of the unintentional murderer to one of the *arei miklat.* Yet the punishment is mixed with compassion. The rabbis point out that Adam ate from the Tree of Knowledge of Good and Bad even though he had been told, "In the day that you eat from that tree, you will die." (Genesis 2:17) Yet God did not put him to death. Instead, say the rabbis, God demonstrates compassion and expels him from the Garden of Eden.

The lesson to be learned here, continue the rabbis, is that human beings are to show compassion upon "the fate of one who commits murder in error. Such a person is to be protected from avengers and exiled from his own home to cities of refuge. . . . Furthermore, you are to establish resting places on the direct roads leading to them, and at each resting place and along the way there are to be signs reading 'To the cities of asylum' so that the person will know how to get there." (*Numbers Rabbah* 23:13)

Rabbi Yitzhak Magriso, author of *Me'Am Lo'ez,* also stresses the compassion shown by Jewish tradition toward the unintentional murderer by creating the *arei miklat.* Their purpose, he maintains, is "to prevent the blood avenger from killing him." Rabbi Magriso adds that the "reason given for the killer having to stay in the city of refuge until the death of the High Priest is that the relatives of the murdered person would then relent. By mourning for the death of a great person, their own anguish would cool since they would come to realize that all human beings die sooner or later, even the greatest of their generation."

Rabbi Magriso recognizes the apparent inequity in connecting liberation from the city of refuge to the death of the High Priest. After all, one unintentional murderer might be confined to the city of asylum for many years while another might be required to stay for no more than a day should the High Priest die just after his assignment to the city by the court. Such disparity in the length of sentences raises questions about the fairness of linking them to the life of the High Priest. Indeed, members of a grieving family whose loved one has been killed could ask: "What kind of justice is this?"

"The answer," argues Rabbi Magriso, "is that, while there are no scales for measuring which willful murder is more terrible and which is less terrible, in the case of unintentional killings there are differences. There may be an inadvertent killing that is close to deliberate murder; for instance, when someone kills another while chopping wood. If he had looked about him, he would have seen the man standing there, and he would not have hit him. By carelessly swinging the ax to split the wood, he hit the man in the head and killed him.

"On the other hand, if the victim was far away and the metal part of the ax flew out of the other's hand and killed him, his guilt is less; in fact, the killing is considered entirely inadvertent.

"God knows the relative guilt of such inadvertent killings. . . . Accordingly, if one killed another accidentally, this could take place close to the High Priest's death, and his punishment would be correspondingly light. While, if it was close to a deliberate killing, it would take a long time before the High Priest died, and the killer's punishment would be correspondingly harsh." (Commentary on Numbers 35:9–15)

Clearly, Rabbi Magriso is establishing the principle that, because the accidental death has a variety of causes, some through carelessness, others through pure coincidence, the release from punishment ought also to be based upon "coincidence" or "fate." The death of the High Priest presents such a happenstance. No one can know the precise timing. It can be considered "God's will," not the intervention of any human being. For that reason, the "timing" of release from one of the *arei miklat,* no matter how close or far from the sentence, cannot be questioned.

Don Isaac Abravanel provides a more psychological explanation of the link between the High Priest's death and the end of exile in the *arei miklat* for the unintentional murderer. He points out that, when the High Priest died, the entire people "trembled and repented for his sins." The sense of sorrow was great. So was the feeling about the uncertainties of life itself. "It could, therefore, be assumed," explains Abravanel, "that the avenger of a person accidentally killed would, under the sad circumstances of the High Priest's death, reconsider his anger, calm himself, and no longer seek to execute vengeance for the killing of a member of his family. . . . Then it would be safe for the accidental murderer to leave the asylum city and return home." (Commentary on Numbers 35:25)

While some interpreters claim that the *arei miklat* are set aside as places of punishment or as a means of containing the "sin of murder" from spreading through the society, most Jewish teachers stress that they are meant to save the person who has committed unintentional murder from death by individuals who might take the law into their own hands and to provide a place where such a person can *live* a protected and productive life. The asylum cities are not "prison cities" or "penal colonies." Quite the opposite. The *arei miklat* are meant to be "rebirth" places where a person tormented by the shame and guilt of having accidentally taken a life would be able to surmount anguish and rebuild a creative human existence.

QUESTIONS FOR STUDY AND DISCUSSION

1. The request of the Gadites and Reubenites for settlement on the east side of the Jordan River troubles Moses. Is a person's first loyalty to his family or to his people? Are there times when we must put aside self-interest for the good of our nation and our people? What are the criteria for such a decision? What can we learn from the example of the Gadites and Reubenites?

2. Several commentators criticize Moses for his reaction to the petition of the Gadites and Reubenites. Could he have listened more sensitively and clarified their fears or desires? Should he have demonstrated more patience and understanding? Was he wrong in linking their behavior to their dead ancestors, who could not defend their reputations? Which of the interpreters explains best Moses' reaction?

3. Some interpreters argue that the *arei miklat* were created to keep the murderer from mixing in society with the result that he could meet members of the family of the person who had died at his hand. Such a meeting could cause great sadness or provoke great anger, leading to his own death at the hands of a family avenger. Is isolation a justified response to accidental murder? Is murder a crime that demands a different level of punishment? Why?

4. How would you compare the treatment of those guilty of accidental murder today with the treatment suggested by the Torah and our interpreters?

THE
TORAH
PORTIONS
OF
DEUTERONOMY

PARASHAT DEVARIM
Deuteronomy 1:1–3:22

Parashat Devarim begins a series of speeches by Moses to the Israelites. They are about to enter the Land of Israel. Moses will die in Moab on Mount Nebo. He reminds the people that they will take possession of the land given to Abraham, Isaac, and Jacob. He recalls the time when he was unable to lead them by himself and how God told him to appoint wise leaders to assist him. Moses also recounts sending scouts to explore the land, resulting in a divisive report that frightened the people with predictions of defeat. Because of the scouts' lies and the people's lack of faith, their whole generation was not allowed to enter the land. Only Caleb and Joshua son of Nun, who brought back a positive report, would lead the new generation of Israelites into the Land of Israel. Moses then recounts their route of travel from Kadesh-barnea southward to Ezion-geber, then northward skirting Edom and Moab to Kedemoth and Heshbon, and their victorious battles with Sihon king of Heshbon and Og king of Bashan.

OUR TARGUM

·1·

In Hebrew, this Torah portion, like the fifth and final book of the Torah, Deuteronomy, is called *Devarim,* or "words," because it contains the last "words" or speeches of Moses to the Israelites. Addressing them from Mount Nebo, overlooking the Land of Israel, Moses commands the people to enter and recover the land promised to Abraham, Isaac, and Jacob. He notes that their borders are to extend from the Mediterranean Sea on the West, to Lebanon on the North, and to the Euphrates River on the East.

·2·

Recalling their forty years of desert wandering, Moses reminds the people of their bickering and complaining. He admits that he was incapable of bearing the burden of their leadership by himself and thus appointed wise judges and experienced

tribal leaders to assist him. He commanded them to hear all differences of opinion among the people and to judge each case fairly and impartially. Matters too difficult for the judges were to be referred to him.

·3·

Moses reminds the people that, when they reached Kadesh-barnea, about fifty miles south of Beer-sheba, he commanded them to go forth and conquer the Land of Israel. When they suggested that spies be sent to scout the land, he agreed. When the scouts returned, ten of the twelve brought back a report that exaggerated the strength of the people of the land and frightened the Israelites. Sulking in their tents, the people refused to go forward, fearing they would be defeated. As a result of their lack of faith, God punished the whole generation by condemning them to die by the sword of the Amorites before reaching the Promised Land.

Only Caleb and Joshua the son of Nun, who brought back a positive report urging the people to conquer the land, were now privileged to lead a new generation into the Land of Israel.

·4·

Moses traces the Israelites' forty-year march through the wilderness. He recalls his warning not to fight the descendants of Esau, who live in Seir, nor to harass the Moabites. Thirty-eight years of wandering passed during their journey from Kadesh-barnea to the wadi Zered. During that period the older generation had died.

Moses instructs the new generation to go to war with Sihon king of Heshbon and Og king of Bashan if they refuse to allow the Israelites to pass peacefully through their countries. When the kings refuse to allow such passage, they are defeated by the Israelites. Their conquered lands are divided among the tribes of Reuben, Gad, and the half-tribe of Manasseh.

Moses concludes this part of his speech by commanding Joshua to conquer the Land of Israel, without fear of its inhabitants.

THEMES

Parashat Devarim contains two important themes:

1. The art of making judgments.
2. The responsibility of leaders and followers.

PEREK ALEF: *Decide Justly in All Cases*

The fifth book of the Torah, *Devarim*, Hebrew for "words," or Deuteronomy, Greek for "repetition of the Law," presents a series of speeches by Moses to the Israelites as they are about to enter the Land of Israel. In his speeches, Moses traces the Israelites' forty-year trek through the desert.

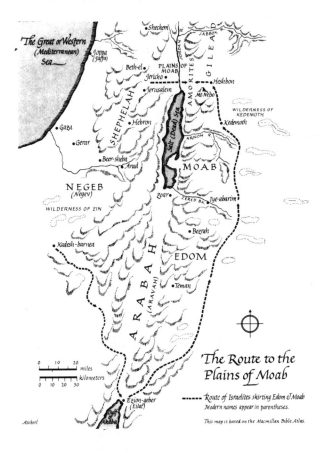

The Route to the Plains of Moab

- - - *Route of Israelites skirting Edom & Moab*
Modern names appear in parentheses.

This map is based on the Macmillan Bible Atlas.

Ascherl

Some scholars claim that *Devarim* was written by an unknown prophet during King Josiah's reign (715–640 B.C.E.) and served as the basis of his consolidation and reformation of the ancient Jewish state. (See II Kings 22–23.) Others dispute this theory, arguing that the text is the work of Moses, that it mirrors the language and laws found within the books of Exodus, Leviticus, and Numbers, and that it presents his last teachings to the people just before his death on Mount Nebo.

While the dispute about dating and authorship persists, the artistry of *Devarim* is acknowledged by all students of Torah. It contains not only reports about the early history and traditions of the Israelites but also a valuable record of the ethical values and laws that guided their society.

Near the beginning of our Torah portion Moses recalls a moment of crisis when he realized that he, by himself, could not lead the Israelites. He remembers saying, "I cannot bear your disputes and bickering by myself." To aid him, he appoints "wise, discerning, and experienced" tribal leaders and judges. "I charged them to hear out the people and to decide justly between them, Israelites or strangers. I commanded them to be impartial in judgment, hearing out low and high alike. I told them to fear no person in rendering a judgment because judgment is God's." (Deuteronomy 1:16–17)

In commenting on the difficult burden of making judgments, the early rabbis, many of whom were presiding court judges, compare the responsibility to dealing with fire. "If you come too close, you will be burnt; if you stray too far, you will be cold. The art of making judgments," they conclude, "is finding the right distance."

Perspective is critical in rendering fair decisions. Independence of outlook and a delicate balance of viewpoint and attitude are essential for arriving at good judgments. Yet how does one achieve independence combined with a balanced viewpoint and attitude? How does one screen out prejudice, bias, and the inclination to favor one person over another?

In his presentation to the Israelites, Moses suggests three significant rules for making judgments: "hear out" those with conflicting views; do not "show partiality to low or high, Israelites or strangers"; and "fear" no one when you are ready to render your decision. Using these guidelines, interpreters of Torah elaborate on the art of achieving justice in human relationships. (*Mechilta* on *Yitro*)

Rabbi Berechiah, quoting his teacher Rabbi Hanina, remarks that "those making judgments must possess seven attributes. They must be wise, understanding, full of knowledge, able, reverent, truthful, and despise corruption." Because for centuries each Jewish community functioned with its own *dayanim*, or "judges," who dealt with all personal and communal problems (e.g., disputes between husbands and wives, children and parents, business partners; business claims; matters of inheritance; ritual matters), it was critical that the reputation of *dayanim* be beyond reproach. Berechiah's seven attributes offer a high standard for judges and others called upon to render judgments. (*Deuteronomy Rabbah* 1:10)

Rabbi Hanina, a wealthy trader and physician who built the second-century academy in the city of Tzporin, or Sepphoris, in the Galilee, also comments about "hearing" a dispute properly. "A judge must not hear the arguments of one person before the arrival of the other person with whom he has a disagreement. Nor should one person seek to pressure the judge into hearing him before the other party is present." A fair, impartial hearing is one where the opponents can correct or object to the impression or facts being presented. To allow a hearing with only one of the parties present could prejudice the judgment. "Hearing," therefore, means listening to both parties together. (*Sanhedrin* 7b)

Within Jewish law, however, "hearing" means even more. If, for instance, one appearing before a judge wishes to bring more evidence or enlarge one's arguments, one must be permitted to do so. A judge must be patient even if the parties are long-winded or the case is tedious. Disputants must not be cut off; they should be heard to the end without intermission. The judge should also ask questions, seeking to "go behind words" and "get to the truth." "Hearing" means paying attention to nuances, inflections, and possible manipulation of facts.

Rabbinic law is also sensitive to how those who make judgments use their eyes. Judges should not look at only one of the disputants. If they do, they may give the impression that one is more important than the other or that one's argument, clothing, gestures, or physical appearance is more pleasing than that of the other. Such an impression could lead to the assumption that the judge is showing favoritism even before a decision is announced. It may also result in a person's leaving a hearing with the conclusion that "the judge's eyes were constantly on my opponent. He favors him. He never paid any attention to me." (*Shulchan Aruch*; *Or ha-Chaim*)

Commenting on the "appearance" of partiality, Rabbi Moshe ben Chaim Alshekh warns against allowing the dress of disputants to influence judgment. "Because one is dressed in fine clothing, the latest fashion, is no reason to favor that person. A person should not go away from a hearing saying, 'Had I worn better clothing, the judge would have heard my case with greater respect and sympathy.' "

Nor, says Alshekh, should judges fear that their reputations will be weakened if, after hearing all the arguments, they decide to refer the dispute to others or to a higher authority. To admit one's inability to reach a fair, knowledgeable judgment is not a sign of weakness but of strength, claims Alshekh. Furthermore, there are times when it is impossible to reach impartial conclusions or when the person called upon to hear the case may not be expert enough to comprehend all of the information necessary for fair and wise judgment. (Commentary to Deuteronomy 1:17)

Commentator Jacob ben Isaac Ashkenazi of Yanov notes that "showing partiality" is not simply a matter of how judges "hear" a dispute but also how they speak to those arguing before them. "If a judge speaks pleasantly to one person and rudely to the other," Ashkenazi warns, "he may influence the emotional state of both disputants, encouraging one and discouraging the other. In fact, such a demonstration of partiality may make it more difficult for the parties to present their cases, especially for the one who assumes that he, for whatever reason, is disliked by the judge. Pressuring or signaling displeasure with disputants may influence the way in which they present facts. . . . [It may] cause them to become so confused that they neglect important elements of their case. Judges, therefore, must do nothing to indicate their preference between contestants." (*Tze'enah u-Re'enah* on Deuteronomy 1:17)

> **Judging others**
> *Judges should see themselves as if a sword were hanging at their necks and as if hell were open at their feet. They should know whom they are judging and that God will punish judges who*

depart from the strict line of justice. . . . Whenever judges render true decisions, it is as if they had put right the whole world. . . . (Sanhedrin 7a; also Tur, Choshen Mishpat 8)

Rabbi Akiba teaches: Do not allow sentimentality in making judgments. (Mishnah Ketubot 9:2)

 Zugot *Rashi*

Hillel says: Do not judge another person until you have put yourself in that person's place. (Avot 2:5) *To which Rashi adds: Do not harshly condemn another for falling into temptation until you have been tempted by similar circumstances and have overcome them.*

Joshua ben Perachyah says: "Judge all people by giving them the benefit of the doubt." Quoting the chasidic teacher Rabbi Bunum, Rabbi Isaac Unterman comments: "It is always good to give everyone the benefit of the doubt. If the person is really innocent, then you acted correctly and in accordance with the truth. If, on the other hand, the person is guilty, your act is not irrevocable." (Pirke Aboth, p. 45)

 Hertz

Rabbi Joseph H. Hertz, quoting a story from the Babylonian Talmud, emphasizes the care judges must take to demonstrate impartiality. Samuel, a revered scholar and judge, was crossing a stream on a narrow plank. A stranger, seeing that the rabbi could use some help, reached out, took his hand, and brought him safely to the other side of the stream. Upon learning the man's name, Samuel realized that the man was scheduled to appear before him for judgment in a few days.

"Friend," Samuel told him, "by your kind favor you have disqualified me as the judge in your dispute."

Favors, even innocent kindness, charity, or the appearance of gestures of generosity, must not be accepted by those making judgments. The integrity of a judge must be above reproach.

The issue of "partiality" also pertains to strangers and noncitizens. Hertz points out that Jewish law makes it clear "there must be no difference between an Israelite and the resident alien." Equal respect and treatment in court is to be given to all persons. They are to be heard and judged on the merit of their case, not by their national, ethnic, religious, or racial heritage. Jewish tradition recognizes how easy it is to discriminate against those whose language, customs, religious beliefs, or skin color may be different. It warns against establishing one standard of justice for citizens and another for strangers. (*The Pentateuch and Haftorahs*, pp. 738–739)

 Hirsch

Interpreter Samson Raphael Hirsch quotes the ancient Torah commentary *Sifre*, which makes the point that those engaged in judgment should "not be quick in giving it but should give each individual case repeated consideration even if it is quite similar to cases that have previously arisen on several occasions." Hirsch emphasizes the danger in reaching quick decisions based on first impressions. Often, there is a tendency to hear the opening arguments and rush to judgment on the basis of previous cases. In making such assumptions, judges overlook critical individual circumstances that should be considered in arriving at just decisions. For that reason, Jewish law demands that each case be heard with care for all its details and that "no preliminary opinion of the case should be formed."

Hirsch also raises the delicate issue of threats against judges by those whose cases they are hearing. According to our Torah portion, judges should "fear no person" when it comes to rendering a decision because "judgment is God's."

What in practical terms does this mean? Should a judge risk his life, or the lives of his family members, by pronouncing a decision that could encourage an act of violence?

Rambam (Maimonides)

Basing his conclusion on our Torah portion's commandment to "fear no person, for judgment is God's," Maimonides says, "It is the judge's duty to render judgment without any thought of the injury the evildoer may cause him." The judge must not say, "I fear this person because he may kill my son or burn my wheat or destroy my plants." (*Sefer ha-Mitzvot*, Negative Commandments #276)

Hirsch agrees with Maimonides, arguing that "in giving judgment you are doing the work of God." He explains that "it is not your affair, which you can decide in accordance with your own ideas; it is God's justice, which is to be made actual through you. Therefore, you are not to hold back your just judgment out of the slightest fear." Quoting the Talmud, Hirsch concludes, "Every judge who by his verdict makes true justice into an actual accomplished truth is considered as if he had participated in God's work of creation." (Commentary on Deuteronomy 1:17)

The emphasis of Jewish tradition upon hearing and judging disputes justly is not simply for judges. The guidelines also apply to all engaged in hearing arguments and helping others solve disputes: friends, couples, parents, children, business partners, colleagues, students, teammates—all who must inevitably deal with the clashing opinions or claims of others. If a third party listens with patience to both sides, does not cut off discussion but asks questions that clarify matters, pays attention to the nuances of each party's claim, and strives to treat both disputants equally, there is a good chance that a reasonable settlement will be reached.

The ethical rules for judging the arguments of others, identified by our Torah portion and expanded upon by our commentators, offer a wise path to justice. Since making judgments about the claims of others is "dealing with fire," these important guidelines may save us from being burned.

PEREK BET: *The Spies: Another View*

Several times within Deuteronomy Moses addresses the people and reviews past incidents. Recalling their history, especially their forty years of wandering in the desert, is an important function of his role as leader. He connects them to their roots, emphasizing their unique identity and experience as a people that has endured slavery and has faced the challenges of creating a community of laws and traditions in a desolate desert. In speaking to them about their history, he is preparing them for their future in the Land of Israel. Each incident becomes a lesson meant to strengthen them for the trials ahead.

It is particularly curious that, when Moses retells the story of sending twelve spies to scout the Land of Israel, his version in Deuteronomy (1:19–45) differs completely from the version we have already discussed in *Parashat Shelach-Lecha*. (Numbers 13:1–14:45)

In *Parashat Shelach-Lecha*, God commands Moses to send a leader from each tribe to scout the Land of Israel. They are instructed to return with information about the geography, people, fortifications, soil, and forests of the land, along with some samples of its fruit. When the scouts return at the end of forty days, they report that the land "flows with milk and honey" but warn that its peoples are giants and its cities well fortified. They spread fear among the people, telling them, "We cannot attack the people who inhabit the land for they are stronger than we."

Only Caleb and Joshua disagree, advising Moses and the people to go forward and take control of the land.

Frightened by the other scouts, the people protest to Moses and Aaron, "Why is *Adonai* taking us to that land to fall by the sword? . . . Let us head back to Egypt." For their faithlessness and fomenting of panic among the people, God punishes the spies by extinguishing their entire generation over the next forty years. Only their children, led by Caleb and Joshua, will enter the Promised Land.

In the Numbers version of the story, the spies are blamed for the people's fear and faithlessness. Their distinguished tribal leaders have misled the people with false reports and exaggerations. "You shall bear your punishment," Moses tell them.

The version of the spy story found in this Torah portion differs significantly. Moses recalls the journey of the people to Kadesh-barnea from Mount Horeb, where he had given them the Ten Commandments. According to Moses' recollection, they are camped on the edge of the Land of Israel, ready to conquer it. The people approach him and say: "Let us send men ahead to check the land for us and bring back word on the route we shall follow and the cities we shall come to."

Moses agrees and selects twelve spies. After touring the land for forty days, they return, declaring, "It is a good land that *Adonai* our God is giving to us." The people, however, do not listen to the report. Instead, they refuse to follow God's command to conquer the land. They complain about conditions in the desert and "sulk in their tents." In response to their lack of faith, God punishes them by announcing that none of them, except Caleb and Joshua, will enter the Land of Israel. "Because of you," says Moses, "God was also angry with me, forbidding me from entering as well."

In this recollection by Moses, it is not God who commands Moses to send the spies but the people, who come to Moses, demanding the spies make the journey. In addition, it is not the spies who are at fault for misleading the people by telling them of giants among the Amorites, but it is the people who misconstrue their report. Indeed, it is the people, not the spies, who "have no faith in *Adonai* your God, who goes before you on your journeys. . . ."

In Numbers, the spies are guilty of misleading the people. They cause a crisis of faith in the community and bring death to their generation. In Deuteronomy, it is not the spies but the people who bear responsibility for the catastrophic episode.

What accounts for these two very different versions of the same event? Do we have here a major contradiction of fact and content within the Torah? Are we dealing here with the failing memory of an aging Moses?

Rashi explains that, in Deuteronomy, in his last speeches to the people of Israel, Moses deliberately indicates how disappointed he was with their ancestors' request that spies be sent into the land. Quoting an earlier interpretation from the *Sifre*, Rashi claims that Moses was upset with the people because "they come before him as an unruly crowd, the young people pushing aside their elders, showing no respect for one another or for him."

Rashi also says that Moses tried and failed to placate them with a parable. He told them: "There was a man who said to a friend of his, 'Sell me your donkey.' When the friend agreed, the buyer asked, 'Will you sell it to me on trial?' Again the friend agreed. Then the buyer asked, 'May I try it out in the mountains, take it out in the hills?' Once again the friend agreed. Finally, the buyer, realizing that his friend had total confidence in the donkey, said, 'I shall take the donkey without any trials.'"

Rashi explains that, after reciting the parable, Moses told the people, "I agreed to send the spies, hoping that you would see that I had total confidence in God and in the land, but you did not! You failed to reconsider your request to send spies. Little wonder that catastrophe followed."

According to Rashi and the *Sifre*, it is the people who force Moses to send the spies, and it is the people who bring ruin to themselves by their lack of faith in the report of Caleb and Joshua. In Moses' Deuteronomy recollection, argues Rashi, he makes clear that accusation against the people. (Commentary on Deuteronomy 1:19–24)

The author of the early rabbinic commentary *Tanna Debe Eliyahu* extends the indictment. Claiming that the people were ungrateful, he points out that, although Moses leads them out of Egypt, provides them with silver and gold booty from the Egyptians, and delivers them from Pharaoh's pursuing army at the Red Sea, they remain stubborn and unfaithful. Distrusting Moses and God, they not only complain bitterly about conditions in the desert but also demand that Moses send spies into the Land of Israel.

The author of *Tanna Debe Eliyahu* illustrates his interpretation by presenting his version of the confrontation between the people and Moses. Reading between the lines of Moses' recollection, he puts his own words into Moses' mouth, claiming that, in addition to what the Torah records of his speech, Moses also told the people: "Each one of you approached me, not just a few of you, but all adults and children, demanding that the spies be sent." In other words, it was the people who should bear the blame for sending the spies.

The author of *Tanna Debe Eliyahu* further maintains that, although they saw the fruit of the land, the grapes, the figs, and the pomegranates, they remained defiant, refusing to go forward and conquer the land. Thus they were punished and prevented from entering the Land of Israel. (29:27, pp. 144–146)

Who is responsible for evil?
Rabbi Judah Aryeh Loeb Alter in his commentary Sefat Emet *asks: Why did Moses agree to send the spies but then blame the people for sending them? Because, answers Rabbi Loeb, the people pressured Moses, forcing him to send them. Their insistence infected him, teaching that the sins of people can infect their leaders as well. (See A.Z. Friedman,* Wellsprings of Torah, *pp. 369–370.)*

Jerusalem was destroyed only because the people did not speak out and criticize one another for their wrongdoings. (Shabbat 119b)

Rabbi Jonah teaches: "Those who refuse to listen to criticism or to give it will die," meaning that "criticism" is the only way out of wrongdoing. (Commentary on Proverbs 15:10)

In his book, The Abandonment of the Jews: America and the Holocaust, 1941–1945 *(Pantheon, New York, 1984), author David S. Wyman examines the failure of leaders of the Western world to rescue Jews from extermination in Nazi death camps, raising the question of responsibility for speaking out in the face of evil. He writes: "Roosevelt, Churchill, and the Pope might have made clear to the Nazis their full awareness of the mass-murder program and their severe condemnation of it. If, in addition, Roosevelt and Churchill had threatened punishment for these crimes and offered asylum to the Jews, the Nazis at least would have ceased to believe that the West did not care what they were doing to the Jews. That might possibly have slowed the killing. And it might have hastened the decision of the SS, ultimately taken in late 1944, to end the extermination." (See pp. 331–340.)*

The punishment suffered by the wise who refuse to take part in the government is to live under the government of bad leaders. (Plato)

A demonstration will not solve the problem of poverty, the problem of housing, the problem in the school. But, at least, the demonstration creates a kind of constructive crisis that causes a community to see its problem and to begin moving toward acting on it. (Martin Luther King, Jr.)

Rabbi Moshe ben Chaim Alshekh argues that the people are not only unfaithful and defiant, but they deliberately deceive Moses. They lead him to believe that they require a strategic plan for conquering the land and for that reason are demanding a spy mission. Alshekh writes that the people also insist that the report of the spies not be given to Moses but to them, signaling their distrust of Moses as a leader. The people, Alshekh concludes, must, therefore, bear full responsibility for their deception of Moses and for rejecting his leadership. They cannot blame the spies for their punishment and exclusion from the Land of Israel. Their dishonesty and subterfuge led to disaster. (Commentary on Deuteronomy 1:7)

Modern Israeli commentator Nehama Leibowitz stresses the same point. Making reference to the interpretative work of biblical critic David Hoffman, Leibowitz explains the differences between the versions of the spy story in Numbers and in Deuteronomy. In Numbers, "Moses speaks as a historian recounting the events as they took place." In Deuteronomy, "He is delivering a moral discourse urging the people to learn the lesson of history.

"In his criticism of the people," Leibowitz writes, "Moses recalls that it was the people who initiated the idea of spying out the land. . . . He does so to be able to draw a moral, to emphasize the direct responsibility of their ancestors for their actions. They had wanted to send the spies in the first place, and their responsibility for what happened afterwards was even greater." Moses, says Leibowitz, "wishes to stress this point forcefully upon the descendants of that generation."

Leibowitz

Following this line of reasoning, Leibowitz also points out that "in the earlier account the spies appear as slanderers and misleaders of the people." However, "in the recounting of this incident . . . the main responsibility for the slander is no longer attached to the spies. Moses speaks of the people and accuses the Israelites as a whole and them alone."

Leibowitz concludes: "The Torah here wishes to teach us an important lesson. Human beings are put to the test by God at every moment of their existence . . . the ears hear and the heart is seduced. The question becomes: Is the listener who is misled by the seducer free from all moral responsibility? The Torah makes each person responsible for his or her actions. The listener has a choice of turning a deaf ear to evil and misleading words. Choice belongs to each of us. We have the duty to resist. . . . Each of us has to be his or her own leader, responsible for every action, and not just a cog in the vast machine called society." (*Studies in Devarim*, World Zionist Organization, Jerusalem, 1980, pp. 16–25)

In their distinction between the two versions of the spy mission into the Land of Israel, Jewish commentators raise critical ethical questions about human responsibility in the face of evil. They emphasize that it is not only the leaders who bear the guilt for the injustices and wrongdoings of society. Ordinary citizens are to be held accountable as well. Moses, they claim, meant to teach that lesson in his review of Israelite history.

The lesson remains an important one today. As British statesman Edmund Burke commented: "All that is necessary for the triumph of evil is that good people do nothing."

QUESTIONS FOR STUDY AND DISCUSSION

1. What are the rules the Torah and Jewish commentators lay down for making "just" judgments between disputing parties? How can these rules be applied to making judgments in arguments between family members, friends, and business associates?

2. Jewish law teaches that "a person who accepts money for acting as a judge renders verdicts that are valueless, and a person who accepts pay for testifying as a witness also renders valueless testimony." (*Mishnah Berachot* 4, 6) Given what the Torah and interpreters say about "showing partiality," what is wrong with accepting "pay" or a small gift for judgments and testimony?

3. In our Torah portion, Moses blames the Israelites for asking to send spies into the Land of Israel and for believing their report of doom about the impossibility of conquering it. Is that a fair accusation? Should the people or the leaders—including Moses and Aaron—bear the guilt? Who is really at fault?

4. In 1943, when the occupying Germans announced the roundup of the Jews of Denmark, an extraordinary rescue operation was set into motion, involving the Danish people and the Swedish government. Jews were hidden and then secretly ferried across to Sweden, where they remained in safety until the

end of the war. Of the 8,000 Jews of Denmark, only 400 were rounded up by the Nazis; 51 of them died in the Theresienstadt concentration camp. Is it possible for ordinary people to make a difference in the face of evil? Clearly, the Danish people did. What other examples are there? What do they have in common?

PARASHAT VA'ETCHANAN
Deuteronomy 3:23–7:11

Parashat Va'etchanan continues Moses' speeches to the Israelites just before his death. He pleads with God to allow him to enter the Land of Israel, but he is refused. He warns the people against falling into idolatry; reminds them to observe all the commandments given to them; and recalls their awesome experience at Mount Horeb, where they received the Ten Commandments. Moses also sets aside Bezer, Ramoth, and Golan as refuge cities for those who commit unintentional homicide. Proclaiming that God made a covenant with the Israelites at Mount Horeb, Moses recites the Ten Commandments. The people are overwhelmed and ask Moses to recite the rest of the commandments, promising to obey them. Afterwards, Moses tells them, "Hear, O Israel: *Adonai* is our God, *Adonai* is One. You shall love *Adonai* your God with all your heart and with all your soul and with all your might." Warning them against repeating their rebelliousness at Massah, Moses tells them, "Do what is right and good in the sight of *Adonai,* that it may go well with you. . . ." Finally, Moses informs the Israelites that they are not to spare the people who occupy their land nor intermarry with them. The Israelites are God's chosen and treasured people who will be loved by God if they remain loyal to God's covenant and commandments.

OUR TARGUM

·1·

Moses continues his last speeches to the Israelites while they are camped in a valley near Beth-peor on the east side of the Jordan River. He tells of pleading with God to allow him to enter the Land of Israel and of his disappointment at being refused. God instructs Moses to view the land from Pisgah, a high place on the east side of the Jordan River, and to advise Joshua about conquering the land.

· 2 ·

Moses tells the Israelites that God has given them laws and commandments by which to live when they enter the Land of Israel. They are to observe them faithfully and to teach them to their children. That will prove that they are a "wise and discerning people . . . a great nation."

He reminds the people of the time they stood with him at Mount Horeb (Sinai). The mountain was "ablaze with flames to the very skies, dark with the densest clouds," and God "commanded you to observe the Ten Commandments" and avoid making or worshiping idols. Moses warns them that failure to observe God's commandments will result in their being driven from their land and scattered among the nations. If they search for God with their hearts and souls, God will not fail them or forsake the covenant made with their ancestors.

Moses speaks of the unique relationship between God and the Jewish people. God spoke to them out of the fire at Mount Horeb, liberated them from bondage, and gave them the Land of Israel. "Know therefore this day and keep in mind that *Adonai* alone is God in heaven above and on earth below; there is no other. Observe God's laws and commandments . . . that you may long remain in the land that *Adonai* your God is giving you for all time."

· 3 ·

Moses sets aside three cities—Bezer, Ramoth, and Golan—as refuge places where those who have committed unintentional homicide may flee for justice.

· 4 ·

Moses continues by declaring that "God made a covenant with us at Horeb . . . out of the fire." He then repeats God's words to the people, the Ten Commandments: (1) I *Adonai* am your God who brought you out of the land of Egypt, the house of bondage. (2) You shall have no other gods beside Me. You shall not make for yourself a sculptured image. . . . (3) You shall not swear falsely by the name of *Adonai*. . . . (4) Observe the Sabbath day and keep it holy. . . . (5) Honor your father and your mother. . . . (6) You shall not murder. (7) You shall not commit adultery.

(8) You shall not steal. (9) You shall not bear false witness against your neighbor. (10) You shall not covet.

Recalling the revelation at Mount Horeb, Moses reminds the people of their fear of the fire and their request that he receive the Ten Commandments for them. He agreed and warned them to follow God's commandments. He told them, "Do not turn aside to the right or to the left: follow only the path that God has given you."

Moses then instructs them: "Hear, O Israel: *Adonai* is our God, *Adonai* is One. You shall love God with all your heart and with all your soul and with all your might. Take to heart these commandments. . . . Impress them upon your children. . . . Recite them when you are at home and when you are away. . . . Bind them between your eyes . . . inscribe them on the doorposts of your house."

To parents he adds, "When your child asks, 'What is the meaning of these laws and commandments?' explain: 'We were slaves to Pharaoh in Egypt and God freed us . . . that we might be given the land promised to our ancestors. We are to observe these commandments for our survival.'"

·5·

Moses speaks of the Israelites entering the Land of Israel and dislodging the Hittites, Girgashites, Amorites, Canaanites, Perizzites, Hivites, and Jebusites. He cautions the Israelites against intermarriage with these foreign people, reminding them that "God chose you to be a treasured people. . . ." Those who observe the commandments will be rewarded and those who do not will suffer destruction.

THEMES

Parashat Va'etchanan contains two important themes:

1. Deciphering the meaning of the *Shema*.
2. Loving God.

PEREK ALEF: *Can We Decipher the Meaning of the Shema?*

Of the 4,875 verses in the Torah, one stands out as the code of faith for Jews. Since the time of the Temple in Jerusalem, the words *Shema Yisrael, Adonai Elohenu, Adonai Echad,* "Hear, O Israel: *Adonai* is our God, *Adonai* is One," have been recited twice daily by pious Jews. They are among the first words taught to a young child and the last words recited at the time of death. Jewish martyrs have proudly pronounced them against forces of tyranny, and, through the centuries, they have constituted the most universally known Hebrew phrase in Jewish tradition.

crown of faith and proven true and enduring in human history." (pp. 1369–1370)

Despite these testimonials to the importance of the *Shema,* commentators of Torah raise questions about its meaning. And, as with other portions of Torah, they differ in their interpretations.

Rabbi Pinchas ben Hama claims that the Israelites first said the *Shema* as they were standing at Sinai; the early rabbis teach that it is an affirmation of the Jewish people's partnership with God. Other rabbis argue that the phrase "*Adonai* our God" means "God is our Source." In other words, human beings derive from God and are made "in the image of God." (*Deuteronomy Rabbah* 2:31, 35)

Hertz

Rashi

In evaluating the words of the *Shema,* Rabbi Joseph H. Hertz, once the Chief Rabbi of the British Empire, writes: "Throughout the entire realm of literature . . . there is probably no utterance to be found that can be compared in its intellectual and spiritual force, or in the influence it exerted upon the whole thinking and feeling of civilized humanity, than the six words that have become the battle cry of the Jewish people for more than twenty-five centuries." (*Authorized Daily Prayer Book,* Bloch Publishing Co., 1948, p. 269)

Rabbi W. Gunther Plaut, author of *The Torah: A Modern Commentary,* characterizes the *Shema* as "a precious gem . . . a diamond set into a

Rashi offers a different approach. Living in eleventh-century France, in a world of conflicting faiths, he hopes that in time human thought will evolve to the point where all human beings embrace one notion of God and achieve peace. For him the words "Hear, O Israel: *Adonai* our God, *Adonai* is One" translate into "Hear, O Israel: *Adonai,* whom we recognize as our God, will one day be accepted by all people as One, and their belief in one God will unite us as one human family."

In this view, Rashi reflects the perspective of the *Alenu* prayer recited at the conclusion of Jewish worship services. In the words of Deuteronomy 4:39, the *Alenu* declares: "Know therefore this day and keep in mind that *Adonai* alone is God in heaven above and on earth below; there is no other." *Alenu* then continues with the hope that all evil will be ended, that the world will be "perfected under God's rule," and that all human beings will acknowledge that "God is One." (Zechariah 14:9)

In *Gates of Prayer: The New Union Prayerbook* (Chaim Stern, editor, Central Conference of American Rabbis, New York, 1975, p. 620), a more modern version of the *Alenu* mirrors Rashi's interpretation: "Eternal God, we face the morrow with hope made stronger by the vision of Your kingdom, a world where poverty and war are banished, where injustice and hate are gone. Teach us more and more to share the pain of others, to heed Your call for justice, to pursue the blessing of peace. Help us, O God, to gain victory over evil, to bring nearer the day when all the world shall be one."

Rambam (Maimonides)

For Maimonides the *Shema* is not a statement of hope that all human beings will eventually agree that "God is One" but a theological declaration that "the Cause of all existence is One." In his "Thirteen Principles of Faith," Maimonides declares that God's unity is eternal and unique, that God creates all that is and continues to create all that will be, and that God has no body or form. In other writings, he holds that God's power may not be compared to any other power known to human beings. "God is not subject to physical limitations or definitions. . . . God's power is endless."

The *Shema,* says Maimonides, affirms the unity of all that exists and will exist. God's power embraces everything. It is the primary Cause uniting the countless stars of the cosmos; the green globe of earth with its complex web of life; and the yesterday, today, and tomorrow of humanity. In the declaration of the *Shema,* Jews acknowledge that God is not mortal, not limited by human frailties, and not a symbol reducible

to stone, wood, or artistic images. God, Maimonides argues, is the One Power that creates all that is. (See Philip Cohen, *Rambam on the Torah,* Rubin Mass Ltd., Jerusalem, 1985, pp. 146–147.)

Ramban (Nachmanides)

Nachmanides sees in the words of the *Shema* a very personal statement by Moses. He points out that, in most other cases where Moses uses the words "Hear, O Israel," he follows them with *"Adonai your* God," not with *"Adonai our* God." Why, asks Nachmanides, does Moses in this particular situation choose to say *our* God?

Nachmanides speculates that Moses is concerned with appearances. God has liberated the people from slavery, has provided for their needs in the desert, and has given them the Ten Commandments. Now, in reminding the people of all God has done, Moses does not want to exclude himself. In declaring God's unity with words of the *Shema,* he makes it clear that he is including himself as a witness to God's goodness and power.

> שְׁמַע יִשְׂרָאֵל, יְהוָֹה אֱלֹהֵינוּ, יְהוָֹה אֶחָד.
> Hear, O Israel: *Adonai* is our God, *Adonai* is One.

Nachmanides bases his interpretation on the actual Torah text. In the Torah text, the last letter, *ayin,* of the first word of the *Shema* and the last letter, *dalet,* of the last word are enlarged. Combined, the letters spell the word *ed,* meaning "witness." In reciting the *Shema,* Jews bear "witness" to God's unity and power. (Comments on Deuteronomy 6:4)

Rabbi Abraham Samuel Benjamin Sofer, a nineteenth-century Hungarian interpreter, also calls attention to the way in which the *Shema* is worded. The verse, says Sofer, could have been written "Hear, O Israel: *Adonai* is our God and is One." Instead, the word *Adonai* appears twice. Why?

Sofer speculates that Moses meant to teach that all human experience comes from God. What we know as good and evil, our moments of joy and sadness, all our successes and disappointments, and our good or bad fortune—all are derived from God. At times, Sofer explains, there is a tendency to believe, as did many other early religious traditions, that there are gods for good and gods for evil. Contradicting this assumption, Moses tells the people: "Hear, O Israel: *Adonai* our God provides all the goodness we experience, and *Adonai* our God is the author of the harsh judgments we endure. *Adonai* is One." (See discussion in B.S. Jacobson, *Meditations on the Torah,* p. 271.)

Contemporary commentator Rabbi Shlomo Riskin holds a view close to Sofer's. Carefully analyzing the Hebrew words *Shema Yisrael, Adonai Elohenu, Adonai Echad,* he notes that two words are used for God. The first is *Adonai;* the second is *Elohenu.* Early Jewish tradition, says Riskin, associates God's qualities of mercy and love with the word *Adonai* and God's qualities of judgment with *Elohim. (Elohenu* means "our God.")

Riskin maintains that, when Moses first spoke the words of the *Shema,* he meant to clarify a significant problem faced by the Israelites and by all people as well: the problem of understanding God's unity and the way God works in our lives and in the universe. "When things go smoothly," Riskin writes, "when one feels a warm glow of love, success, and good health, one naturally attributes this to the good, compassionate nature of God *(Adonai).* But, when sudden tragedy strikes, the death of a loved one, national calamity, an earthquake, one feels the awesome and inexplicable power of God *(Elohim).* The holy *Zohar* teaches that this seeming split in God's character is a result of our imperfect vision. If we could see more clearly, we'd understand that everything God does is done for the good of humanity. Perhaps we can't always perceive it, but how can a finite creature be expected to fathom the Infinite Will?"

The message of the *Shema,* Riskin adds, "is that, if our eyes (and ears) were truly opened, we would comprehend that everything in the world, both the things we think of as being clearly good and those other things that frighten us with their might, emerges from a compassionate and loving God; in other words, '*Adonai* is One.' " Within Jewish tradition, Riskin concludes, we teach that "just as we praise God for the good so must we praise God for the evil. If we truly understand what the *Zohar* teaches, then we will understand that there is no evil." (*Jerusalem Post,* week of August 12, 1989, p. 23)

What the Shema is for and against
The Shema *"is against the plurality of small gods and half-gods and no gods; it is against the fragmentizing idolatry of worshiping a part for a whole. . . . It is a unity against the duality that would neatly package life into good and evil compartments and assign evil to a lesser scapegoat god, leaving to the chief god the dignity of presiding over unalloyed good. . . ."*

The Shema *"is for the common parenthood of God . . . the unity of humanity. It is for that diversity found in a family. . . . The* Shema *says: Hear, thou! God is One; therefore, God's children must be one."* (Jacob J. Weinstein, The Place of Understanding, *Bloch Publishing Co., New York, 1959, pp. 126–127)*

"Hear, O Israel . . ." means that every Jew is a member . . . of a community that extends not only in many lands but throughout history.

"Adonai our God . . ." means whatever be our condition . . . we will not . . . deny life, despair of the ultimate vindication of righteousness. . . .

"Adonai is One . . ." means this is not a universe in which evil has a chance of winning. . . . The ultimate authority, the final sovereign is not the force of army and legion but the God who in time will assert sovereignty. (Morris Adler, The Voice Still Speaks, *pp. 372–373)*

Can we truly believe, however, that "there is no evil" and that this is the message of the *Shema?* Rabbi Leo Baeck, leader of German Jewry during the Holocaust years, probes this significant question. "The Jewish spirit has always sought to grasp the oneness of all reality. All reality, whether unfolding itself in one sphere or in the other, expresses one great unity to the Jewish spirit. . . . Only the One God exists, and, therefore, there is only one order, no matter how manifold its appearances, how contradictory its representations. . . . Within every thing, therefore, there exists an inner reality—unique, one, concealed, unfathomable, infinite, eternal—that is its foundation. . . . Everything proceeds from the One God; everything returns to the One God." (*This People Israel: The Meaning of Jewish Existence,* Albert H. Friedlander, translator, Jewish Publication Society, Philadelphia, 1965. pp. 7, 14, 23)

Baeck's view seems to differ from Riskin's. It is not that there is "no evil" or suffering. Quite the contrary. The suffering of human beings and the evil they experience is real and from God. "Suffering becomes a test of human power to overcome afflictions," says Baeck. He concludes, "The wisdom of Judaism—its very history so devised it—is that it sees life as a task imposed upon human beings by God. Suffering is part of that task; every creative individual experiences it. Through suffering human beings experience those conflicts that give tragic significance to their will to fulfillment." In other words, not only is evil real but in the battle against it human beings test their strength. In reciting the *Shema,* Jews set their energies toward resolving conflicts and transforming them "into unity and harmony." (*The Essence of Judaism,* Schocken Books, New York, 1948, pp. 136–138)

While Baeck does not deny the "reality" of evil, his solution argues that God, who is all-powerful and all-knowing, actually causes evil so that human beings will be tested to triumph over it. Modern Jewish philosopher Rabbi Mordecai M. Kaplan disagrees. He points out that, if we say that God is responsible for evil, then we must accept that God brought on all the atrocities of history and that God is responsible for earthquakes, famine, floods, and other natural catastrophes. Such a conclusion, argues Kaplan, makes God into an evil monster!

Instead, Kaplan believes that we can resolve this difficult problem by "assuming that God's omnipotence [all-powerfulness] is not an actually realized fact at any point of time but a potential fact." If we take into consideration that God is eternal (exists forever), then it is possible to understand "that the evil that now mars the cosmos will ultimately be eliminated" by human beings who, as God's creation, are seeking to "reduce the amount of evil in the world." Evil, therefore, is not, as Baeck says, deliberately and knowingly placed by God in our lives or in the universe as a test for human beings, but, rather, it represents an obstacle to the good that God is seeking to achieve.

Kaplan clarifies his point by answering the question: "Why did God make polio?" He writes: "God did *not* make polio. God is always helping us human beings to make this a better world, but the world cannot at once become the kind of world God would like it to be. When human beings make use of the intelligence God gives them, they learn more and more of the laws of health, by which all kinds of illness can be prevented or cured." In this way, concludes Kaplan, human beings help God eliminate the "evil that now mars the cosmos." For Kaplan, the *Shema* is an expression of the special partnership between God and the Jewish people in the battle against suffering and in the triumph of good over evil. (*Questions Jews Ask,* pp. 115–120)

Rabbi David Hartman also speaks of the *Shema* as an expression of the partnership between the Jewish people and God. He writes: "In reciting the *Shema,* we hear God addressing the community. The emphasis, so to speak, is 'Hear, O Israel: study, reflect, and be attentive to the revelatory message of Torah.' It is the moment of commitment of the community to God and to God's Torah. In the *Shema* . . . one captures the felt immediacy of the revelatory moment of Sinai. God invites the community to enter into the covenant."

Hartman's explanation places Moses in the position of using the words of the *Shema* to remind the people of their experience with God at Mount Sinai, where they received the Ten Commandments. Since that time, Hartman says, Jews recall standing at Sinai when they recite Moses' words. In saying the *Shema* they reenter the covenant of ritual and ethical mitzvot, pledging themselves to God "who commands a total way of life." (*A Living Covenant,* The Free Press,

New York, 1985, pp. 164–165)

Rabbi Jacob ben Isaac Ashkenazi of Yanof, author of *Tze'enah u-Re'enah,* compares reciting the *Shema* to receiving a cherished love letter. "When you say the *Shema,*" he writes, "it should be as if you are reading a letter from the king, which was written to you only today and which you cherish. You listen to each and every word. So should you pay careful attention to each and every word of the *Shema.*" (Comment on Deuteronomy 6:6)

Throughout the centuries, Jews have recited the *Shema* as the most important expression of their faith. They have regarded the words as "love letters," but they have also argued over their meanings, deciphering various messages as if these words contained clues to understanding their relationship to God. Today, the explorations and debates continue. The declaration of Jewish faith remains a source of inspiration and challenge.

PEREK BET: *Is It Possible to Love God?*

In defining "love," psychologist Erich Fromm asserts that it is "an activity, not a passive affect; it is a 'standing in,' not a 'falling for.' " Fromm goes on to explain that "the active character of love can be described by stating that love is primarily *giving,* not receiving. . . . Giving is the highest expression of potency [power]. In the very act of giving, I experience my strength, my wealth, my power. This experience of heightened vitality and potency fills me with joy. I experience myself as overflowing, spending, alive. . . . Giving is more joyous than receiving, not because it is a deprivation, but because in the act of giving lies the expression of my aliveness." (*The Art of Loving,* Harper and Row Publishers, Inc., New York, 1974, pp. 18–19)

Following the statement of the *Shema* in Deuteronomy 6:4, Moses commands the Israelites: "You shall love *Adonai* your God with all your heart and with all your soul and with all your might." This commandment is a cornerstone of Jewish tradition. It is recited together with the *Shema* at worship and is considered by rabbinic tradition as one of the 613 mitzvot, the commandments of Jewish practice.

The statement, however, raises serious questions. Given Erich Fromm's definition of love, is it possible to love God? What could Moses have meant by this commandment? Can "love" for either a human being or God be commanded? How is such love expressed?

Early rabbinic interpreters also struggled with these questions. In the *Tanna Debe Eliyahu* (pp. 139–141), they claim that the mitzvah "to love God" is "the most important commandment of the Torah" and that it entails causing others to love God. For instance, if one studies Torah and acts honestly and fairly in business dealings, then others will say: "Look at the caring and ethical behavior of those who say they love God. Seeing the direct results of such love, they will be inspired to become lovers of God and to teach their children to study Torah and follow its commandments."

Furthermore, say the rabbis, loving God means making no distinction between the way Jews deal with Jews and the way Jews deal with non-Jews. To love God means to treat every human being with respect and to act honestly, justly, and kindly to all. Those who, by their actions, show their love for God set an example for others. It is God's influence on their lives that makes them witnesses to God's power.

Another issue raised by rabbinic commentators is the distinction between loving and fearing God. To show this distinction, they relate the story of a king with two servants. One loved the king; the other feared him. Once the king went on a year-long voyage. The servant who loved him started a beautiful garden, tended it carefully, and, when the king returned, presented him with heaping platters of fruits. The king was delighted and filled with gratitude. Seeing the grateful response of the king, the servant who feared him quickly found some dry fruits and brought them before him. Realizing that this gift was an afterthought, the king was displeased.

To love God means to know the joy of "generosity." Love leads to giving, to sharing one's creativity with another. Fear cripples our capacity to share. It drains our energies from positive efforts to efforts to protect and serve the self. In the act of loving we concentrate all our efforts to provide thoughtful contributions. We use our talents to create "heaping platters of fruits." Loving God, say the ancient rabbis, is like all true loving, an expression of joyful and creative gratitude. (*Yoma* 86a)

Rashi also seeks to define the meaning of loving God. On the basis of comments in the *Sifre,* he argues that the Torah itself offers an explanation: To the commandment "to love God" it adds the words "with all your heart, with all your soul, and with all your might." "With all your heart" means we should serve God with all our powers for goodness, compassion, and charity, as well as with our powers for competition, success, and physical strength. "With all your soul" means we should be ready to give our lives, if necessary, for the principles of our faith. "With all your might" means we should be willing to use our property and wealth to perform acts of charity that promote the survival of our people. Rashi concludes that "lovers of God" see the commandments of Torah as neither antiquated nor out of touch with reality; they see them as always relevant and challenging to their times. (Commentary on Deuteronomy 6:4–6)

While Maimonides agrees with the rabbis of the *Tanna Debe Eliyahu* and Rashi on many points, he clearly views the commandment "to love God" from another perspective. Charity and compassion are sufficient. For him, "loving God with all your heart" is an intellectual commitment. It is a matter of study and critical contemplation. "In the act of contemplation," Maimonides argues, "you come closer to understanding God and to reaching that stage of joy where love of God is bound to follow."

Maimonides has in mind the study of not only the commandments of Torah but also the sciences, including philosophy. "Love of God depends upon knowledge," he says. "Therefore, we should devote ourselves to understanding and becoming knowledgeable in the skills and sciences through which we develop appreciation of God and of our ethical responsibilities. It is only when we comprehend the real nature of our world and universe that we can penetrate the wisdom of God and attain to the love of God."

Loving God, however, is more than the pursuit of knowledge about Torah and "the nature of our world." Recalling the work of Abraham, the founder of Jewish tradition, Maimonides points out that Abraham took upon himself the teaching to potential converts of the Jewish view of God and morality. In this way he brought them to a love for the one God and welcomed them as a part of the Jewish people. "He made God beloved of many people." For Maimonides it is not enough to study or perform the mitzvot with devotion. Loving God means reaching out to those without faith and bringing them in as converts to Judaism. (*Mishneh Torah, Teshuvah* 3, 6, 10; *Sefer ha-Mitzvot,* Positive Commandments #3)

 Luzzatto   *Leibowitz*

Loving God

Those who set God before them and are exclusively concerned with doing God's pleasure and observing God's commandments will be called lovers of God . . . the love of God is not a separate commandment but an underlying principle of all the commandments. The love itself cannot be the subject of a command. (Samuel David Luzzatto. See Nehama Leibowitz, Studies in Devarim, *p. 65.)*

Psychologist Erich Fromm observes that "the basis for our need to love lies in the experience of separateness and the resulting need to overcome the anxiety of separateness by the experience of union. The religious form of love, that which is called the love of God, is, psychologically speaking, not different. It springs from the need to overcome separateness and to achieve union." (The Art of Loving, *p. 53)*

The only way to attain to a real fear and love of God, to a genuine longing for God through worship, to a comprehension of God is through prayer offered with self-sacrifice and burning enthusiasm. (Rabbi Kalonymus Kalmon, as quoted in Louis Jacobs, Hasidic Prayer, *Schocken Books, New York, 1978, p. 20)*

An individual unable to pray is permitted to engage in telling jokes to awaken a sense of love in his mind. Perhaps, the individual will then say: "If I have laughter from such nonsense, how much more should I appreciate the delights God has given me." As a result, such a person will recite the prayers in love and awe. (Maggid of Meseritch. See Louis Jacobs, Hasidic Prayer, *p. 51.)*

Bachya ben Joseph ibn Pakuda, the author of *Duties of the Heart,* agrees with Maimonides that one achieves a love of God through "contemplation and study" and that the love of God is expressed by reaching out to instruct and welcome converts. He differs, however, in his emphasis. "This love," he writes, "requires that a person should contemplate the basis and principles of the commandments . . . [such contemplation] will bring much delight."

Pakuda argues that worldly concerns often prevent a person from such "contemplation" and "delight." To overcome the stress and temptations of daily concerns and the pursuit of riches, which prevent us from achieving the "love of God," he maintains that we must "retreat from worldliness, from the pleasures of the material world, and from physical desires." Those who seek the true love of God must "commune with God in solitude, dedicate themselves to God alone, trusting, craving, and serving God without any other interests." (See chap. 3; also B.S. Jacobson, *Meditations on the Torah,* pp. 263–274.)

Modern commentator Rabbi W. Gunther Plaut rejects Pakuda's notion of retreating from the world to commune "with God in solitude" as the means to loving God. Instead, Plaut returns to the suggestion of the early rabbinic interpreters that the love of God is expressed through mitzvah-deeds. "It is our attention to the mitzvot that will make us as well as others aware of the One in whose name they are performed, and, the greater our devotion and concentration upon the mitzvah and its Giver, the more likely we will be to enter into the context of pure love. . . ." Plaut concludes: "Each mitzvah done in the right spirit is an act of loving God. It can be done everywhere and anywhere, wherever the opportunity for mitzvot exists, and it is, therefore, not exclusively the consequence of spiritual contemplation." (*The Torah: A Modern Commentary,* pp. 1370–1371)

 Peli

Pinchas Peli agrees with Plaut's emphasis on doing mitzvot as the primary expression of our love for God. He maintains, however, that, while the love of God results "from the awareness of the oneness of God," it is proven in the way it influences us to set an example for others.

Peli calls attention to Moses' command "to take to heart these words that I command you this day. Teach them diligently to your children. . . ." He explains that "the teaching with which we are concerned here is not done by passing on information or by preaching or issuing orders but by personal example, which by its sheer sincerity and passion should be qualified to impress our children or students. . . ." Peli writes, "Your children will be taught by the fact that you yourself practice your religion. . . . Action and thought must go together in the life of the truly religious person." ("Torah Today," in the *Jerusalem Post,* August 10, 1985, p. 10)

Defining the meaning of love and the way it is expressed among human beings continues as a major subject of debate among students of human behavior. Is love a matter of trust, mutual respect, a sense of responsibility for one's self and others, a means of surmounting the fear of loneliness, a biological drive to maintain human survival? Is it a magical, awesome gift of God? And, if it is difficult to explain the meaning of love among human beings, the notion of loving God is equally perplexing.

For that reason, Jewish commentators continue the struggle of deciphering Moses' command to the Israelites: "You shall love *Adonai* your God. . . ." In all their discussions, however, they fail to recognize that love is not static, but dynamic. It evolves, grows, matures. The love expressed by a child is not the same as that felt by a young adult or that achieved by an elderly person who has a life filled with experience. Love is a construct of many feelings: respect, knowledge, loyalty, caring, mercy. It is expressed in uplifting the needy, in the pursuit of justice, in the nurturing of others, in the warmth of an embrace, and in the passion shared by two human beings.

Perhaps Moses, the wise and aged leader of the Israelites, understood that love is not a single expression but rather a mysterious and wonderful gift evolving from human beings and expressed in a variety of ways. That understanding may account for his command: "You shall love *Adonai* your God with all your heart, with all your soul, and with all your might." Moses may have meant that the love of God is achieved only when we develop our emerging powers of mind (heart), spirit (soul), and physical strength (might). Love of God grows, changes, and ripens. As with love among human beings, it is the achievement of a lifetime, not of a moment. For that reason, Moses commands that its cultivation be given the highest priority in every aspect of our lives.

QUESTIONS FOR STUDY AND DISCUSSION

1. Rabbi Milton Steinberg observes: "In proclaiming the oneness of God . . . the prophets . . . were bent on establishing the principles that reality is an order, not an anarchy; that humanity is a unity, not a hodgepodge; and that one universal law of righteousness holds sway over all human beings." (*Basic Judaism,* Harcourt Brace, 1947, pp. 42–43) Given the discussion of the *Shema* by our interpreters, what is the continuing importance of monotheism set forth by Moses and the prophets of Judaism?

2. Rabbi Leo Baeck comments: "In Judaism, love towards God is never a mere feeling; it belongs to the sphere of ethical activity." *(The Essence of Judaism,* p. 129) Do the interpreters of Moses' statement "You shall love *Adonai* your God . . ." agree? Which definition of the "love of God" makes most sense? Why?

3. Given Moses Maimonides' views on loving God, should Jews proselytize?

PARASHAT EKEV
Deuteronomy 7:12–11:25

Parashat Ekev continues the speeches of Moses to the Israelites. He tells them that, if they maintain their covenant with God by observing all the commandments, God will make them fruitful and victorious over their enemies. Reminding them of their forty years of wandering through the wilderness, Moses tells them: "God subjected you to the hardship of hunger . . . then gave you manna . . . in order to teach you that human beings do not live on bread alone. . . ." He then warns them that after settling in their land and enjoying its fruits, they should not arrogantly assume: "My own power and the might of my own hand have won this wealth for me." Nor, continues Moses, should they conclude that it is for their virtue that God allows them to defeat their enemies and conquer their land. Rather, it is punishment of the inhabitants for idolatry, and it is God's fulfillment of the covenant made with Abraham, Isaac, and Jacob. Moses recalls the disloyalty of the people; how they built the golden calf when he was receiving the Ten Commandments on Mount Horeb; how they rebelled at Kadesh-barnea; and how he intervened with God to save them, granting them another set of the tablets on which the Ten Commandments were engraved. Moses recounts the death and burial of Aaron. He also tells the people that God wants them to "cut away the thickening about their hearts," observe the commandments, and learn from their history how God freed them from Egyptian slavery and led them through the desert. If you keep the commandments, Moses promises, God will dislodge all nations before you. No one will stand before your power.

OUR TARGUM

· 1 ·

Continuing his speeches to the Israelites before they enter the Land of Israel, Moses warns them that "if you obey these laws and observe them faithfully" God will keep the covenant made with Abraham, Isaac, and Jacob. He informs the people that their land will be fruitful and without disease, and he tells them they will be victorious over their enemies.

He reminds the people of their journey through the wilderness. God, Moses explains, tested them with hardships to determine if they would keep the commandments. They received manna to eat, "in order to teach you that human beings do not live on bread alone, but they may live on anything that *Adonai* decrees."

Moses cautions the Israelites against arrogance, advising that, when eating from the land, "give thanks to *Adonai* your God for the good land that has been given you."

He warns: "When you have eaten your fill, and have built fine houses to live in, and your herds and flocks have multiplied, and your silver and gold have increased, and everything you own has prospered, beware that you do not grow boastful and forget *Adonai* your God—who freed you from the land of Egypt, the house of bondage; who led you through the . . . wilderness . . . who fed you with manna." Be careful not to say: "My own power and the might of my own hand have won this wealth for me. Remember that it is *Adonai* your God who gives you the power to get wealth, in fulfillment of the covenant that God made on oath with your ancestors (Abraham, Isaac, and Jacob), as is still the case."

· 2 ·

Moses also warns the Israelites: After you have been victorious over your enemies, do not say that "God has enabled me to occupy this land because of my virtues." Moses points out that God has enabled the Israelites to possess the land by dispossessing their enemies because of their "wickedness." God has also given them the land in fulfillment of the covenant with Abraham, Isaac, and Jacob.

· 3 ·

Recalling the time when he climbed Mount Horeb [Sinai] and brought back the Tablets of the Covenant with the Ten Commandments, Moses reminds the Israelites that their ancestors built a golden calf. He tells the people that God said to him: "I see that this is a stiffnecked people. Let Me alone and I will destroy them and blot out their name from under heaven, and I will make you a nation far more numerous than they."

Moses reports that after shattering the Tablets of the Covenant, he sided with the people, arguing with God: "Do not annihilate Your very own people. . . . Else the country from which You freed us will say, 'It was because *Adonai* was powerless to bring them into the land that was promised them, and because God hated them, that God brought them out to have them die in the wilderness.'" (See discussion of parallel text in *A Torah Commentary for Our Times*, Volume II, *Parashat Ki Tisa*, Exodus 30:11–34:35, pp. 77–85.)

Moses relates that God gave him new Tablets of the Covenant with the Ten Commandments and told him to resume the journey toward the Land of Israel. Moses also recounts the death and burial of his brother, Aaron.

· 4 ·

"And now, O Israel, what does *Adonai* your God demand of you?" Moses eloquently asks the people. God, he declares, demands that they keep the commandments. "Mark, the heavens to their uttermost reaches belong to *Adonai* your God, the earth and all that is on it! Yet it was to your ancestors that *Adonai* was drawn in love for them, so that God chose you, their direct descendants, from among all peoples."

For those reasons, Moses continues, "Cut away the thickening about your hearts and stiffen your necks no more. For *Adonai* your God is God supreme . . . upholding the cause of the fatherless and the widow, befriending the stranger . . . with food and clothing. You too must befriend the stranger. . . . You must revere *Adonai* your God."

THEMES

Parashat Ekev contains two important themes:

1. Arrogance and gratitude.
2. "Circumcising" the heart.

PEREK ALEF: *Warning against Arrogance*

Moses raises important ethical considerations in these speeches to the people before they enter the Land of Israel and before he goes to die on Mount Nebo. Recalling their difficult years of wandering through the desert, he tells them that God has tested us with hunger, long days of hot sun, and long cold nights. All that we were given to eat was manna. The years were filled with harsh trials.

Moses, however, does not focus only on the past. He worries about the future. He foresees a time when the Israelites will be comfortable, prosperous, and secure in their land. They will have defeated all their enemies and will be enjoying a flourishing economy. He wonders what the state of their spiritual health will be in such a future era of victory and abundance. Unsure of what they will choose to do, Moses presents them with four guidelines:

Guideline One: Remember the hardships of your past and how you were tested for forty years in the desert to teach you that human beings do not live on bread alone but on what God commands.

Guideline Two: God is bringing you into a good land where you will lack nothing. When you have eaten your fill, give thanks to *Adonai* your God for the good land that has been given you.

Guideline Three: When you are satisfied, have built fine houses, and have increased your herds, gold, and silver, beware of your heart growing haughty, of forgetting God's commandments, of saying: "My power and the might of my own hand have won this wealth for me!"

Guideline Four: After you have defeated your enemies and you occupy the land, do not say to yourselves: "God has enabled me to occupy this land because of my virtues."

Several commentators note Moses' concern as expressed in his guidelines and ask: Why this anxiety about how the Israelites will deal with their future victories and prosperity? Why does Moses focus on their response to success?

Early rabbinic interpreters provide a clue in their discussion of *Guideline Two* in which Moses commands the people: "When you have eaten your fill, give thanks to *Adonai* your God for the good land that has been given you." Explaining this guideline, talmudic commentators point out that it was the catalyst that led the rabbis of the Great Assembly in Jerusalem to create the *Birkat ha-Mazon,* the blessing recited at the end of each meal. Concerned with fulfilling their "debt" to God, they reasoned that "whoever eats and enjoys fruits from God's world without pronouncing a prayer of gratitude steals God's property."

Rabbinic interpreters believed that Moses was deeply worried about the Israelites after their entering the Land of Israel. He feared they would settle in their land, enjoy its fruits, and conclude that they owed nothing to God. Moses presumed they would forget about all that God had done for them and reach the conclusion that they alone were responsible for their harvest of plenty.

For this reason, say the rabbis, Moses warns the Israelites not to eat without pronouncing blessings of thanksgiving, not to enjoy the fruits of the land without acknowledging God with words of gratitude. He compares "eating" and "drinking" without reciting a prayer of thanks to "stealing." (*Berachot* 33a–35a)

Rabbi Nachman and Rabbi Yochanan connect ingratitude not only to the dangers of "stealing from God" but also to "forgetting" and "denying" God. Moses, they argue, is concerned that the Israelites will enter the land, enjoy great prosperity, and forget all the commandments God has given them. Surrounded by abundance, they will grow arrogant and deny God's claim on them. Such "forgetting" will lead to abandon-ing both their moral and ritual traditions. It will bring an end to the sacred society they are seeking to create. (*Berachot* 49b and *Sotah* 4b)

Ramban (Nachmanides)

Nachmanides also underscores the importance of Moses' emphasis upon "remembering." He claims that the Israelites, about to conquer the Land of Israel and enjoy its fruits, will assume that they alone have brought about all of their victories and are responsible for the bountiful harvests of their fields. Such a conclusion will be logical. After all they are strong men, people of courage and determination. They will have prevailed in war, and the produce of the land will convince them that they alone are the creators of their destiny. For that reason, says Nachmanides, Moses instructs them: "When you are about to say, 'My power and the might of my own hand have won this wealth for me!' *remember. . . .*"

Nachmanides points out that, for Moses, "remembering" is an antidote to arrogance. He explains that the great leader understands the tendency of human beings to take credit for their accomplishments and victories. Self-congratulations are always a dangerous temptation. So Moses warns them to recall their history and cool their pride by remembering that it is God who liberated them from the slavery of Egypt, where they had no power; and it is God who sustained them in the desert wilderness, where they were helpless and hungry. When they are dwelling in comfortable homes, celebrating the bounty of harvests and their wealth, they are advised to recall that it is God who gives the power to accumulate riches. And, when they are about to boast of their victories and gloat about their virtues, they are to recall that it is God who gave them the power to destroy their enemies.

> **The dangers of pride**
> *The people of Israel are compared to a vine to teach us that just as a vine has large and small clusters of grapes, the larger ones hanging lower*

than the smaller ones, the greater a person is (the heavier his wisdom), the profounder his humility.

King Solomon teaches that pride causes a person to speak dishonestly. It forces a person to deviate from the truth and to make accusations that are unfounded. God weeps over those who are filled with pride. (Bachya ben Asher, Kad ha-Kemach, Encyclopedia of Torah Thoughts, *Charles B. Chavel, translator, Shilo Publishing House, Inc., New York, 1980, pp. 130–136)*

Nachmanides maintains that such recollections, precisely at the moment of celebration, place pride into perspective. They moderate human claims to glory and the dangers of self-centered flattery. History humbles human beings. It prevents arrogant assumptions about human power by setting victories and defeats into the larger and more mysterious context of all life. In his warnings to the Israelites, Moses seeks to teach them that all their bountiful harvests, their wealth and amazing triumphs are not the work of their hands alone but are gifts of God. (Comments on Deuteronomy 8:18–9:4)

By bread alone
Human beings do not live from physical bread . . . but only by God's power, which went forth at the time of creation and which caused bread to come into existence. It is from this spiritual essence that human beings live because it is the food that provides nourishment for the soul. (From Likutei Torah, *as found in A.Z. Friedman,* Wellsprings of Torah, *p. 387)*

Rabbi Moshe ben Chaim Alshekh agrees with Nachmanides. He comments that "the person who enjoys exceptional wealth and apparent good fortune" must deal with powerful temptations. It is difficult, he explains, not to "incline toward arrogance" and "the feeling that one is the architect of one's own good fortune independent of God." The danger of such feelings, says Alshekh, is that they often lead a person away from following God's commandments.

The process of moving away from God's commandments, Alshekh argues, "is gradual, almost imperceptible in its progress." It begins "by observing the commandments with the expectation of some material reward. Next, one eats without giving thanks or credit to God. Finally, one takes the credit for successes and bounty and then rejects God and turns to idol worship." Moses, says Alshekh, understood these dangers, and this explains his guidelines to the people. (Commentary to Deuteronomy 7:4–8:14)

Leibowitz

Modern commentator Nehama Leibowitz echoes the conclusions of both Nachmanides and Alshekh. She points out that Moses' observations focus on the tendency of human arrogance and the resulting dangers in forgetting human reliance upon God. "In blindness," she writes, "human beings tend to detect the guiding hand of God only when it is visible in miracles, as had been the case with Israel during the whole of their progress through the wilderness. They fail to see the hidden miracles performed for them continually, even when the world around them . . . seems to be going on as usual."

Moses, Leibowitz seems to be saying, is intent on warning the Israelites against such "blindness." He is anxious that they retain their sense of awe about the world and their unique history. This explains his reminder to them of God's power at work in their past. "Recollection of visible miracles," she concludes, "is designed to open our eyes to the hidden ones that are the foundation of the whole Torah . . . to awaken our faith in the direct intervention of God." (See *Studies in Devarim*, pp. 90–96.)

Rabbi Morris Adler sees in Moses' guidelines something beyond that suggested by previous commentators. He suggests that the awareness that "human beings do not live on bread alone" is "the highest objective of all religious enterprise and aspiration." Adler argues that, in this "great primary statement," Moses is claiming that human beings are "not only body, but also mind."

They are capable of thought and do not realize their potential unless their intellectual powers are awakened to ask questions and seek answers. "Intellectual curiosity is one of the most stirring and significant aspects of human life. . . . When this capacity develops to its fullest, you get scientific knowledge; you get the understanding of the world about us. . . ."

Moses seeks to stress the importance of the human mind by warning the Israelites that feeding the body bread is not enough. Human beings require intellectual nourishment as well. Education must be given highest priority in human affairs because it is the way the intellect is cultivated and evolves.

Adler, however, believes that, when Moses warns "human beings do not live on bread alone," he also means to emphasize that human beings are seekers both of good and of faith. They cannot live without exercising their sense of justice, their sensitivity to what is right and fair. Nor can they exist without acknowledging that "there is mystery in this world; there are vistas of which our limited human understanding can have only the faintest and vaguest of comprehension."

Moses, Adler seems to be suggesting, means to counter the arrogance of those who declare, "My own power and the might of my own hand have won this wealth for me," or who assume that their victories and harvests are of their own proud making. He senses the dangers of their "moral callousness," their selfish concerns, their "loss of obligation" to use their talents and abilities to benefit others, and their impaired understanding that human beings are "dependent upon cosmic forces" that sustain all life. Through his warnings, Adler argues, Moses is urging upon the Israelites the wisdom of gratitude and humility that ultimately leads to responsibility. "True gratitude," he concludes, "always flowers in obligation."

Nearly all of our commentators see in Moses' guidelines significant lessons. They single out arrogance and pride as dangers that lead to moral insensitivity, corruption, and the denial of God. Moses, they believe, is suggesting that the antidote to arrogance is both gratitude and the power of recollection. Our interpreters extend his view, concluding that an appreciation of history puts all human accomplishments into perspective. It roots us in gratitude and a sense of obligation for the gifts of God.

PEREK BET: *Cutting Away Thickness about the Heart*

In these speeches to the Israelites, Moses not only recalls the past but speaks eloquently about the challenges of the future. He recalls how he climbed Mount Sinai to bring the Ten Commandments to their parents' generation and how they rebelled by building a golden calf. Then he recounts his intervention to save the people and his return to Sinai to bring them a second set of the tablets, having shattered the first upon seeing them dancing around their golden idol.

All that history, says Moses, is a prelude to obligations for the future. Having reminded the people of how easily, after just forty days, their parents had given up on him and enthusiastically donated their gold to create an idol, Moses puts a hard question to them: "And now, O Israel, what does *Adonai* your God demand of you?"

He allows no pause between the rhetorical question and his answer. "Only this," he tells them, "to revere *Adonai* your God, to walk only in God's paths, to love and serve *Adonai* your God with all your heart and soul, keeping God's commandments and laws, which I enjoin upon you today, for your good." Seeking to enlarge their understanding of God, perhaps to break the dangerous tendency toward reducing God to an object or an idol, Moses points his finger to the heavens. "Behold, the heavens and infinite stars, the earth and everything on it belongs to God." In other words, God is greater than any *thing* a human being might make, even greater than the sum of all the wonderful aspects of creation. God is the Source of everything in the heavens and on the earth.

Yet, Moses does not conclude his description of God with this observation about God's creation of all aspects of the cosmos. He stretches the imagination of the Israelites by declaring, "And with it all, God was drawn in love to your ancestors and chose you, their direct descendants, from among all peoples."

One can sense the satisfaction and pride felt by the Israelites listening to Moses. His declaration makes them feel special, selected for privileges denied to others. It is satisfying to believe that God "loves" them and will protect and provide for them. "To be chosen by God," one can almost hear the Israelites whispering to one another, "means to be designated from all that exists in the heavens and on the earth for special treatment! We're the lucky ones!"

Moses, however, does not allow the people time to relish such conclusions. Instead he uses tough language to stun them into another dimension in their relationship to God. He tells them, "Cut away the thickening about your hearts and stiffen your necks no more. For *Adonai* your God is God supreme . . . the great, the mighty, and the awesome God, who shows no favor and takes no bribe, but upholds the cause of the fatherless and the widow, and befriends the stranger, providing them with food and clothing.—You too must befriend the stranger, for you were strangers in the land of Egypt. . . . Love, therefore, *Adonai* your God, and always keep God's charge, laws, rules, and commandments."

It is a powerful statement. Moses intends to stir the Israelites before him. He uses the language they know in an entirely novel way. They are familiar with the commandment to circumcise their newborn infant sons, but now Moses is commanding them to "circumcise their hearts." What can he mean? Does Moses really have in mind some kind of grizzly ritual of cutting flesh?

Within Jewish tradition, circumcision, which consists of "cutting away" the foreskin of the penis and exposing the glans, is not only a surgical procedure. From the time of Abraham it has also been a ritual for identifying a Jew with the *berit*, or "covenant," between the Jewish people and God. The ceremony is called *berit milah*, or the "covenant of circumcision." Traditionally, the ritual is performed on the eighth day after the birth of males, or as a part of the male conversion ceremony, in fulfillment of the Torah's commandment: "Every male among you throughout the generations shall be circumcised . . . that shall be the sign of the covenant between Me and you." (Genesis 17:9–14)

While circumcision of the penis is a "mark" of being a Jew and has been a significant force for Jewish identity and survival, one wonders why Moses draws a parallel between "circumcising" the penis and the heart. A clue may be found in the speeches of the prophet Jeremiah to the leaders and people of Jerusalem during the reign of King Josiah (639–609 B.C.E.). Seeing the unjust treatment of the poor and outraged by the corruption of the rich and the absence of morality throughout Judean society, Jeremiah calls the people to return to their faith. Speaking in the name of God, he commands them: "Circumcise your hearts to *Adonai*. Cut away the thickening about your hearts, people of Judah and inhabitants of Jerusalem, lest My anger break forth like fire and burn, with none to quench it, because of your wicked acts." (Jeremiah 4:1–4)

Commenting on Jeremiah's message, modern interpreter Rabbi Sheldon Blank writes that the "symbol" of Jeremiah's concern is the "uncircumcised heart." He explains that "biblical psychology localizes feelings and emotions in the body and looks to the heart as the organ of comprehension—an uncircumcised heart is 'a closed mind.'" Blank points out that Jeremiah draws an analogy between the human heart and a field where crops are planted. "A farmer does not plant an untilled land that weeds have taken over. To make the soil productive, first he plows it and rids it of weeds. So it is with human beings; the human mind as well must be cleared of noxious growth and made receptive. Only then can ideas strike root and grow. This," Blank concludes, "is the obvious meaning of the figure in its first appearance: the uncircumcised heart is the unreceptive mind." (*Jeremiah: Man and Prophet,* Ktav, New York, 1961, pp. 193–207)

According to Blank and other modern interpreters, Jeremiah warns the people of Judah that, unless they change their ways and "return" to carrying out the commandments of Torah, they will encounter "disaster after disaster." Their nation will be destroyed by nations sweeping in from the north. "Wash your heart clean," the prophet admonishes them. But all he encounters is stubbornness, "the unreceptive mind." As a result, he complains bitterly in the name of God: "For My people are stupid,/They give Me no heed;/They are foolish children,/They are not intelligent,/They are clever at doing wrong;/But unable to do right." (Jeremiah 4:14, 22)

Jeremiah's definition of the uncircumcised heart is moral insensitivity. It is acting cleverly; conniving to cheat others; taking advantage of them; oppressing the poor, homeless, and hungry; turning away from those who require healing and help. The uncircumcised heart is a form of stubbornness that leads to callous and cruel treatment of others.

The cure for such a hard heart is to "circumcise" it, to "cut away the thickening" that causes the insensitivity and produces the "closed mind" and the inability to choose right from wrong. Yet, how is that to be accomplished? How do you prevent the heart from hardening again into dangerous and selfish habits? Jeremiah suggests that the human heart, or "mind," must be nurtured like a crop-bearing field. It requires plowing, constant weeding, and seeding. For Jeremiah "circumcising the heart" begins with the acknowledgment of God's covenant with Israel. By conscientiously integrating the commandments of Torah into every aspect of what we do, we uplift our awareness of good and evil, of what improves the quality of human society, and of what harms the common good. The sensitive heart for Jeremiah is synonymous with a wise, just, and caring heart.

 Rashi

Jeremiah's use of Moses' command to the Israelites to "cut away the thickening about your hearts" also seems to form the basis of Rashi's interpretation. He argues that Moses is telling the Israelites to "remove the closure and cover on your hearts that prevent My words from gaining entrance." Rashi does not identify how the heart, which for him is the center of human affection and intelligence, is covered and closed. What he makes clear is that, once a person's heart is sealed, God's wisdom cannot enter; God's words of Torah are locked out. Whatever barrier is blocking access to the heart must be cut away

to restore understanding, seeing, hearing, and sensitivity.

How shall that be done? Rashi suggests that the remedy for dissolving the membrane that, from neglect, grows around the heart is constant study, self-scrutiny, and performance of the ethical and ritual mitzvot of Torah. This, presumably, is what Moses means when he shocks the Israelites with the words: "Circumcise your hearts." Study of Torah, says Rashi, is the way Jews "cut away the thickness" about their hearts. (Comments on Exodus 6:10 and Deuteronomy 10:16)

Rashi may have had in mind a comment by Rabbi Avira or Rabbi Yehoshua ben Levi, both of whom identify the "thickening about the heart" with the *yetzer ha-ra*, or the human "inclination for wrongdoing." The *yetzer ha-ra* is our tendency to self-centeredness, to weighing all decisions by how they will benefit us. It is evident in our uncaring attitude about the feelings and needs of others. The rabbis claim that unless the *yetzer ha-ra* is carefully balanced by the *yetzer ha-tov*, our "inclination for doing good," it will clog the heart, causing an "occlusion." It will prevent us from doing the will of God. Moses, the rabbis conclude, understands this danger and, therefore, cautions the Israelites to remove the "occlusion," or *yetzer ha-ra*, from their hearts. (*Sukah* 52a)

 Hirsch

Make your heart obedient . . .
Rabbi Samson Raphael Hirsch suggests that by telling the Israelites "to circumcise their hearts," Moses meant "to make your heart obedient to yourself and to your God . . . to do away with the intractability, the insubordination of your heart, to bring your heart with its feelings and desires under your mastery . . . [and] not to allow yourselves to be detracted from the service of God by any uncontrolled thinking or willing and by no stubbornness and self-willed obstinacy." (Comment on Deuteronomy 10:16)

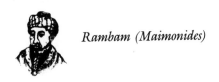

Rambam (Maimonides)

Moses Maimonides sees in Moses' statement a warning against "obstinacy" or "stubbornness." He argues that the whole purpose of the Torah is to put human desires and creativity into human hands. Freedom of choice is given to us. The Torah helps direct our choices. It encourages us to realize that we make mistakes; stubbornness and selfishness often overwhelm our best intentions and confuse us.

Moses, says Maimonides, understood this. For that reason he warned that the Israelites would settle in their new land and sink into self-centered obstinacy. They would forget about God, who had liberated them from slavery. They would abandon God's Torah and commandments, making decisions based on selfishness and greed rather than on the Torah's laws of justice, kindness, and love. Maimonides maintains that, sensing the danger, Moses commands them to "circumcise their hearts." By this he meant: In making decisions, keep your hearts open to the teachings of Torah, to the anguish of others, to the mistakes you will make and the need to rectify them. (*Guide for the Perplexed* 33)

Not satisfied with Maimonides' rational interpretation, some chasidic rabbis suggest that Moses was not referring to human stubbornness or the painful plight of others when he told the Israelites to "circumcise the thickening about your hearts and stiffen your necks no more." Instead, say these chasidic teachers, Moses suspected that the Israelites would begin to question the Torah and its commandments. They would raise doubts about the ethical behavior commanded, pointing out that by following the Torah we must give charity to the poor and, therefore, take less for ourselves. Questions, say the chasidic rabbis, can lead to dangerous answers and choices. Proof that Moses realizes this lies in his statement, "Circumcise the thickening about your hearts," which when punctuated with some minor adjustments means, "If you wish to circumcise the

thickening about your heart and your neck, then ask no more questions."

Supporting their view, these chasidic interpreters recall how Rabbi Shneur Zalman of Liadi was constantly besieged for answers to difficult questions about the meaning of various Torah commandments. Wherever he traveled, Jews would crowd about him. As he finished his prayers in the synagogue, they would approach him with their most difficult questions. One day, when he apparently recalled Moses' speech to the Israelites, he told them, "Ask no more questions! Instead, join with me in singing this melody. Hum it if you do not know the words." As the people sang, their spirits were renewed and their minds cleared. They were able to look upon the Torah and uncover answers for their questions. (See S. Y. Zevin, *A Treasury of Chasidic Tales,* Volume Two, Mesorah Publications, New York/Hillel Press, Jerusalem, 1980, pp. 512–515.)

The chasidic masters are concerned with the attitude of cynical rationalism, which assumes that if you ask enough of the right questions you will understand everything—all the mysteries of creation, heaven and earth, life and death. Such a presumption leads, they believe, to arrogance and dangerous assumptions of superiority and insensitivity. Moses, say the chasidic teachers, feared such attitudes. He identified them with what he called the "thickness about your heart." He knew that human beings are incapable of answering all questions and that there is much about our universe and ourselves that will always remain shrouded in mystery. So, say the chasidic teachers, he tells the Israelites: "If you wish to circumcise the thickening about your hearts and your neck, then ask no more questions. Be satisfied with what the Torah teaches and with the vast mysteries and wonders of life."

Clearly the command to "circumcise the heart" is a strange and baffling one. As we can see, interpreters reach a variety of opinions about its meaning. On the face of it, "cutting away the thickening about the heart" is a frightening, even grizzly, suggestion. Yet the aging Moses knows that he must attract the attention of the young Israelites as they ready themselves to follow Joshua into the Land of Israel. Perhaps that explains why he uses such a shocking metaphor. Human sensitivities for justice, truth, honesty, and kindness can easily be calloused. "See enough violence," psychologists observe, "and you begin to get used to it. You begin to tolerate it, even excuse it."

After leading his people for forty years, Moses knew their hearts and his. He understood human strengths and weaknesses and the dangers of anger, pride, self-centeredness, habit, callous insensitivity, and stubbornness. These needed to be "cut away," not unlike the foreskin, as a sign of the covenant between God and the Jewish people.

The purpose of the covenant between God and the Jewish people is to raise human life to levels of sacred behavior, justice, caring, honesty, and love. Anything that prevents Jews from such an accomplishment must be removed. Thus, Moses warns the Israelites with a powerful metaphor. Using the ritual of circumcision, he commands them: "Cut away the thickening about your hearts and stiffen your necks no more." Achieving the Promised Land requires heightened moral sensitivity and integrity.

QUESTIONS FOR STUDY AND DISCUSSION

1. The Book of Proverbs contains several warnings about pride and arrogance. We are told: "In the mouth of a fool is a rod of arrogance,/ But the lips of the wise protect them." (14:3) "Pride goes before ruin,/Arrogance, before failure./Better to be humble and among the lowly/Than to share spoils with the proud." (16:18–19) "A person's pride will humiliate him,/But a humble person will obtain honor." (29:23) Would you agree with these ancient observations? Why do Jewish commentators see dangerous ethical consequences in pride? Can the act of giving thanks curb arrogance? What else do our commentators suggest as antidotes to pride?

2. Our commentators define the "uncircumcised heart" as the unreceptive, thoughtless, and insensitive mind, clogged by habit and stubbornness. Chasidic tradition argues that the way to open such a mind is through quiet meditation or song, not through debating questions and answers. Would you agree? Are there other "better" means of "circumcising" the heart for the purpose of achieving sensitivity, compassion, and wisdom?

PARASHAT RE'EH
Deuteronomy 11:26–16:17

Parashat Re'eh continues Moses' speeches to the Israelites. Warning that they face the choice between a life of blessings or a life of curses, he urges them to observe God's commandments in the land west of the Jordan, where they will settle. He tells them to destroy all idolatrous altars and to worship at the place designated by God. Rules about sacrifices, tithes, and care for the Levites are discussed along with regulations for slaughtering and eating meat. Moses warns the people not to be lured into idolatry by false prophets, family members, or friends. He commands them not to disfigure themselves or eat anything harmful to their health. He clarifies which animals are permitted and which are forbidden for eating and details regulations for setting aside a tenth part of one's produce (tithe) for the stranger, fatherless, and widow. Moses also defines the sabbatical year as a time for canceling all debts and for extending care to the needy, promising that those who help the poor will be blessed with no regrets. In addition, he instructs the Israelites in the treatment of slaves and reviews the three Pilgrimage Festivals of Pesach, Shavuot, and Sukot.

OUR TARGUM

· 1 ·

Moses declares that God is giving the Israelites a choice of making life a blessing or a curse. He urges them to choose the way of blessing by carrying out God's commandments. When they enter the Land of Israel, they are to pronounce a blessing at Mount Gerizim and a curse at Mount Ebal, located across from each other near Shechem. Moses emphasizes that when the people settle in the land, they are to destroy all sites of idol worship and bring their sacrifices, tithes, and gifts to the Levites in the place chosen by God.

Moses informs them that they may follow their desire to eat meat from any of the sheep and cattle given to them, including the deer and gazelle, but the blood is forbidden. It is to be poured on the ground like water. Offerings of flesh and blood may be burnt on the altar.

·2·

Moses warns against adding or subtracting from the commandments. He cautions the Israelites not to be tempted to worship the gods of other nations, telling them that false prophets, diviners, and even family members and friends will seek to divert them from their faith. They should reject all invitations to idolatry. Those who mislead Israelites into idolatry, says Moses, are to be shown no pity. They are to be stoned to death for causing Israelites to stray from loyalty to God and the commandments of Torah.

·3·

Moses tells them, "You are a people consecrated to *Adonai* your God: *Adonai* your God chose you from among all other peoples on earth to be God's treasured people." Reviewing the meaning of "God's treasured people" (see also *Parashat Shemini, A Torah Commentary for Our Times,* Volume II), Moses reminds them that they are forbidden to harm their bodies or to shave their heads when loved ones die. They may eat meat from the ox, sheep, goat, deer, gazelle, roebuck, wild goat, ibex, antelope, mountain sheep—animals that have cleft hooves and chew cud. All other meat is forbidden, including camel, hare, daman, and pig. Anything in the water with fins and scales is allowed. Clean birds are permissible, but the eagle, vulture, black vulture, kite, falcon, buzzard, raven, ostrich, nighthawk, sea gull, hawks of any kind, owl, pelican, buzzard, cormorant, stork, heron, hoopoe, and bat are forbidden. All winged swarming things are also forbidden, as is anything that has died a natural death. Also, they are not permitted to boil a kid in its mother's milk.

·4·

Moses sets out rules concerning the yearly tithes, a tenth part of all the crops of the fields. He tells the people that they are to put aside their pro-

duce, or the value of their produce in cash, for their festival celebrations and for the Levites, who have no fields. Every third year the entire tithe is to be left for the Levite, the stranger, the fatherless, and the widow. Every seventh year they are to forgive all debts.

Expressing concern for the poor, Moses tells the Israelites, "Do not harden your heart and shut your hand against your needy kinsman. Rather, you must open your hand and lend him sufficient for whatever he needs. . . . Give to him readily and have no regrets . . . for in return *Adonai* your God will bless you. . . . For there will never cease to be needy ones in your land."

·5·

Furthermore, Moses deals with the treatment of Hebrew slaves: They must be freed after seven years; they must not be sent away empty-handed but given food from the flock, threshing floor, and vat; slaves who refuse liberation are to have an awl put through their ears at the doorpost, indicating they have chosen to be slaves forever.

·6·

Moses repeats the laws for celebrating the three Pilgrimage Festivals—Pesach, Shavuot, and Sukot. (See also *Parashat Emor, A Torah Commentary for Our Times,* Volume II, pp. 138–146.)

THEMES

Parashat Re'eh contains two important themes:

1. Slaughtering animals and eating meat.
2. The meaning of being an *am segulah,* "a treasured people."

PEREK ALEF: *Shechitah: Regulations for Slaughtering Animals and Eating Meat*

Addressing the Israelites about their future in the Land of Israel, Moses emphasizes the critical importance of observing all the mitzvot, or "commandments," of Torah. If the people do so, they will be blessed; if they do not, they will be cursed. The choice is theirs.

An important part of that choice has to do with what they eat. Moses predicts that once they settle in their land and begin to prosper, the people will have an urge for meat, saying, "I want to eat meat." Moses encourages them, "You may eat meat whenever you wish."

Earlier, when they were wandering through the desert, the only meat permitted for food was cut from animals sacrificed on the altar of the sanctuary. Aside from that, the people ate only the manna that was provided for them each day, with a double portion on Fridays for Shabbat. Now Moses presents a new possibility. When they settle the Land of Israel, they will be allowed to satisfy their craving for meat.

Moses makes it clear, however, that there are important limitations they must follow: "You

may slaughter any of the cattle or sheep that *Adonai* gives you, *as I have instructed you;* and you may eat to your heart's content in your settlements. . . . *But make sure that you do not partake of the blood.*" As the Torah makes clear in Leviticus 6:1–8:36, eating blood is forbidden. It must be removed from the animal, poured on the ground, and buried. Since it is considered the sacred substance of life, it may not be consumed. (See discussion in *Parashat Tzav, A Torah Commentary for Our Times,* Volume II, pp. 108–109.)

Moses also suggests that there exists a required means of slaughter. He tells the Israelites to slaughter meat "as I have instructed you." However, there is no record of such instructions in the Torah. Later, during the talmudic period, rabbinic leaders and interpreters set out rules for the *shechitah,* or the "ritual slaughtering," of animals and birds for food. (See *Hullin.*) These rules are to be carefully followed by the *shochet,* or "slaughterer," who is responsible for the preparation of meat for the Jewish community.

The *shochet* must study and become expert in slaughtering. His hands must be steady. The knife used for slaughter must be regularly examined for sharpness by passing it over a thread or fingernail. The knife must be clean, smooth, and without a dent or nick. It must be at least twice the length of the diameter of the animal's neck and not pointed at its end.

Before slaughtering, the *shochet* is to pronounce the blessing: "Be praised, *Adonai* our God, Ruler of the universe, who sanctifies us with commandments and commands us regarding the act of *shechitah*." Slaughtering is to be performed with a horizontal cut across the throat, severing the trachea and the esophagus. The knife must be drawn quickly back and forth with no *shehiyah*, "pausing"; *derasah*, "pressing"; *hachladah*, "burrowing"; *hagramah*, "cutting out"; or *agirah*, "tearing out." The *shochet* is to spill the blood of the animal upon the ground or upon a bed of dust, pronouncing the blessing: "Be praised, *Adonai* our God, Ruler of the universe, who sanctifies us with commandments and commands us to cover the blood with earth." (See Isaac Klein, *A Guide to Jewish Religious Practice,* Jewish Theological Seminary, distributed by Ktav, New York, 1979, pp. 307–312.)

What is the purpose of these carefully developed regulations regarding the slaughtering of animals?

Rambam (Maimonides)

In his *Guide for the Perplexed,* physician and philosopher Moses Maimonides discusses the importance of diet and the proper means of slaughter. Apparently aware of those who claim that a vegetarian diet is superior to one with meat, he counters that a balanced human diet requires "vegetables and the flesh of animals." He writes: "No doctor has any doubts about this."

Given the requirement for meat, Maimonides expresses concern about the manner of killing animals. Jewish tradition teaches us that the death of the animal should be as painless as possible. It is forbidden to torment the animal by cutting the throat in a clumsy manner, by sawing it, or by cutting off a limb while the animal is still alive. It is also prohibited to kill an animal with its young on the same day. . . . There is no

difference in this case between the pain of a human being and the pain of other living beings since the love and tenderness of the mother for her young ones are not produced by reasoning, but by instinct, and exist not only in human beings but in most living beings." Maimonides adds: "For the same reason, the Torah commands us to let the mother bird fly away when we take her young, or her eggs . . . for when the mother bird is sent away, she does not see the taking of her young ones and does not feel any pain." (3:48)

In stressing compassion for animals, Maimonides uses the talmudic ethical category known as *tza'ar ba'alei chayim,* or concern for the "pain of living things." Nothing should be done that needlessly causes pain to an animal. The procedure of *shechitah,* which uses a razor-sharp knife on an area of the throat with very few sensory cutaneous nerve endings, insures that the incision itself causes no pain. With the instant severing of the carotid arteries and jugular veins, there is a massive loss of blood, resulting in unconsciousness within a few seconds. The procedure of *shechitah* has been recognized for centuries as the most humane method of slaughter now in use.

The concern of Maimonides and other commentators for the principle of *tza'ar ba'alei chayim,* the "pain of living things," is not simply a matter of compassion for animals. The same principle is applied to human relations. These laws are set out, says Maimonides, "with a view to perfecting us so that we should not acquire habits of cruelty and should not inflict pain needlessly, but [we] should be kind and merciful even with animals."

To eat or not to eat meat
Rabbi Judah Ha-Nasi declares that a person should be careful not to eat meat. Rabbi Yochanan says that our generation is physically weak, and, if a person has only one gold coin, he ought to buy meat with it. Rabbi Nachman says that our generation is so weak that a person should borrow money to buy meat so that he will be strong in doing God's service. (Tze'enah u-Re'enah, Devarim, p. 912)

Hirsch

Rabbi Samson Raphael Hirsch writes: "The eating of meat is one of the purposes for which God has given you your herds and your flocks." (Comment on Deuteronomy 12:21)

For the sake of self-discipline, it is far more appropriate for human beings not to eat meat. Only if they have a strong desire for meat does the Torah permit it, and even this only after the trouble and inconvenience necessary in order to satisfy the desire. Perhaps because of the bother and annoyance of the whole procedure, people will be restrained from such a strong and uncontrollable desire for meat. (Kelei Yakar, in Abraham Chill, The Mitzvot, *p. 400)*

Agreeing with Maimonides, Aharon Halevi of Barcelona observes in his *Sefer ha-Hinuch* that the "root purpose" of all these regulations about animals and their slaughter "is to teach us that our souls must be beautiful, choosing fairness and pursuing loving kindness and mercy. In training our souls to such behavior with regard to animals, which are not created other than to serve us . . . we train ourselves to do good for human beings and to watch over them lest they cross the boundary with regard to that which is proper and bring pain to others. This is the proper path for the holy, chosen people." (596)

The prevailing motive behind the regulations dealing with the slaughter of animals has to do with the effect that butchering other living beings has upon humans beings. Jewish teachers fear that taking the life of animals promotes insensitivity, even cruelty. To counter this danger, they insist upon blessings before and after the slaughter, care for the sharpness of knives, and the quickest, least painful method of death—all means of teaching compassion in the midst of animal slaughter.

Modern interpreter Rabbi Abraham Isaac Kook differs from this view. He argues that the slaughter and eating of animals is morally wrong and that the rules of *shechitah* do not represent a

means of perfecting human behavior. Instead, they are a compromise with physical needs that one day will be overcome.

Kook maintains that at creation (see Genesis 1:24–28) human beings are told to be fruitful and multiply "and rule the fish of the sea, the birds of the sky, and all the living things that creep on earth." However, human beings are not commanded to slaughter animals for meat. While the eating of meat is allowed to Noah and the generations after him, Kook points out that the Israelites are permitted to eat meat slaughtered only for the purposes of sacrifices on the sanctuary altar at the time of their wandering through the desert. He also explains that the permission to eat meat mentioned in this Torah portion arose out of Moses' realization that the people could not control their appetite for it.

For that reason, says Rabbi Kook, rules for the compassionate slaughter of animals were created. They are meant to stress that, despite the human need for meat, killing animals is morally wrong—an act of cruelty and shame. Kook argues that the rules of *shechitah* will ultimately lead human beings to reject afflicting any pain on animals and, therefore, to abandon the consumption of meat. "These regulations will ultimately educate human beings. The silent protest will, when the time is ready, be transformed into a mighty shout and succeed in its purpose. The aim of *shechitah* is designed to reduce pain and to create a realization that one is not dealing with an inanimate object but with a living being." (See Nehama Leibowitz, *Studies in Devarim*, pp. 137–142.)

Rabbi Kook's view that the ideal relationship between human and animal species precludes the slaughter of animals and the eating of meat is one with which most vegetarians would agree. While Kook believed that humanity eventually would adopt that ideal and that the regulations of *shechitah* actually promoted such a conclusion, he did not argue against continuing the slaughter of animals or for a strictly vegetarian diet.

All the regulations of *shechitah* are part of Jewish ritual. They are meant to function within the lives of Jews as a means of bonding the community by sharing standards of behavior. They are meant to uplift ordinary moments into sacred ones. When the *shochet* pronounces a blessing before the act of slaughtering, or as the blood is covered with dust, he is reminded that his work—even the grizzly duty of putting an animal to death for the consumption of meat—must fulfill God's commandments. His skill must be placed in the service of compassion for the pain of animals and reverence for all life. In treating the slaughter of animals as ritual, Jewish tradition seeks to prevent it from becoming a cruel and callous function of human behavior.

Today, the technologies of animal slaughter and the health risks associated with meat consumption are major topics of controversy. Many argue that slaughter houses employing stun guns in an assembly-line killing of animals is extremely cruel; in comparison, the regulations and procedures of *shechitah* are far superior. They introduce important ethical and ritual considerations into the grim butchery of animals—of living beings.

PEREK BET: *Am Segulah: Can Israel Be God's "Treasured People"?*

Several times in the Hebrew Bible the people of Israel are referred to as God's *am segulah,* "treasured people."

In the third month after their liberation from Egypt, Moses climbs Mount Sinai. There, according to the Torah (Exodus 19:4–6), God tells Moses: "You have seen what I did to the Egyptians, how I bore you on eagles' wings and brought you to Me. Now then, if you will obey Me faithfully and keep My covenant, you shall be My *am segulah,* 'treasured possession,' among all the peoples . . . you shall be to Me a kingdom of priests and a holy nation."

In our Torah portion, *Re'eh,* Moses declares to the Israelites: "You are a people consecrated to *Adonai* your God: *Adonai* your God chose you from among all other peoples on earth to be God's treasured people." (Deuteronomy 14:2) In another speech to the people, Moses expands the idea, clearly indicating the mutuality of the commitment between God and the people of Israel. He says, "You have affirmed this day that *Adonai* is your God, that you will walk in God's ways, that you will observe God's laws and commandments and rules, and that you will obey

God. And *Adonai* has affirmed this day that you are, as God promised you, God's *am segulah,* 'treasured people,' who shall observe all God's commandments, and that God will set you, in fame and renown and glory, high above all the nations that God has made; and that you shall be, as God promised, a holy people to *Adonai* your God." (Deuteronomy 26:17–19)

This idea that God selects or designates the people of Israel as an *am segulah* remains a central belief in Jewish tradition. The prophet Malachi (3:17) uses the term. So does the Psalmist who, singing in the Jerusalem Temple, praises God for having "chosen Jacob—Israel—as a treasured possession." (135:3–4)

In daily, Shabbat, and festival worship, just before Jews recite the *Shema,* "Hear, O Israel: *Adonai* is our God, *Adonai* is One," they say: "Be praised, O God, who in love has chosen Israel as God's people." The identical notion is a part of the *aliyah* blessing chanted before the reading of the Torah: "Be praised, O God . . . who has chosen us from all peoples by giving us the Torah."

Clearly the idea of the people of Israel as a "chosen people," as an *am segulah,* a "treasured people," is central to Jewish faith. Yet, what does this assertion mean? How does the Torah understand it? How has it been interpreted throughout the ages?

Early rabbinic commentators speak of the mystery of love between God and the people of Israel. God, they say, discovers the oppressed and beaten people in Egypt, liberates them, leads them through the desert, and gives them the Torah at Mount Sinai. God's love for Israel is "eternal." It is a love of rescue and protection, a love of deep mutual affection and commitment. Quoting the Song of Songs as love poetry between God and Israel, the rabbis claim that God says of Israel, "My beloved is mine and I am my beloved's," and the people of Israel respond, "God is our God, and we are God's people."

This sense that God's mysterious and eternal love for Israel leads to its being chosen as an *am segulah* is expressed by Moses, who tells the people that they are "consecrated" to God, who has selected them not because they are powerful or because they are numerous but because God "loves" them. It is for that reason, Moses tells them, that God freed them from Egypt and made a covenant with them. (See *Exodus Rabbah* 99:1; *Tanna Debe Eliyahu*, p. 31; *Song of Songs Rabbah* 2:16, and Deuteronomy 7:6–11.)

The nature of love, whether between God and Israel or between human beings, cannot be explained. No one knows the secret of what attracts one person to another or what sustains a relationship through years of sad and happy times, through celebrations, achievements, disagreements, and disappointments. If the capacity and power of human love remain a riddle, so does the mystery of the relationship between God and human beings. The origins of life, the sources of human curiosity, and the urge to create, care, seek justice, and love are all beyond explanation. We are more sure of our astonishment than of our tentative theories. For many early rabbinic interpreters, God's choice of Israel as an *am segulah,* God's liberation of Israel from Egypt, and Israel's exile and return to its land could only be explained as an expression of such powerful and mysterious love.

Other rabbinic commentators, however, define the relationship, with a sense of humor, as one of mutual desperation. God and Israel treasure each other and love each other because they cannot do otherwise. These interpreters argue that at precisely the time Israel is wandering on the Sinai desert, God is searching for a people to accept the Torah. Each of the great nations of the world is asked if it will take the Torah, and each refuses, saying that the Torah's teachings are not suitable or compatible with its beliefs and culture. Finally, say these rabbis, God sees the tattered and desperate Israelites making their way across the desert. Lifting Mount Sinai over their heads, God asks threateningly, "Will you accept my Torah or be buried by this mountain?" Seeing that they have no choice if they wish to live, the Israelites respond: "It is a tree of life to all who grasp it. . . ."

For these rabbis, the Israelites choose life by choosing the Torah. It is a desperate choice of a desperate people singled out by a desperate God. God requires an *an segulah,* a "treasured people," not for special favors but for a special burden. They are to be responsible for carrying the Torah and its commandments into the world. The survival of the world and all within it depends upon the truths of Torah and the loyalty of those who carry out its ethical and ritual commandments. Israel is beloved by God when it chooses to be God's partner and when it lives by Torah. To the extent that they "choose" to live by the commandments they guarantee their survival. (*Numbers Rabbah* 14:10; *Avodah Zarah* 2b–3a)

Rashi

Rashi offers his own interpretation of what it means for Israel to be called an *am segulah.* He suggests that the people of Israel are like a precious golden cup or gem among a larger collection of cups and gems belonging to a ruler. They are precious, special, but not exclusive. All peoples and nations belong to God, writes Rashi. No people, including Israel, can claim that it alone is God's people.

Israel's special relationship with God, Rashi holds, derives from its historical and mutual covenant and from its commitment within that covenant to abandon idolatry and pagan practices and to become a holy people through its practice of all the mitzvot of Torah. God chooses them for that purpose. They are a "treasured people" to God if they uphold their part of the covenant. (Comments on Exodus 15:5; Deuteronomy 14:2)

Ramban (Nachmanides)

Nachmanides connects Rashi's view with those of the Jewish mystics who speak of God's love for Israel and of Israel's love for God. They teach that *if* the people of Israel are loyal in carrying out the mitzvot, they are God's treasure, *am segulah,* or they are "a treasure in God's hand." Nachmanides agrees, emphasizing the conditional nature of the relationship. God loves Israel for its love, its attention, and its loyalty. Every mitzvah performed proves that loyalty. Love promotes love; loyal deeds engender loyal rewards. That is the test of love. It is demonstrated through the doing of mitzvot. Anything else is disloyalty. (Comments on Exodus 19:5)

Dangers and challenges

Israel was elected for the purpose of *entering into a covenant relationship with the God of the whole world* in order to *be God's "kingdom of priests." Without the Torah, and without the commandments, the "chosen people" ceases to be a meaningful concept and is liable to degenerate into pagan notions of chauvinism and racism.* (Jakob J. Petuchowski, Ever Since Sinai, B. Arbit Books, Milwaukee, 1979, p. 64)

Israel did not discover God. Israel was discovered by God. Judaism is God's quest for man. *The Bible is a record of God's approach to Israel. . . . There is no concept of a chosen God, but there is the idea of a chosen people. The idea of a chosen people does not suggest the preference for one people over another. We do not say that we are a superior people. The "chosen people" means a people approached and chosen by God. The significance of this term is genuine in relation to God rather than in relation to other peoples. It signifies not a quality inherent in the people but a relationship between the people and God.* (Abraham Joshua Heschel, God in Search of Man, Farrar, Straus and Cudahy, New York, 1955, pp. 425–426)

In seeking to understand the contemporary meaning of being a "chosen people," Rabbi W. Gunther Plaut suggests: "Perhaps it is the destiny of the Jew today to maintain the possibility of minority and diversity . . . to be acculturated yet not assimilated; to be totally in this world yet also beyond it; to be loyal to nations of many countries yet the earth's true internationalists; to be the bearers of many cultures yet never to be known by them; to be acceptable yet never quite accepted for kodesh is invisibly engraved on the forehead of every Jew. (The Case for the Chosen People, Doubleday, New York, 1965, pp. 120–121)

Philosopher Yehudah Halevi proposes a different view in his book, *The Kuzari.* He presents an imaginary discussion between a rabbi and the king of the Kuzars. Writing in eleventh-century Spain, Halevi advances the idea that the people of Israel are "the heart of the nations." When they are sick or suffer, all peoples are sick and suffer. They are an *am segulah,* a people "distinguished from other people by godly qualities, which makes them, so to speak, an angelic caste. Each of them is permeated by the divine essence . . ." with the result that "the human soul becomes divine. It is detached from material senses and joins the highest world, where it enjoys a vision of the divine light and hears the divine speech."

For Halevi, being a part of this "treasured people" is to sense God's influence and to be shaped by it. Living within "the divine light" brings wisdom and sensitivity, justice, and love to the human heart. Hearing "the divine speech" within one's mind opens the way to doing God's will by fulfilling the commandments of Torah.

Halevi's view of being a part of the "treasured people" does not promise a life after death in pleasant and beautiful gardens but rather a life "among angels on earth." The Jewish people are "the heart of the nations," Halevi argues. What they do, how they carry out the commandments of Torah has consequences not only for them but for the entire human family. (See *The Kuzari,* Schocken Books, New York, 1964, pp. 70–76, 109–115.)

Modern philosopher Martin Buber reflects Yehudah Halevi's view but adds his own emphasis. Calling the Jewish people a *res sui generis,* a unique people molded by their history and by "a great inner transformation" through which they became "an anointed kingdom" representing God, Buber seeks to define "the idea of election." He warns against the slogans of nationalism built on empty pride and dangerous assumptions about superiority. Buber maintains that the notion of Israel as a chosen people "does not indicate a feeling of superiority but a sense of destiny. It does not spring from a comparison with others but from the concentrated devotion to a task, to the task that molded the people into a nation."

"The prophets," Buber continues, "formulated that task and never ceased uttering their warning:

If you boast of being chosen instead of living up to it, if you turn election into a static object instead of obeying it as a command, you will forfeit it!" In specific terms, Buber challenges Zionists with the message that "Israel be a nation that establishes justice and truth in its institutions and activities" and that summons all peoples "to walk in the light of *Adonai*."

For Buber, the people of Israel is no ordinary nation. The people have a mission, a prophetic purpose. They are to bring about the time when justice and compassion will rule all personal, national, and international endeavors and when humanity will be redeemed from cruelty, deceit, and war. The people of Israel is God's instrument to bring about such an era of understanding, truth, and peace. So is Zionism. "True Zionism," Buber concludes in an essay to Zionists in the Land of Israel and throughout the world, is "the desire to establish something like 'the city of the great king. . . .' We need 'Zionists of Zion' here and abroad." (*Israel and the World: Essays in a Time of Crisis,* Schocken Books, New York, 1963, pp. 223–224 and 258 ff.)

Differing with Buber and most of the interpreters on the meaning of Israel as an *am segulah* is the creator of the modern Reconstructionist movement, Rabbi Mordecai M. Kaplan. For Kaplan the concept of "being chosen" grows out of four "entirely unwarranted" assumptions: first, that Jews possess hereditary traits that make them religiously and ethically superior to others; second, that Jews were the first to receive these religious and ethical conceptions and ideals; third, that Jews possess the truest form of religious and ethical ideals; and fourth, that Jews have the historic task of teaching these ideals to the world.

Such assumptions, says Kaplan, are "unproved." He argues that "national traits" are more a product of "historical circumstances . . . geographic environment, and social institutions" than of "heredity." "For Jews to claim sole credit for having given mankind those religious and ethical concepts that hold out the promise of a better world smacks of arrogance." Few modern Jews, Kaplan continues, believe that they have "the truest form of truth" when it comes to religion or ethics. The idea that God selected Israel to "fulfill the mission of making God known to the nations" is not central to Jewish tradition but is found only in "less than a dozen passages in the second part of Isaiah."

Kaplan advances the idea that each nation and people has a special "vocation." He writes: "No nation is chosen or elected or superior to any other, but every nation should discover its vocation or calling as a source of religious experience and as a medium of salvation to those who share its life. . . ." For the Jewish people this means using all of its traditions, historical experience, ethical wisdom, and culture to advance its survival and enrich all peoples with its unique way of life. (*The Future of the American Jew,* Macmillan, New York, 1948, pp. 211–130)

Kaplan's rejection of the idea of the Jewish people as "chosen," or as an *am segulah,* has received wide criticism. Scholars have pointed out that the concept is not confined to the prophetic pronouncements of Second Isaiah but is found sprinkled generously throughout the Torah, in other biblical writings, and in the Talmud and Midrash. Others claim that, except for Yehudah Halevi's interpretation of Israel as "the heart of the nations," the concept of *am segulah* has never been interpreted to mean that the people of Israel considered itself superior to other peoples. Instead, its meaning is precisely what Kaplan has in mind when he uses the term "vocation." In other words, the people of Israel has a special task, a responsibility, a unique role to play in the history of nations.

The business of Israel
The business of Israel is not to vaunt itself as the historical possessor of a priceless heritage but to live and serve and teach in the sight of all the world as becomes the bearers of a great name and of a glorious tradition . . . to live as seekers after God, doers of justice, ever fanatical for social righteousness, possessed of childlike purity of heart. Whether the heritage is to be carried on depends upon the life of the Jew today, here and everywhere upon the capacity of the individual Jew to give himself to those noble and consecrated ends of life. (Rabbi Stephen S. Wise, quoted in A Modern Treasury of Jewish Thoughts, *Sidney Greenberg, editor, Thomas Yoseloff, New York, 1964, p. 285)*

It is this "task" that modern interpreter Rabbi Leo Baeck attaches to the idea of being "chosen." Israel, he writes, "is elect if it elects itself." Baeck, like other commentators, sees the concept of being an *am segulah* as conditional. If the people obey God's commandments and are loyal to their covenant with God, they will survive and prosper as a "chosen" people. "Israel, though chosen by God, can remain so only if it practices righteousness; sin separates it from God," says Baeck. "Election," he continues, "is a prophetic calling of an entire people. This mission goes beyond Israel itself; it is an election for the sake of others . . . (as the prophet puts it) . . . 'I *Adonai* have called you in righteousness, and will hold your hand, and will keep you, and give you for a covenant of the people, for a light to the nations; to open the blind eyes, to bring out the prisoners from the prison, and them that sit in darkness in the prison house.'" (Isaiah 42:6ff.) Baeck concludes that "this classical idea, of which the essential core has been retained, could only have arisen from the consciousness of election." (*The Essence of Judaism,* pp. 65–68)

The majority of Jewish commentators seem to agree that the Jewish people in its covenant with God sensed that their relationship was more than self-serving. They bore the unusual task of being God's instrument for extending truth, justice, righteousness, compassion, and peace on earth among all peoples. The awareness of this responsibility grew in them and, as Baeck explains, became a "consciousness of election." Nothing in this view claims superiority. On the contrary, being an *am segulah* means the people of Israel must measure its existence by the values and demands of Judaism. To be chosen by God means to be responsible, not only for your own survival, but for the survival of all peoples.

Struggling to determine the meaning of being an *am segulah,* a "treasured people" of God, interpreters to this day must deal with the significant question: "What is the purpose of Jewish existence?" It is out of such exploration that ancient ideas are confronted and new understandings and responsibilities are born.

QUESTIONS FOR STUDY AND DISCUSSION

1. Why does Jewish tradition put such emphasis upon the manner in which an animal is slaughtered? Are there considerations beyond concern for the pain of animals?

2. The laws of *shechitah* are part of Jewish ritual. Ritual is meant to uplift life with special meanings, to enhance it with ethical values and sensitivities, and to celebrate it with joy. How do the rituals and regulations of *shechitah* perform such a function?

3. Some interpreters argue that the claim that the people of Israel is an *am segulah* leads to arrogance and feelings of superiority. How does the historic notion that being "a treasured people" means being selected for carrying out the commandments of Torah and for being "a light to the nations" answer this objection?

4. There are many contemporary thinkers who argue that surviving as a nation is sufficient and that no nation or people needs to justify its existence, traditions, or culture. Given Jewish history and experience, is mere survival enough? Do the people of Israel and all peoples need to think about life beyond the borders of their own self-interests? Can Yehudah Halevi's view of being an *am segulah* still motivate Jews to stretch their concerns beyond the survival of their people?

PARASHAT SHOFETIM
Deuteronomy 16:18–21:9

Parashat Shofetim opens with the command to appoint judges and legal officials to carry out justice within the society and with a warning against the worship of other gods. Two witnesses must be heard before a court can impose the death penalty. Cases of homicide, civil law, or assault too difficult to decide in one court must be transferred to a higher court. Regulations for choosing a king/leader are presented, including a warning that this leader should follow the laws of Torah faithfully. The offerings for priests are again set forth; also set forth is the difference between a true and false prophet. Cities of refuge for those guilty of manslaughter are described, with laws forbidding the movement of landmarks. The portion concludes with regulations to be observed during war and with assessments of communal responsibilities when the body of a murder victim is found beyond city limits.

OUR TARGUM

·1·

Moses tells the people to appoint judges in their settlements so that they may be governed with justice. These judges must show no partiality and are forbidden to take bribes. "Justice, justice shall you pursue, that you may thrive and occupy the land that *Adonai* your God is giving you."

A person may receive the death penalty only on the testimony of two witnesses. The testimony of one witness cannot be used to validate guilt. If witnesses give false testimony, they shall be punished. If a case dealing with homicide, civil law, or assault proves too complex for the court hearing it, it is to be sent to a higher court of priests or judges whose verdict must be carried out.

·2·

The people are forbidden to set up places for idols, to offer defective sacrifices, or to engage in moon or sun worship.

· 3 ·

Upon entering the Land of Israel, the people may choose monarchy as a form of government. The king must not be a foreigner, may not keep many horses or send servants back to Egypt to purchase additional horses, may not have many wives nor amass silver and gold to excess. The laws of Torah, which he is to study throughout his life, will insure that he is humble and never arrogant toward his people.

· 4 ·

Moses repeats that the levitical priests, the entire tribe of Levi, will not be allotted any land. They are to be given the shoulder, cheeks, and stomach of offerings; first fruits of new grain; wine; oil; and the first shearing of sheep. In this way they will be compensated for their service in the Temple.

He again warns the people against such forbidden religious practices as offering children to fire or following soothsayers, diviners, sorcerers, casters of spells, or those who claim to consult with spirits, ghosts, or the dead. Such people should be banished from the community.

· 5 ·

Moses predicts that other prophets like him will rise to lead the people and that they should be followed. However, he warns the people not to follow those who speak in the name of other gods or those who make untrue predictions in God's name. He declares them "false prophets."

Preparing them to enter the land, Moses reviews the importance of establishing refuge cities for those accused of causing the accidental death of another person. He explains that if a person cutting wood swings an ax to cut down a tree and the ax-head flies off the handle killing a person, the unwitting killer should be allowed to flee to a refuge city for justice, spared from the revenge of the victim's relatives. In this way, explains Moses, innocent blood will not be shed.

He also forbids moving landmarks, a form of stealing property allotted by God to the people entering the Land of Israel.

·6·

Anticipating the wars for reconquering the land, Moses orders the priests to encourage the people with the following formula: "Hear, O Israel! You are about to join battle with your enemy. Let not your courage falter. Do not be in fear, or in panic, or in dread of them. For it is *Adonai* your God who marches with you . . . to bring you victory."

He continues by instructing them to exempt from battle those who have built a new home but not dedicated it, planted a vineyard but not harvested it, become engaged but not married, or are anxious and afraid.

The tactics of war also concern Moses. He tells the people that a town approached for attack must be offered terms of peace. If its citizens respond peaceably, they can be taken to serve as forced labor; if they do not surrender, the city should be besieged and everything in it taken as booty.

When you capture a city, says Moses, do not destroy its trees. You may eat their fruit, but you may not cut them down. Because trees are not human, they cannot withdraw before you. Only trees that do not yield fruit may be cut down and used for constructing siege mounds from which to attack the city.

·7·

Moses declares that when a dead body is found outside a city and the murderer is unknown, the elders and officials from nearby towns should measure the distance between each town and the corpse. When it is determined which city is nearest the corpse, its elders will sacrifice a heifer and declare: "Our hands did not shed this blood, nor did our eyes see it done," and they will be absolved of guilt.

THEMES

Parashat Shofetim contains two important themes:

1. The guarantee and pursuit of justice within the society.
2. Concern for trees and the ecological balance of the world.

PEREK ALEF: *"Justice, Justice Shall You Pursue"*

The pursuit of justice is one of the most frequently repeated concerns, not only of the Torah, but of Jewish tradition. The Israelites are commanded to use "just weights and honest measures" in their business dealings and to hear and "decide justly in disputes between any persons, Israelites or strangers." They are forbidden to take bribes or to favor persons in judgment because they are rich or poor.

Society is to pursue justice in dealing with social, political, and international matters. The prophet Amos declares in the name of God: "Let justice well up as waters, and righteousness as a mighty stream." Isaiah proclaims: "Seek justice, relieve the oppressed." The Psalmist poses the question, "Who is worthy to dwell in God's sanctuary?" and answers, "Those who live without blame, act justly, acknowledge the truth, do not slander others, harm others, hold grudges against their neighbors." The mother of Lemuel, king of Massa, advises her son: "Speak up for those who are silent, for the rights of the unfortunate. Speak out, judge justly, champion the poor and the needy." (See Leviticus 19:36; Deuteronomy 1:16; Amos 5:24; Isaiah 1:17; Psalms 15:2; and Proverbs 31:8–9.)

The emphasis of the biblical tradition upon the pursuit of justice influences later rabbinic teachers as well. Commenting on our Torah portion's command to appoint judges and for those judges to "pursue justice," Rabbi Simeon ben Gamaliel, who served as president of the Sanhedrin in the middle of the first century, C.E., warns his generation: "Do not ridicule or scorn the doing of justice for it is one of the foundations of the world. For the world is balanced on three things—on justice, on truth, and on peace." (*Deuteronomy Rabbah* 5:1; also *Avot* 1:18)

Other rabbinic commentators claim that the guarantee of justice in the courts and in all dealings between human beings is more important than all the sacrifices offered at the Temple in Jerusalem. Justifying their view, they quote a verse from Proverbs, which declares: "To do righteousness and justice is more desired by God than sacrifices." The rabbis maintain that sacrifices had value during the limited historical period of the Temple. By contrast, the doing of justice is always crucial to society's welfare.

To seek justice

To seek justice is to relieve the oppressed. But how else are the oppressed to be relieved if not by judging the oppressor and crushing the ability to oppress! History is not a Sunday school where the question is to forgive or not to forgive. The toleration of injustice is the toleration of human suffering. Since the proud and the mighty who inflict the suffering do not, as a rule, yield to moral persuasion, responsibility for the sufferer demands that justice be done so that oppression be ended. (Eliezer Berkovits, Man and God: Studies in Biblical Theology, *Wayne State University Press, Detroit, 1969*)

Rabbi Nachman offers an example of the importance of justice within society by singling out the accomplishments of King David. "He judged others justly, acquitting the blameless and condemning the guilty, making the robber restore his stolen property." As a result, the kingdom he

built was a strong and secure one. People trusted one another and lived in cooperation and peace. (See Proverbs 21:3; *Deuteronomy Rabbah* 5:3.)

This emphasis upon justice within Jewish society is particularly evident within the early biblical and rabbinical judicial systems. *Parashat Shofetim* begins with Moses commanding the people to "appoint judges and clerks for your tribes, in all your settlements." Elders are to appoint judges for these courts and give them power to carry out hearings, trials, and judgments. If they, for any reason, cannot reach a decision, the case is to be turned over to a higher court of priests.

Rabbi Judah Ha-Nasi, author of the *Mishnah*, provides a description of the courts and cases before them. Each city had its local *bet din*, or "house of justice," comprised of three or seven judges with two levitical attendants. In Jerusalem there was a Small Sanhedrin of twenty-three judges and a Great Sanhedrin, which was not only the final arbiter of the law but also responsible for determining the religious calendar and defining matters of religious tradition. The Great Sanhedrin was comprised of seventy-one members, a number chosen because of God's command to Moses to choose seventy elders to help him with the leadership of the people. Adding Moses to the seventy, the rabbis held that the Great Sanhedrin should have a total of seventy-one members.

Rabbi Judah describes the work of each of these courts. The local *bet din* dealt with cases of property and personal injury. The Small Sanhedrin adjudicated criminal and capital cases. The Great Sanhedrin heard all exceptional matters and resolved those cases sent to it by the lower courts.

The system of justice also included regulations for appointing judges, examining witnesses, and hearing and deciding cases. Excluded from acting as judges were relatives, dice-players, those who loaned money on interest, pigeon-flyers, and those who sold produce grown during the sabbatical year. Relatives were also forbidden from serving as witnesses. Witnesses were to be examined one at a time without hearing the testimony of others so the court could compare their reports and reach a just decision.

In noncapital cases representatives were permitted to present arguments for dismissal or conviction in any order; in capital cases, however, the court first heard arguments for acquittal and then for conviction. The eldest judges were required to declare their opinion first when discussing a noncapital case. In capital cases, the youngest were required to speak first so that their opinions would not be influenced by the older judges.

A simple majority determined the verdict in noncapital cases; in capital cases a majority of one was sufficient for acquittal, but a majority of two was necessary for conviction. A higher court could reverse the decision of a lower court on noncapital matters, but in capital cases a higher court could only reverse a case from conviction to acquittal. Finally, the verdict on a noncapital case could be rendered on the same day as the hearing. In capital cases, if the verdict was acquittal, it could also be given on the same day, but if the court decision was conviction, the announcement could be made only the next day. Trials were never permitted on Shabbat or on festivals. (*Mishnah Sanhedrin* 1–5)

Clearly the issue of fair treatment in all cases was central to the Jewish court system of justice. Biased testimony and influence of one judge on another were to be avoided to guarantee fair trials. Decisions seemed to tilt toward acquittal and dismissal rather than conviction.

Commenting on the Torah's command to appoint judges who will promote justice, the *Sifre* emphasizes the importance of appointing judges with expert knowledge of the *halachah,* or "law," and with records of unquestionable integrity, honesty, and righteous behavior.

Rashi

Rashi notes that dispensing justice means not accepting bribes and never showing favor or preferential treatment to witnesses or those seeking judgment before the court. (Comments on Deuteronomy 16:18–20)

Several commentators ask the question: "Why does Moses repeat the word *tzedek,* or "justice," in his statement: "Justice, justice shall you pur-

sue, that you may thrive and occupy the land that *Adonai* your God is giving you"? Pointing out that the commandment could stand without the repetition since the Torah does not often repeat words, interpreters offer a number of explanations.

Some modern scholars suggest that the repetition is simply the way in which the ancient text forms an exclamation point or emphasizes an idea. By repeating the word *tzedek,* Moses underscores the importance of pursuing justice as a means of community survival.

Others argue that the term is repeated to convey the idea that the pursuit of justice is not only the responsibility of government, of judges within society, but also a mitzvah—an imperative—for each individual. One may not say, "Let the courts worry about right and wrong or justice and injustice. I will remain silent."

This may have been what Rabbi Aha meant when he quoted Rabbi Tanhum, son of Rabbi Hiyya, who said, "Though a person may be a scholar of Torah and a teacher of great renown, careful in observing all the ritual commandments, if such a person is able to protest wrongdoing and neglects to do so, he is to be considered cursed." Hearing this observation, Rabbi Jeremiah quoted Rabbi Hiyya who taught: "If a person is neither a scholar, nor a teacher, nor known for observing all the ritual commandments but stands up to protest against evil, such a person is called a blessing."

For rabbinic interpreters of Torah and for the prophets, the pursuit of justice in society was paramount. Correcting the evils originated by human beings was considered the highest ethical priority. Moses' repetition of "justice, justice" was understood to mean: "Don't be satisfied with observing wrongdoing. Stand up and protest against it!" (*Leviticus Rabbah* 25:1)

Why I protest

Author Elie Wiesel tells the story of the one righteous man of Sodom, who walked the streets protesting against the injustice of his city. People made fun of him, derided him. Finally, a young person asked: "Why do you continue your protest against evil; can't you see no one is paying attention to you?" He answered, "I'll tell you why I continue. In the beginning I thought I would change people. Today, I know I cannot. Yet, if I continue my protest, at least I will prevent others from changing me." (One Generation After, *Random House, New York, 1970, p. 72)*

Set the example

Levi Isaac taught that the meaning of the commandment "Set judges . . . in all your settlements" is that you must set justice in your gates, your high places, which you carry out and which you assure with your deeds. Each Jew is to be an example of the doing of justice for God. (See David R. Blumenthal, God at the Center, *pp. 154–155.)*

The mandate to go out of your way to guarantee justice is also seen in a rabbinic discussion comparing Abraham to Job. Job suffers great personal agony. He loses his riches; he endures the death of his children. Seeking an explanation, justice from God, he asks: "Did I not feed the hungry, give drink to the thirsty, clothe the naked? Why has all this evil come upon me?"

The rabbis claim that God answers: "True, you did all those just acts, but don't count yourself as having fully pursued justice. Compare your deeds with those of Abraham. Where you invited hungry guests into your home and greeted them when they came to the door, he ran out to greet them and invited them inside. Where you gave meat to those who normally ate meat, Abraham gave meat to those who were unaccustomed to eating meat. Where you provided wine and beds for those who were accustomed to drinking wine and sleeping on cots, Abraham built roadside inns to provide for thirsty and tired travelers."

From the rabbinic point of view, Job's pursuit of justice is halfway. He sits and waits. He gives only what is required. He does what is right but does not extend himself to do more. By contrast, Abraham goes beyond what is necessary. He generously greets tired travelers and gives them hospitality. He is not content to help the needy; he wants to prevent the root causes of the difficulties they face. By building roadside inns, he makes the extra effort. He practices the double

emphasis of *tzedek, tzedek tirdof,* or "justice, justice shall you pursue." (*Avot de-Rabbi Natan 7*)

Simeon ben Lakish, who lived and taught in Tiberias during the third century C.E., interprets the repetition of *tzedek, tzedek* as a special lesson in judgment. Lakish urges caution and careful probing. The repetition of *tzedek,* he teaches, is to remind us to make the extra effort to review and examine the evidence by listening carefully to what is said and by seeking out deception. There should be no rush to judgment. (*Sanhedrin 32b*)

Other commentators claim that the repetition of *tzedek* attached to the verb *tirdof,* or "pursue," means to emphasize that there are two forms of justice that must be fulfilled: the *tzedek* of "righteous" action and the *tzedek* of "just compromise." For example, what should be done when two ships meet at the same moment at the entrance to a narrow waterway? Each claims that it arrived first and, therefore, should enter first. Each has *tzedek* on its side. However, if both enter the channel at the same time, they will crash and sink.

The rabbis conclude that in such a case the best solution is to effect a compromise. The repetition of *tzedek* teaches us that when two fully justified claims clash with each other, the just solution is for the parties to find a compromise between them. (*Torah Temimah.* See commentary on Deuteronomy 16:20.)

Rambam (Maimonides)

Moses Maimonides suggests an additional interpretation of the repetition of *tzedek.* It is there, he says, to emphasize the need to reach judgments through a process of consultation. Individuals and judges should not make decisions based on their own impressions. They should discuss a case thoroughly, review it carefully, listen to varying opinions and perspectives, and reach judgments with open eyes and minds. Pursuing justice means going out of your way to make sure that you have gathered all the facts, have consulted with all the experts, and have taken no short cuts. (Comment on Deuteronomy 16:20)

Obviously, the pursuit of justice is a critical and central concern of Jewish society. Within the Hebrew Bible and imbedded within rabbinic commentary, the accomplishment of justice is a requisite for truth and peace. Jews are commanded to pursue justice because no human community can survive without it. The cornerstone of Jewish ethics is to "be deliberate and careful in judgment" because "where justice is done, peace and truth prevail." (*Avot* 1:1; *Pesikta de-Rav Kahana* 140b)

PEREK BET: *Don't Destroy the Environment, God's Precious Gift!*

If the pursuit of justice discussed above is meant to preserve the delicate relations of human beings within society, Moses' instruction concerning the treatment of trees is meant to preserve the delicate relations of human beings to the environment of the earth. Moses tells the people: "When in your war against a city you have to besiege it a long time in order to capture it, you must not destroy its trees, wielding the ax against them. You may eat of them, but you must not cut them down." Then, as if to create sympathy for the trees, he adds the question: "Are trees of the field, like human beings, capable of withdrawing before you into the besieged city?" (Deuteronomy 20:19)

While the commandment deals specifically with cutting down trees during a siege, Jewish interpreters extend it to cover all forms of wasteful destruction under the principle of *bal tashchit,* or "do not destroy." (See discussion of this principle as it relates to the treatment of animals in *Parashat Re'eh.*)

Accordingly, they forbid shifting the course of a stream that could cause the roots of trees to dry up. When asked for the justification for such a law, the rabbis explain that our Torah portion forbids destroying trees, not only by chopping them down with an ax, but "by all means of destruction," including the diversion of water from their roots. Rabbinic commentators also extend Moses' prohibition of cutting down trees during a siege to a prohibition of cutting them

down during times of peace. Wasteful destruction is condemned. "Anyone who deliberately breaks dishes, tears clothing, wrecks a building, clogs up a fountain, or wastes food violates the law of *bal tashchit.* (*Hullin* 7b; *Tosafot Baba Kamma* 115b; *Avodah Zarah* 30b; *Kiddushin* 32a)

Aversion to vandalism
Rabbi Joseph Karo in his Shulchan Aruch *declares: "It is forbidden to destroy or to injure anything capable of being useful to human beings."* (Hilchot Shemirat Guf va-Nefesh 14)

Rabbi Robert Gordis comments: "The principle of bal tashchit *entered deep into Jewish consciousness so that the aversion to vandalism became an almost psychological reflex, and wanton destruction was viewed with loathing and horror by Jews for centuries."* (Congress Bi-Weekly, *April 2, 1971, p.10*)

Teach your children what we have taught our children—the earth is our mother. Whatever befalls the earth befalls the children of the earth. If human beings foul the ground, they foul themselves. This we know. The earth does not belong to humanity; humanity belongs to the earth. This we know. All things are connected like the blood that unites one family. All things are connected. Whatever befalls the earth befalls the children of the earth. Humanity did not weave the web of life; it is merely a strand in it. Whatever humanity does to the web, it does to itself. (Chief Seattle, as quoted in The Earth Speaks, *edited by Steve Van Matre and Bill Weiler, Institute for Earth Education, Warrensville, Illinois, 1983, p. 122)*

While all commentators seem to agree with the emphasis against wasteful destruction, there are differences of opinion on the justification for such a prohibition. The differences reveal at least two foundations for the Jewish concern about the environment.

Moses ibn Ezra, for example, takes a very pragmatic view about chopping down trees. He argues that fruit trees yield food; human beings require their produce for existence. Therefore, we are prohibited from cutting them down because, in doing so, we are injuring ourselves. "The life of human beings," he writes, "derives from trees." One does not destroy the environment because destruction of the environment results in self-destruction.

Hirsch

Rabbi Samson Raphael Hirsch agrees with this pragmatic—human-centered—approach. He emphasizes that "the tree of the field is the human being; the products of the soil are the condition for human existence." For Hirsch, as for ibn Ezra, destroying fruit trees or wasting precious resources endangers human life. It wastes that which we require for survival. God gave us the world to enjoy, with its fruits to nourish and sustain us. We are commanded "to rule the fish of the sea, the birds of the sky, the cattle, the whole earth," not to pollute its waters and air or waste its precious resources and beautiful forests. Such careless destruction endangers not only our planet but human life as well. (Comments on Deuteronomy 20:19)

A story about Honi Ha-Ma'agal, who lived during the first century C.E. in the Land of Israel, dramatically exemplifies the dependency of human beings on trees. Out walking one day, he sees an old man planting a carob tree. He asks him: "How long does it take for a carob tree to bear fruit?"

The old man replies, "Seventy years." Surprised, Honi asks: "Old man, do you expect to live another seventy years to eat from its fruits?" The old man laughs. "When I came into the world, I found carob trees planted by others. Now I am planting new ones for my children and their children." (Ta'anit 23a)

Contemporary environmentalists raise the same concern as the old man, seeing the need to plant fruit trees for the future. Restoring our planet's diminishing resources is a critical issue—one that affects our present and will certainly shape our future on earth. Destruction of tropical forests,

which contain between 50 percent and 80 percent of the earth's species and countless genetic materials for curing diseases and improving crops, endangers the future of life on earth. Lumbering without a policy of reforestation has reduced forests in the United States, Europe, Africa, and Asia, leaving huge expanses of land open to erosion. The burn-off of these lands introduces millions of tons of greenhouse gases and pollutants into the atmosphere.

The ethical concerns of Jewish commentators about preserving and replenishing the critical resources of the earth have clear implications for life on this planet. Caring about trees is a matter of life and death. Perhaps that was the motivation behind the teaching of Rabbi Yochanan ben Zakkai, a student of Hillel, who headed the Sanhedrin during the siege of Jerusalem by the Romans in 70 C.E. Rabbi Yochanan taught that if you are in the midst of planting a tree and are told that the Messiah, the messenger bringing a new era of peace to the world, has arrived, you must not stop planting. "First," says Rabbi Yochanan, "finish planting the tree, then go out and greet the Messiah."

In other words, the duty of insuring the future through replenishing the earth is more important than promises of peace, even if they are brought by the Messiah. Work done to preserve and protect the environment serves to promote human survival.

Blessings for trees

Rabbi Judah said: "When you go out during spring and see the trees budding, you should say, 'Be praised, O God, who has caused nothing to be lacking in the world and has created beautiful creations and beautiful trees from which human beings derive pleasure.'" (Berachot 43b)

When you see handsome or beautiful people or lovely trees, you should say: "Be praised, O God, who creates beautiful creatures in the world." (Mishnah Berachot 7:7)

Let us begin to think about the mystery of life and the links that connect us with the life that fills the world, and we cannot but bring to bear upon our own lives and all other life that comes within our reach the principle of reverence for life. (Albert Schweitzer)

taught, "The heavens are the heavens of God; but the earth God has given to humanity." (Psalms 115:16)

There is, however, another interpretation of Moses' command against cutting down trees. Beyond justifying the prohibition from a pragmatic—human-centered—point of view, there is also a spiritual foundation for not destroying trees and the environment. Jacob ben Isaac Ashkenazi of Yanof, author of *Tze'enah u-Re'enah,* presents such a point of view. He suggests that there is good reason for the Torah text not only to forbid cutting down trees but to ask the question: "Are trees of the field, like human beings, capable of withdrawing before you into the besieged city?" It does so, says Rabbi Jacob, to focus attention on the sacred "life" within trees.

Jacob ben Isaac asks, "Why does the Torah compare a tree to human beings? Because, just as human beings have the power to grow within them, so do trees. And just as human beings bear children, so do trees bear fruits. When a human being is hurt, the painful cries are heard throughout the world, and when a tree is chopped down, its cries are heard from one end of the earth to the other." (Comment on Deuteronomy 20:19)

Using the tree as an example, Rabbi Jacob means to create a sympathy and awareness that all living things—human beings, animals, trees, or vegetation—are formed by God, the sacred Source of life. For that reason all existence must be respected and nurtured.

It is remarkable that Jewish tradition's concern for the environment originates in an ancient time when fears about exploiting or endangering the planet were remote. Nonetheless, Torah interpreters sensed the danger of damaging God's creation by polluting and wasting precious natural resources and potentials. They saw the earth as a gift to humanity and human beings as partners with God in sustaining the delicate ecological balance of earth. With the Psalmist they

QUESTIONS FOR STUDY AND DISCUSSION

1. Rabbi Ephraim Lunshitz, who died in Prague in 1619, asked, "Is it possible for a man to act justly, and yet unrighteousness can be involved in what he does?" Take the case of a businessman who secretly cheats by adjusting his scales so they will underweigh his product, at the same time providing an incentive to his customers by advertising that product at a better price than that of his competitors. How do the principles of justice discussed by the commentators apply to such a case?

2. Jewish tradition claims that without justice there can be no truth or peace in human society. Do you agree? What examples from history or contemporary life can you give to prove this ancient argument?

3. Rabbinic commentators claim that when God created the first human beings, all the trees in the Garden of Eden were placed before them. God said: "Behold all that I have created, how beautiful and excellent it all is! I have created it all for you. Think upon this. Do not corrupt or ruin My world for there will be no one to repair it after you." (*Ecclesiastes Rabbah* 7:28) What are the lessons we can learn from this ancient rabbinic warning?

4. Scientists have identified four major threats to the earth's environment: (1) destruction of forests and life species; (2) overpopulation; (3) global warming; and (4) waste disposal. Given the discussion about forbidding the destruction of trees, how do you think Jewish tradition deals with these "threats"?

PARASHAT KI TETZE
Deuteronomy 21:10–25:19

Parashat Ki Tetze contains a mixture of seventy-two commandments, dealing with such diverse subjects as the treatment of captives, defiant children, lost animals, birds' nests, roof railings, divorce, rights of aliens, loans, vows, protection of works, parental guilt, charity for the poor, regulations for inheritance, and fair weights and measures. The portion concludes with a warning to remember how the Amalekites attacked the weary Israelites in the desert.

OUR TARGUM

· 1 ·

M oses sets out rules for the fair treatment of women captives. If they are taken as wives and then divorced, they are to be set free.

The rights of inheritance for the firstborn apply although a father may have multiple wives and many other children.

A disloyal and defiant son who does not obey his parents is to be brought for judgment before the town elders. If he is guilty, they are to stone him to death. A person put to death must be buried on the same day.

· 2 ·

If a neighbor's animal or garment is lost, it must be returned when it is found. If an animal has fallen on the road, it must be helped. One must not remain indifferent.

Men and women must not dress in each other's clothing.

If a bird's nest with fledglings or eggs is found, the mother bird must not be taken with her young.

Railings must be placed on roofs.

A vineyard must not be sown with a second kind of seed. One may not plow with an ox and ass together nor muzzle an ox while it is threshing. One may not wear garments mixed with the fibers of wool and linen. *Tzitzit,* or "fringes," are to be worn on the four corners of garments.

If a man marries a woman and later charges she was not a virgin, but her parents prove her virginity with stained sheets from the wedding night, the man is to be punished and fined for ruining the reputation of the woman. He may not divorce her. However, if the charges are true, she is to be stoned for bringing shame on the people of Israel.

The penalty for adultery is death. If a man has sex in a city with a woman engaged to another man, both are to be put to death—she because she did not cry out for help; he because he violated her. If, however, he rapes her in an open field, only he shall be put to death for he is like a murderer. If a man lies with a virgin who is not engaged and they are discovered, he is to marry her and he may never divorce her.

·3·

A man is not permitted to marry his father's former wife. Children of adulterous or incestuous relationships, along with Ammonites or Moabites, are not to be admitted to the people of Israel. Edomites, however, are to be considered as brothers and sisters.

All human waste is to be disposed of outside the camp.

Slaves seeking refuge must be taken in and treated kindly. Israelites are forbidden to become cult prostitutes, nor can money from whoring be used as gifts to the sanctuary.

·4·

It is forbidden to take interest from other Israelites but permissible to do so from foreigners. Promises must be fulfilled.

When entering your neighbor's vineyard or fields as a laborer, you may eat grapes and pluck ears of corn with your hands, but you may not place grapes in a container or cut grain with a sickle.

A man may not remarry a woman he has divorced, who then married another man who divorced her or died.

A newly married man is exempt from army service for one year.

When a loan is made to a neighbor, it is forbidden to enter his house to claim his pledge. If he is needy, the pledge must be returned to him at sundown. Abuse of needy, destitute laborers is forbidden. Wages should be paid by sundown of each day.

Uphold the rights of the stranger. Do not take a widow's garment as a pawn. Leave all sheaves overlooked during the harvest for the stranger, the fatherless, and the widow. Do not shake your olive tree twice or pick your vineyard a second

time. Instead, allow the needy to eat what is left after the harvest.

·5·

When a court renders a decision, the punishment of the guilty party is to be carried out before the innocent party. The punishment is not to exceed forty lashes.

When brothers live together and one of them dies leaving no son, it is the duty of a living brother to marry his brother's widow and to father a child in his brother's name. If the brother refuses, the widow may publicly declare: "He refuses to build up his brother's house."

You must employ honest weights and measures in all business dealings. Those who deal dishonestly are hateful to God.

Finally, Moses reminds the people how Amalek attacked the weak and weary Israelites on their journey through the desert. "Remember Amalek," he warns. "Blot out the memory of Amalek from under heaven."

THEMES

Parashat Ki Tetze contains two important themes:

1. A warning against indifference.
2. Marriage and divorce.

PEREK ALEF: *You Shall Not Remain Indifferent*

Parashat Ki Tetze contains seventy-two commandments, the largest number in any Torah portion. Among these are the obligation to return lost property and the responsibility to help those in need.

Regarding lost property, the Torah commands us to return anything we find that belongs to another person, be it an ox, a sheep, a garment—anything that may have been lost. The Torah adds the warning, "You must not remain indifferent." (Deuteronomy 22:1–3)

The Torah is also quite clear concerning the obligation to aid someone in need. Our responsibility is to help others with their burden. If, for example, while traveling along a road, we come upon the fallen ox or donkey of a friend, the Torah says, "Do not ignore it; you must help him raise it."

What obligations, however, do we have if the lost property belongs to an enemy or the animal in distress belongs to someone we dislike?

In a parallel passage found in *Parashat Mishpatim* (see Exodus 23:4–5), Moses makes it clear that the lost property of enemies must be returned and an animal in distress belonging to an enemy must be helped. Are we then to assume that the Torah teaches that we have the same ethical responsibility to both friends and enemies when it comes to returning lost property or offering help? Would not such a command contradict normal human emotions?

Early rabbinic interpreters insist that, whether the lost item belongs to one's enemy or friend, it must be returned. Furthermore, if the person finding the property makes a profit with it before returning it to the owner, that profit belongs to the owner and must be paid back when the lost property is restored. If the property cannot be returned and its care costs money, the owner must pay the amount when the property is restored. (*Baba Metzia* 26a–30a)

> **The status of lost property**
> *Some found articles become the property of the finder immediately, and others have to be advertised.*
>
> *The following become the property of the finder: scattered fruits, scattered coins, small sheaves of corn lying in a public road, cakes of pressed figs, bakers' loaves, strings of fish, pieces of meat, fleeces of wool in their natural state. . . .*
>
> *The following found articles must be advertised so that the owner may repossess them: fruit in a vessel or an empty vessel; money in a purse or an empty purse; heaps of fruit; heaps of*

coins; three coins, one on top of the other; small sheaves lying on private property; homemade loaves of bread; fleeces of wool that had been removed from a workshop. . . . If someone finds something in a store, it belongs to him; but, if he finds it between the counter and the store-keeper's seat, it belongs to the storekeeper. (Mishnah Baba Metzia 2:1, 2, 4)

For example, rabbinic interpreters tell of a man who, passing the door of Rabbi Hanina ben Dosa, accidentally left some of his hens. "We must not eat their eggs," Rabbi Hanina told his family. However, the eggs and hens quickly multiplied, and there was no place to keep them. So Rabbi Hanina sold them and purchased goats. Sometime later, the man who had accidently left his hens returned, asking about them. Rabbi Hanina inquired if he had some identification to prove his ownership. He did. Rabbi Hanina immediately gave him the goats.

They also tell of Rabbi Pinchas ben Yair who was once visited by men who brought with them two measures of barley. They deposited the barley with him and then apparently forgot about it. Rabbi Pinchas sowed the barley for several years, harvesting it and storing it. When, after seven years, the men returned, Rabbi Pinchas told them: "Take your storehouses filled with grain." (Ta'anit 25a; Deuteronomy Rabbah 3:5)

Leibowitz

Both incidents above emphasize not only the ethical responsibility of returning to others what they have lost but also the principle that the person finding lost property should not profit from it. In her discussion of both rabbinic stories, modern commentator Nehama Leibowitz points out an additional ethical dimension. "The mitzvah of restoring lost property . . . involves, not only the passive taking charge of the article until the owner claims it, but also an active concern with safeguarding a neighbor's possessions so that they remain intact and constitute something

worth restoring." Jewish law is clear about the obligation of returning that which has been lost. The finder must care for the property, may not profit from it, and, if it is invested, owes all earnings when it is restored. (*Studies in Devarim,* p. 214)

The issue of returning lost property raises other important considerations about the way human beings deal with one another and the trust required to make human society secure. Bachya ben Joseph ibn Pakuda argues that such ethical concerns relate to other matters raised by the Torah. Restoring property, says Bachya, is a fulfillment of the Torah's instruction to "love your neighbor as yourself." (Leviticus 19:18) Property is an extension of each individual. It is like the limb of one's body. Loving one's neighbors means taking care of all that is important to them as you would want them to safeguard all that is important to you. Returning lost property is a demonstration of love and concern for one's neighbors. (See Abraham Chill, *The Mitzvot,* pp. 452–454.)

Aharon Halevi in his *Sefer ha-Hinuch* extends Bachya's view, arguing that the commandment to return lost property is "fundamental" and that "all society depends upon it." It is not just a matter of one person taking care of another's possessions or of "loving" another. What is important here is the critical matter of "trust" among human beings. A society depends upon the faith people place in one another. Without people feeling that they can rely upon one another—that others are looking out for what belongs to me and that I must look out for what belongs to them—society collapses into suspicion, selfishness, and bitter contention. Whether people return or keep lost articles, says Halevi, is a significant indication of a society's health. (538)

You shall return it
A man once visited Rabbi Aaron of Chernobyl and told him about his nightmares. In one dream he picked up a wallet containing a fortune. When he pursued its owner in the crowd, he could not find him. With the funds he found he grew wealthy. On the other hand, the man who had lost the money fell on terrible

misfortune, losing his businesses and the trust of others. He died leaving his wife and children in poverty, with no one to support them and no one to finance the education of his children.

The man who had prospered told Rabbi Aaron of Chernobyl that he suffered from terrible recurring dreams about taking the wallet and being responsible for the harm its loss had brought upon others. He pleaded for the rabbi to advise him what to do.

The rabbi commanded him to find the family of the man, to give them half of what he had accumulated, and to see to it that the man's children were educated. When he did so, his recurring nightmares ceased. (S.Y. Zevin, A Treasury of Chasidic Tales, pp. 561–563)

What about returning that which you may have to go out of your way to rescue? If you have restored lost property once to its owner, must you do so again if you find it? What if the lost property belongs to an enemy? What if you find an enemy's property in danger? What obligations do you have?

Ramban (Nachmanides)

Nachmanides makes it clear that the mitzvah of returning lost property supersedes any inconvenience to the finder. The finder is obligated to announce the discovery of the lost item so that others will know he possesses it, and the loser's anxiety will be shortened.

Carrying out the mitzvah of restoring lost property applies to friends, strangers, and even to enemies. If one encounters a person whose property is in danger—a donkey who has fallen while carrying a heavy load, a runaway animal, or a broken vehicle—one's ethical responsibility is to help save the property. This applies also to the property of an enemy. Nachmanides puts it this way: "Assist others. Remember the bond of humanity between you and forget the hatred." (Comments on Deuteronomy 22:1–2)

Benno Jacob

Benno Jacob builds upon Nachmanides' interpretation. He explains that "when you see the animal of your enemy fallen on the road, it is natural for you to think, 'I will ignore it. I will not lend a helping hand. After all, why should I do a good deed for someone who hates me and has treated me badly?' But the Torah teaches us to overcome our hatred and to do everything possible to be of help."

Jacob sees the act of helping an enemy as a means of arriving at reconciliation. First, one sees the fallen animal and understands that help must be given. One is likely to say, "I'll help to relieve the pain of the animal." Yet, once involved, words of concern for the animal are exchanged. This leads to other words and finally to forgiveness between those who are angry with each other. In this way, the mitzvah of turning aside to aid an animal brings about renewed trust and friendship. (Comment on Exodus 23:4–5)

Peli

You must not remain indifferent
From the moment one notices an animal gone astray or an object lost by someone, one may not "hide oneself." Whether he is busy with something else or whether he chooses to get involved, a person is in fact involved and duty-bound to bring the object to his home, keeping it there safely until it can be returned to its owner. . . . While some legal systems require returning or handing over found property to the authorities, none enjoins the finder from ignoring the lost object in the first place. (Pinchas H. Peli, Jerusalem Post, September 7, 1985)

People often value possessions as much as life itself. Therefore, when they lose something that has a special distinction, they are likely to feel great pain as if a life has been lost. Those finding the lost object and failing to return it are contributing to the distress and mental anguish of others. (Rabbi Menachem ben Benjamin Recanati, 13th century, Italy, as found in Abraham Chill, The Mitzvot, *p. 454)*

Rambam (Maimonides)

*Moses Maimonides comments: We are forbidden to shut our eyes to lost property; we must pick it up and return it to its owner. This prohibition is what is meant by the words: "You must not remain indifferent." (*Sefer ha-Mitzvot, *Positive Commandments #269)*

Malbim

Nehama Leibowitz, basing her interpretation on that of Malbim, suggests that the command to turn aside and help an enemy whose property is in danger is an example of how the Torah deals with the real world. It does not present a world where all people get along with one another or rush to care for one another's property. Instead, it "takes into account the grim reality that people do not achieve the desired observance of 'you shall not hate others in your heart.' "

Leibowitz stresses that the Torah "lays down rules of behavior even for such an admittedly immoral situation where two people are hostile to each other, enjoining such acts of assistance as relieving the ass of an enemy of its burden and the returning of his lost property. These small deeds of goodwill," Leibowitz concludes, "would, it is hoped, eventually lead to the removal of hatred. . . ." Indeed, as Leibowitz

makes clear, the rabbinic commentators of the Talmud state the moral standard to be followed and the reason for it. "If you are faced with the situation of your friend requiring help with his animal and also your enemy, your first duty is to aid your enemy. For in this way we train and discipline our instincts." (*Studies in Shemot,* World Zionist Organization, Jerusalem, 1980, pp. 428–434; *Baba Metzia* 32b)

After the Torah clarifies the duty to return lost property or to keep it safe until it can be restored to its owner, it concludes with the words *lo tuchal le-hitalem,* or "you must not remain indifferent." Many interpreters point out that this phrase may also be translated literally as "you shall not hide" or "you shall not act as if you were blind."

This powerful phrase puts forth the ethical demand of Torah. Upon encountering a lost object, a fallen animal in pain under its burden, the property of friends or enemies in danger, one's duty is to help. We are not permitted to look the other way, to pass by without paying attention, or to continue with our business as usual. Hiding the truth from ourselves and not acting to help others is immoral. Indifference is intolerable. Responsible caring is at the heart of Jewish ethics.

PEREK BET: *Marriage and Divorce*

Parashat Ki Tetze discusses both the institution of marriage and the process of divorce. In the Torah, men choose their wives and have the right to divorce them. If a wife lies about being a virgin at the time of marriage, she may be stoned to death. If a woman "fails to please her husband because he finds something obnoxious about her," he may divorce her. There are few hints that affection is the basis of marriage relationships; there is no indication of mutuality or equal rights for women in choosing a husband or seeking a divorce. (See Genesis 24:67.)

In interpreting the Torah's description of marriage and divorce, the commentators raise significant questions. They inquire about the purpose of marriage, explore its emotional and legal consequences, and examine the appropriate conditions and rituals for divorce. As with other subjects, it is the interpreters who, over the centuries, unlock new understandings and initiate new rituals. In doing so, they adapt the commandments of Torah to new conditions of society and to new moral sensibilities. Marriage and divorce are important examples of such dynamic change and evolution within Jewish tradition.

After describing the creation of heaven and earth, the Torah reports that God comments, "It is not good for man to be alone. I will make a fitting helper for him." In answer to loneliness, God creates woman and declares: "A man will leave his father and mother and cling to his wife so that they become one flesh." Within this early description, the Torah advances the view that marriage provides mutual support, total trust, caring, and companionship. Husband and wife are "helpers" to each other; they are to be inseparable—"one flesh"—both physically and spiritually. Together they form a sacred new world through which they create a family. (Genesis 2:18–24)

Early rabbinic commentators stress the importance of marriage. Rabbi Akiba remarks that "a man who does not marry impairs the divine image," meaning that love and marriage are the will of God. Rabbi Jacob teaches that "he who does not have a wife lives without joy, without blessing, without a helper, without goodness, and without atonement. Some add, without Torah and moral protection." Rabba ben Ulla adds, "without peace." (*Genesis Rabbah* 17:2; *Yevamot* 62a–63b)

The author of the mystical commentary the *Zohar* underscores the centrality of marriage by claiming that, since finishing the creation of the world, God has been busy with creating "new worlds" by bringing together bridegrooms and brides. Since marriage perpetuates life and fills it with love, nothing has greater value. Marriage, concludes the author of the *Zohar*, keeps God in the world because God's Presence dwells in the love between husband and wife. (*Zohar* 1:89a; 3:59a)

While the Torah makes reference to "a man marrying a women," it does not describe any ceremony or ritual. Later rabbinic tradition defines three aspects of the marriage ritual: *sheduchin,* or "engagement"; *erusin,* or "betrothal";

and *nisuin,* or "marriage vows." Originally, these three rituals were celebrated at different times. Later, *erusin* and *nisuin* were merged into the wedding ceremony called *kiddushin,* or "holiness."

Just before the wedding ceremony a *ketubah,* or "written agreement" between husband and wife, is signed. The *ketubah* functioned throughout the centuries as a prenuptial agreement, spelling out the obligations assumed by the husband in marriage. These included support, food, clothing, shelter, and sexual relations. It also specified fixed financial arrangements should the couple divorce. Many Jews continue to use the ancient formulas for their *ketubah;* others choose a *ketubah* that is more egalitarian in its language, making clear the mutual responsibilities and commitments of husband and wife.

After signing the *ketubah,* the bride and groom are led to the *chupah,* or "wedding canopy," symbolizing the Jewish home they are about to establish. Beneath the *chupah,* the *birkat erusin,* or "betrothal blessing," is recited, including the blessing, "Be praised, O God, who sanctifies Your people Israel through the celebration of *chupah* and marriage." The groom then places a wedding ring of precious value, but without jewels, upon the bride's finger and says to her: "With this ring be consecrated to me as my wife in accordance with the law of Moses and the people of Israel." Among Reform, Conservative, and Reconstructionist Jews, brides often exchange a ring and a similar vow with their bridegrooms.

The exchange of rings is followed by the recitation of the *sheva berachot,* or "seven wedding blessings." These thank God for the creation of man and woman and the desire to perpetuate life; ask God to provide bride and groom with the happiness of Adam and Eve in the Garden of Eden; and express the hope that the rejoicing of bride and groom will soon be heard in the Land of Israel. The rabbi then presents the couple with their *ketubah,* and the ceremony is concluded by breaking a glass. According to some rabbis, breaking the glass commemorates the destruction of the Jerusalem Temple in 70 C.E. Others say that the ritual is meant to remind the bride and groom that they have obligations to the "shattered" within society, the poor, hungry, homeless, and helpless. Still others see in the ritual a symbolic expression of the triumph of truth, hope, and love over the persecution and suffering of the Jews throughout the ages.

All the prayers and rituals of *kiddushin* are meant to uplift and celebrate the love shared by bride and groom. However, the marriage ceremony is not only a public acknowledgment of their special love relationship, but it also marks the establishment of a Jewish home, which guarantees the Jewish future. Through their commitments to celebrate Shabbat and holy days, to maintain their Jewish community and the welfare of their people throughout the world, and to elevate their relationship through Jewish study and charity, bride and groom strengthen the Jewish people. Rabbinic interpreters understood that marriage was not only an institution through which human satisfaction might be achieved, but they praised it as one of the "most important ingredients of the magic potion that has strengthened the Jew to survive." (Trude Weiss-Rosmarin, quoted in *A Modern Treasury of Jewish Thoughts*, p. 149)

Despite such regard for the institution of marriage, however, rabbinic commentators were realists. They knew that some partnerships between husband and wife begin in rapture and happiness but end in disappointment and bitterness. Rabbi Akiba observes that "if a husband and wife are worthy, then God dwells between them. If they are not worthy, fire will consume them." Akiba, whose marriage to Rachel was one of passion, sacrifice, mutual support, and respect, may have been speaking from his own experience. He and Rachel endured hardship in order for him to acquire a Jewish education. Their devotion to each other was a model for their students. Akiba observed that without such shared priorities, without trust and an affection that accommodates differences, marriage turns into a battleground—into a consuming fire. (*Sotah* 17a)

Because Jewish tradition does not rule out incompatibility between husband and wife, it accepts the tragedy and necessity of divorce. "Many marry," comments a rabbinic teacher, "some succeed, some come to grief." Others express the matter of compatibility in a powerful image.

"When love is strong, a husband and wife can make their bed on the edge of a sword's blade. When love diminishes in strength, a wide, soft bed is never large enough." Couples may marry with great expectations, feeling that they share enthusiasms, mutual passion, and a will to create a home and family. Yet, with all their good intentions, differences surface. Stress from work and unresolved tensions often lead to great unhappiness and a decision to divorce. (*Numbers Rabbah* 9:4; *Sanhedrin* 7a)

The Torah treats divorce as an occurrence that must be regulated by law and the traditions of the community. The Torah says, "If a wife fails to please her husband, if he finds something obnoxious about her, he may write her a *sefer keritut*, or a *get*, as it is called in the Talmud, a "document of divorce." (Deuteronomy 24:1) Rabbinic commentators insist that a wife also has the right to initiate divorce if she is unhappy with her spouse. Grounds for initiating divorce by either husband or wife may be sexual or social incompatibility, distasteful feelings in the presence of the other person, infertility, one spouse's refusal to have children, a refusal to work or provide support, mental illness, a chronic disease that makes sharing physical intimacy impossible, unfaithfulness, conversion to another religion, abandonment, or abuse. (See Isaac Klein, *A Guide to Jewish Religious Practice*, Jewish Theological Seminary, distributed by Ktav, New York, 1979, chap. XXXIII, pp. 466–473.)

While the Torah speaks only of the husband giving his wife a "document of divorce," later rabbinic tradition defines the process of the divorce proceedings: The husband arranges for a *sofer*, or "scribe," to write a *get*, a document especially for the wife that includes the declaration: "I release you . . . to go and be married to any man you may desire. . . ." The *get* is given to the wife by the husband before two witnesses who sign it. Where distance separates a couple, the husband may send the *get* to his wife through an agent authorized by him to present it. For a divorce to be valid, both parties must agree willingly, without pressure, to give and to accept it. (*Shulchan Aruch* 140–141)

Despite the realistic acceptance of the necessity of divorce, Jewish interpreters underscore the tragedy it represents. "If a man divorces his wife," they teach, "even the altar of the Temple sheds tears." Rabbi Yochanan is more harsh in his judgment: "Whoever divorces his wife is hated by God!" Undoubtedly such commentators saw in divorce not only the sad defeat of all the hopes of bride and groom but also a severe blow to the vitality and future of the Jewish community. (*Gittin* 90b; *Avot de-Rabbi Natan* 30)

No marriage is without its periods of satisfaction and frustration. A medieval rabbi has observed that "the honeymoon lasts for a month, the troubles for a lifetime." Jewish tradition wisely counsels that husband and wife facing irreconcilable differences should seek counseling and the mending of their love. Marriage expert, author, and psychologist Dr. Aaron T. Beck writes that "mates need to cooperate, compromise, and follow through with joint decisions. They have to be resilient, accepting, and forgiving. They need to be tolerant of each other's flaws, mistakes, and peculiarities." Beck concludes that as these "virtues" are developed over time, "the marriage develops and matures." (*Love Is Never Enough*, Harper and Row Publishers, Inc., New York, 1988, p. 4)

With major changes in the roles of men and women in the workplace and in marriage, the mutual commitment to work at such maturation of love is critical. As a part of that process, Jewish tradition can play an important role. Celebrating sacred times and seasons together can bond a couple, as can shared commitments to enhance the community through volunteer service and charity. Love suffocates when it is not shared. It evolves into mutual satisfaction, support, and fulfillment when its power is allowed to flower in all our relationships.

The talmudic rabbis comment that "it is as hard to arrange and sustain a good marriage as it was for God to divide the Red Sea before the escaping Israelites." The recognition that love between husband and wife is truly an unfathomable mystery and a delicate gift is at the heart of Jewish tradition's view of marriage and divorce. To build their relationship into blessings remains the challenge of every husband and wife.

QUESTIONS FOR STUDY AND DISCUSSION

1. The Torah and nearly all of the commentators place great emphasis upon restoring lost property. Why is this important to the stability of a society? Are there other commandments that are equally critical?

2. Do you agree with those commentators who argue that when we reach out to help our enemies, it is likely we will end up as friends? Can you cite some examples from your own experience or from history?

3. If you were writing a *ketubah* today, what would you have a bride and groom pledge to do in their marriage to assure its success? If you were putting together a modern *get,* what would the divorce document say?

4. Commenting on the significance of Jewish commitment and practice as a means of strengthening a marriage, Benjamin Kaplan writes: "A religiously motivated home can bring a sense of belonging . . . it can be the major buffer in easing the tensions that beset couples . . . it can absorb the shocks and tempers . . . in this frightfully competitive society." (*The Jew and His Family*, Louisiana State University Press, Baton Rouge, 1967, p. 189) Do you agree? What advice would you give couples about Jewish celebrations in their homes and involvement in their Jewish community?

PARASHAT KI TAVO
Deuteronomy 26:1–29:8

Parashat Ki Tavo addresses the time when the Israelites will settle in the Land of Israel. Moses instructs them to place in a basket the first fruits they have harvested and present them, together with a prayer, to the priest at the sanctuary. Their prayer is to be a formula recalling they were slaves in Egypt, liberated by God, and given the land whose first fruits they now enjoy. They are also to set aside a tenth part of their yield for the Levite, the stranger, the fatherless, and the widow, and they are to keep all the commandments given to them. In this way they will be a treasured people to God. Moses and the elders tell them, when they have settled in the land, to write the commandments on large plastered stones and set them up on Mount Ebal, where they are also to build an altar to God. Then representatives of the tribes of Simeon, Levi, Judah, Issachar, Joseph, and Benjamin are to stand on Mount Gerizim to hear the blessing describing the good times that will come as a result of observing God's commandments. Facing them on Mount Ebal, representatives from the tribes of Reuben, Gad, Asher, Zebulun, Dan, and Naphtali are to stand to hear the curse resulting from disobeying the commandments. God promises the Israelites blessings of plenty, security, and peace if they observe faithfully the teachings of Torah. Curses of destruction, agony, want, and exile will befall them if they spurn the teachings of Torah. "Observe faithfully all the terms of this covenant," Moses warns, "that you may succeed in all that you undertake."

OUR TARGUM

· 1 ·

Moses instructs the people, when they enter the Land of Israel and complete their harvest, to take their first fruits in a basket for an offering at the sanctuary. When the priest places the basket on the altar, the people are to declare: "My father was a fugitive Aramean. He went down to Egypt with meager numbers and sojourned there. . . . The Egyptians dealt harshly with us. . . . We cried to *Adonai* . . . *Adonai* heard our plea. . . . *Adonai* freed us from Egypt . . . and gave us this land. . . . Wherefore I now bring the first fruits of the soil which You, *Adonai,* have given me."

In the third year, after setting aside a tenth of the yield for the Levite, the stranger, the father-less, and the widow, the Israelites are commanded to declare: "I have cleared out the consecrated portion from the house; and I have given it to the Levite, the stranger, the fatherless, and the widow, just as You commanded me. . . . Look down from Your holy abode, from heaven, and bless Your people Israel and the soil You have given us, a land flowing with milk and honey, as You swore to our ancestors."

Moses reminds the people they are commanded to observe God's commandments faithfully. He tells them they are God's treasured people and, because of their faithfulness, God "will set you, in fame and renown and glory, high above all the nations . . . and you shall be, as God promised, a holy people to *Adonai* your God."

·2·

Moses provides instruction for them after they have crossed the Jordan. They are to set up large stones on Mount Ebal, plaster them over, and write upon them all the commandments of the Torah. In addition, they are to build an altar to God of uncut stones for offerings.

Moses describes a special ceremony where representatives from the tribes of Simeon, Levi, Judah, Issachar, Joseph, and Benjamin will stand on Mount Gerizim while words of blessing are spoken. Representatives from the tribes of Reuben, Gad, Asher, Zebulun, Dan, and Naphtali will stand on Mount Ebal while the curse is spoken. The ceremony is to dramatize to the Israelites the critical importance of living according to the laws of Torah.

Among the curses mentioned are those directed at Israelites who make idols; insult their parents; move a neighbor's landmark; mislead a blind person; subvert the rights of the stranger, the fatherless, or the widow; practice improper sexual relations; hurt another in secret; accept a bribe; or fail to live according to the terms of the Torah.

Ignoring God's commandments, Moses says, will cause calamity, panic, and misfortune. Enemies will bring destruction. God will strike Israel with sickness, scorching heat, and drought. "The skies above you shall be copper and the earth under you iron . . . you will be wiped out." Furthermore, you will be driven into exile; others will harvest your fields; nothing you plant will succeed. "The cricket shall take over all the trees and produce of your land." Plagues and chronic diseases will afflict you. "You shall find no peace. . . . The life you face shall be precarious; you shall be in terror, night and day, with no assurance of survival."

Conversely, abundant blessings are promised to the people if they are faithful to the laws of the Torah. They will be blessed with victory over their enemies and plenty in their harvests and all their undertakings. "*Adonai* will make you the head, not the tail; you will always be at the top and never at the bottom . . . if you do not deviate to the right or to the left from any of the commandments that I enjoin upon you. . . ." Your children will be blessed, all your property will prosper, so will your basket of charity, all your comings and goings.

Because of your faithfulness to the commandments, Moses tells the people, "*Adonai* will open for you a bounteous store, the heavens, to provide rain for your land in season and to bless all your undertakings. You will be creditor to many nations, but debtor to none." These are the terms of the covenant Moses concludes with the Israelites.

THEMES

Parashat Ki Tavo contains two important themes:

1. Reliving history.
2. Facing the consequences of our actions.

PEREK ALEF: *The Drama and Meaning of Reliving History*

In these speeches to the Israelites in the desert, Moses focuses on the future when the people have already conquered the Land of Israel and are enjoying its harvests. At that time, he tells them, they are to take "every first fruit of the soil . . . put it in a basket and go to the place where God's name will be established." Once at the sanctuary, they will present the basket to a priest, saying: "I acknowledge this day before *Adonai* our God that I have entered the land that *Adonai* swore to our ancestors to give us."

As the priest takes the basket, the Israelites are to continue the ritual drama with the following declaration: *Arami oved avi.* . . . "My father was a fugitive Aramean. He went down to Egypt with meager numbers and sojourned there; but there he became a great and very populous nation. The Egyptians dealt harshly with us and oppressed us; they imposed heavy labor upon us.

We cried to *Adonai,* the God of our ancestors, and *Adonai* heard our plea and saw our plight, our misery, and our oppression. *Adonai* freed us from Egypt by a mighty hand, by an outstretched arm and awesome power, and by signs and portents. God brought us to this place and gave us this land, a land flowing with milk and honey. Wherefore I now bring the first fruits of the soil that You, O *Adonai,* have given me."

One can easily imagine participating in such a ritual: filling the basket with first fruits, presenting it at the sanctuary, and reciting the declaration. But what is the purpose of this ceremony?

Several commentators point out that the ritual of declaration constitutes one of the only prayers found in the entire Torah. Its meaning, however, is a matter of dispute.

Rashi

Some interpreters, including the author of the *Sifre* and Rashi, insist that the translation of *Arami oved avi* is "an Aramean sought to destroy my father," meaning that Laban, for whom Jacob worked twenty years, intended to destroy him. This interpretation, as we shall see, is followed by those who authored the first Pesach *haggadot.*

Rashi's grandson argues that the Aramean mentioned is not Laban but Abraham, who was born and raised in Aram-naharaim.

Ibn Ezra

Others, following Abraham ibn Ezra, point out that it makes no sense to identify Laban or Abraham as the Aramean. Instead, ibn Ezra claims Moses is referring to Jacob, whose mother had come from Aram-naharaim, who was persecuted there by Laban, and who fled from the oppression of famine into Egypt, where Joseph was in power and could assure the survival of Jacob's family.

Given the variety of interpretations of the words

Arami oved avi, the ritual prayer could mean: "My father was a fugitive (wandering or persecuted) Aramean," referring to Abraham or Jacob. Or the text could mean: "An Aramean sought to destroy my father." In other words, Laban schemed to destroy Jacob and his family. Most modern biblical scholars agree that the identification of either Abraham or Jacob as the "fugitive" Aramean is correct.

The *Mishnah* describes the colorful celebration of offering the first fruits at the Temple in Jerusalem. In each town throughout the Land of Israel, prayer groups would gather. They would celebrate during the evening; in the morning they would commence their pilgrimage to Jerusalem, led by a flute player, followed by an ox with horns overlaid with gold and a wreath of olive leaves on its head. When they reached Jerusalem, they sent messengers to the Temple and prepared their first fruits for offering. As they marched through the city, the people of Jerusalem would greet them, saying: "Welcome to Jerusalem." When they reached the Temple, the Levites would break into song.

Inside the Temple, holding their baskets, they would recite: "I acknowledge this day. . . . My father was a fugitive Aramean. . . . Wherefore I now bring the first fruits of the soil that You, *Adonai,* have given me." The long walk up to Jerusalem, the parade through the streets, the musical entrance into the Temple, and the drama of reciting their declaration with basket in hand must have made a powerful impression and filled them with memories for a lifetime. (*Bikkurim* 3)

Is this what Moses had in mind when he defined the ritual drama of the first-fruits offering? Did he envision a musical parade? Why was a fixed formula of declaration put into the mouth of the worshiper? Why wasn't the prayer a spontaneous declaration or a prayer of thanks to God for the abundant fruits of the harvest? Why was the prayer about the past, about suffering, misery, and oppression?

Moses Maimonides addresses such questions in his *Guide for the Perplexed.* (3:39) Offering the first fruits of the harvest, he says, is a way people "accustom themselves to being generous" and a means of "limiting the human appetite for more consumption, not only of food, but of property."

Maimonides views the ritual drama as an antidote to materialism and overindulgence. "People who amass fortunes and live in comfort," he observes, "often fall victim to self-centered excesses and arrogance. They tend to abandon ethical considerations because of increasingly selfish concerns." Bringing a harvest basket of first fruits and reciting the prayer "promotes humility."

Rambam (Maimonides)

Maimonides also points out that "it is essential . . . to recall previous experiences of suffering and distress in times of ease." Such recollections remind us that human experience is a mixture of successes and failures, of joys and disappointments. History, like the life of a human being, is complex and often frustrating. People often become cynical and abandon their hopes and dreams.

The triumph of freedom over oppression often evolves slowly through pain, setbacks, and strong determination. Jacob suffers, his children endure hunger and homelessness, his grandchildren and subsequent generations are oppressed, tortured, and enslaved in Egypt. Without faith in God's liberating power, the Israelites would not have achieved freedom. It sustained them through the darkest hours. In offering the first fruits with a declaration recalling their stormy history, the people underscore the importance of taking nothing for granted. This ritual, concludes Maimonides, "helps us keep God's miracles fresh in memory and perpetuate faith."

For Rashbam the ritual is much more than a means of recalling the past and the Jewish people's reliance upon God's miracles. Rashbam points out that each participant, standing inside the Temple with the basket of first fruits, becomes a part of a significant drama—a highly personal confession. Identifying with Abraham, the worshiper declares: "*My* father [Abraham] was a wandering Aramean." By this he means to say that "*my* parent, not someone else's but *mine*, was lost, and *my* relatives suffered in Egypt, were liberated, and fought to conquer the Land of Israel. They were victorious and I hold this basket of fruits because of God's help."

Rashbam believes that for the pilgrim this ritual is a life-transforming moment of identification with one's ancestors and with the truth that the fruits in the basket and the liberation from Egypt are not the accomplishments of human beings alone. It is God's will that transforms seed into fruits; it is God's will that frees the captive. Rashbam sees each participant in the Temple ritual arriving at this conclusion: "*My* parents came from a strange land where they were slaves to this good and prosperous land. Now, in gratitude, I am bringing the first fruits of the land to the Temple because I realize that this bounty is not of my doing, but I enjoy it through God's mercy." (Comments on Deuteronomy 26: 3–11)

Words count

Rabbi Aharon Halevi argues that the Israelites are commanded to recite the prayer "My father was a fugitive Aramean. . . . Adonai freed us from Egypt. . . . Wherefore I now bring the first fruits . . ." because "the mind and imagination of people are deeply impressed by what they say." This prayer "arouses the heart, prompting the minds of those who say it to believe that all they enjoy came to them from the God of the universe." (Sefer ha-Hinuch 606)

Against conceit

Rabbi Jacob J. Weinstein comments: "Each Israelite was religiously commanded to recall in the time of prosperity that his [her] father was a wandering Aramean, a hobo, a sojourner, a rootless and homeless refugee. The intention of this admonition was to curb the conceit of the self-made person. He [she] was reminded that it required more than industry, skill, ambition, and contriving to rise from poverty to affluence.

It required also the help of God. . . . True piety, philosopher Santayana said, is a sense of reverence for the sources of our being." (The Place of Understanding, pp. 136–138)

Modern philosopher Martin Buber comments that this declaration of the Israelite at the sanctuary is unique because it is a very personal, individual expression. Instead of saying, "Our fathers were fugitive Arameans," one says, "My father. . . ." What we have here, says Buber, is a "merging of the people and the individual into one." The drama of the worship identifies the individual with Israel's history. It roots him in the past by allowing him to make the claim that he is a direct descendant (my father . . .) of those who came out of Egyptian slavery and forty years of desert wandering into the Land of Israel.

This identification is not casual. It deliberately links Jews to their historical experience and to the responsibilities of carrying out the commandments. Each year, explains Buber, the worshiper comes to the sanctuary and, in effect, says: "I as an individual feel and profess myself as one who has just come into the land, and, every time I offer its first fruits, I acknowledge who I am and renew my identity." (Israel and Palestine, Farrar, Strauss and Young, New York, 1952, pp. 3–5)

Buber's interpretation of the pilgrim's declaration as a means of identity with one's history may be compared to a similar declaration in the Pesach haggadah. After completing the narration of the liberation from bondage, which begins with the words "In the beginning our ancestors were idol worshipers" and includes a rabbinic commentary on the statement "My father was a fugitive Aramean," each person at the seder says: "In every generation a person is to see himself as if he were going out of Egypt. . . ." The drama of the seder, like the drama of presenting the basket of first fruits, bonds the individual to the Jewish people. Such rituals banish loneliness by placing us in the company of others who are celebrating shared ethical aspirations, heroes and heroines, tragedies and triumphs. Participating in the seder transports the individual back "home" to ancient ties of faith and tradition.

What about those who are not born into the people, whose past is non-Jewish but who convert to Judaism? Is it appropriate for converts to say Arami oved avi, "My father was a fugitive Aramean"?

According to the Mishnah, converts may bring their baskets of first fruits to the sanctuary, but they are forbidden to recite the prayer. The prayer includes statements that, for converts, are untrue: "I acknowledge this day before Adonai our God that I have entered the land which Adonai swore to our ancestors to give us," and "My father was a fugitive Aramean." Rather than recite a ritual prayer that is technically untrue, as one's birth parents were not Jews, the convert may bring the basket without saying the ancient prayer. From the Mishnah's point of view, the ritual is not to be trivialized by inviting people to falsify their pasts. (Bikkurim 1:4)

The Mishnah's view, however, is challenged by other authorities. Rabbi Judah claims that converts are not only permitted to say the words "My father was a fugitive Aramean," but they are also encouraged to recite all prayers that include the phrase "Our God and God of our ancestors, God of Abraham, God of Isaac, and God of Jacob." Rabbi Judah bases his view on the belief that Abraham was also a convert, and God promised to make him "father of a multitude of peoples." The promise, he argues, legitimately makes Abraham the "father" of all non-Jews who choose to become Jews, making it appropriate for them to address Abraham as their parent. (Jerusalem Talmud, Bikkurim 1:4)

In the eleventh century, Moses Maimonides signaled his agreement with Rabbi Judah. He ruled that it was permissible for converts to recite the prayers of the first fruits. His view became the acceptable practice of the Jewish community. Interestingly, this is the only case where Maimonides challenges the Mishnah. (Mishneh Torah, Bikkurim 4:3)

Later, a famous convert by the name of Obadiah wrote to Maimonides asking for a clarification of his ruling. "Should a convert," he asked, "recite prayers with the words 'Our God and God of our ancestors,' or 'who has commanded us,' or 'who has chosen us,' or 'who has brought us out of Egypt . . .'?"

Referring to Obadiah as "our teacher and master . . . the scholar and understanding one, the righteous convert," Maimonides answered: "You should recite all the prayers just as they are formulated in the liturgy. Change nothing! But, just as every born-Jew prays and recites benedictions, so you should do so whether in private or public as a leader of the congregation. . . . The reason for this is that Abraham our father taught all humanity. . . . Consequently, everyone who accepts Judaism until the end of all generations . . . is a descendant of Abraham. . . . There is absolutely no difference whatsoever between us and between you." (Jacob S. Minkin, *The World of Moses Maimonides,* Thomas Yoseloff, New York, 1957, pp. 375–376)

Leibowitz

Commenting on Maimonides' letter, modern interpreter Nehama Leibowitz concludes that "the letter utterly repudiates any racial theory that would evaluate human character in terms of ethnic origins. Maimonides well and truly bases human merit in the eyes of God upon our conduct and deeds."

Peli

Pinchas Peli agrees but widens the point of view. "By joining the Jewish religion, the convert joins the Jewish people and its history. Abraham, Isaac, and Jacob, to whom the land was promised, are also ancestors of the convert. [One] can rightly say, therefore, the full text of the first-fruits offering." (*Torah Today,* B'nai B'rith Books, Washington, D.C., 1987, pp. 227–228)

The ritual drama of the first-fruits offering was meant to express gratitude to God for liberation from bondage, for the Land of Israel, and for the bounty of the harvest. The ritual, however, is more than words of prayerful thanksgiving. The power of the experience on the individual was enormous. In recalling Abraham's struggle and the suffering of the Israelites, the worshiper

made Israelite history his or her own. The ceremony, for a born-Jew or a convert, confirmed the bond of the individual to the people of Israel. Through this ceremony one became a proud participant in Judaism's challenges and future.

PEREK BET: *Blessings and Curses; Who Is Responsible for Them? Are They Just?*

In these speeches by Moses to the Israelites, we find a powerful idea—an idea that has occurred earlier in the Torah. Some would argue that it is the greatest challenge put before the Israelites. They are told that if they faithfully observe the mitzvot, or the "commandments," they will be blessed. If they do not practice the mitzvot, they will be cursed. The choice is theirs.

This proposition of blessings and curses is also presented in Leviticus, *Parashat Behar-Bechukotai.* (See *A Torah Commentary for Our Times,* Volume II.) Now the Torah returns to it. This time, however, it is presented partially in the form of a ritual formula to be pronounced by tribal leaders and then proclaimed by the Levites to the people.

The ritual contains twelve curses, each beginning with the words "Cursed be the one who." The curses condemn (1) creating images; (2) insulting parents; (3) moving a landmark; (4) misleading a blind person; (5) subverting the rights of the stranger, the fatherless, and the widow; (6) having sexual relations with one's father's wife; (7) having sexual relations with animals; (8) having incestuous relations; (9) having sexual relations with one's mother-in-law; (10) secretly harming a neighbor; (11) accepting a bribe; and (12) failing to uphold the laws of Torah.

Conversely, Moses assures the people that if they observe faithfully all the commandments of Torah, they will enjoy four special blessings, each beginning with the words "Blessed shall you be." The blessings shall come upon the people (1) in their cities and in the country; (2) in the numbers of their children, herds, and produce; (3) in their basket and kneading bowl; and (4) in their comings and goings.

After articulating these curses and blessings, Moses adds a list of additional rewards if the Israelites observe all the commandments God has given them. These include victory over their enemies, productivity of their herds and crops, abundant prosperity, and leadership among all the nations.

Moses adds, if the people fail to practice the mitzvot, they will be punished with such catastrophes as calamity, frustration in all that they undertake, sickness, blight, skies that turn to copper and earth that turns to iron, destruction by their enemies, madness, blindness, dissolving of family ties, exile, ruthless rule by strangers, terrible famine, and a return to Egyptian slavery and oppression.

The Torah concludes these curses and blessings, these rewards and punishments, with the statement: "These are the terms of the covenant that *Adonai* commanded Moses to conclude with the Israelites. . . ."

One ponders these blessings and curses and asks: What did Moses think? Did he really believe that refusal to follow the commandments would bring about such frightful punishments? Or did he make the result of following the commandments so pleasant and the consequence of deliberate or careless rejection so calamitous because he believed that only "fear of God" would bring compliance? In our modern society, is there anything to be learned from this list of curses and blessings?

Knowledge brings responsibility
Rabbi Simeon ben Halafta taught that if one becomes knowledgeable of Torah and its commandments but then does not fulfill them, the punishment will be more severe.

Other rabbis teach that benefits, even peace, come into the world on account of the merits of those who live according to the commandments.
(Deuteronomy Rabbah 7:4,7)

Several early rabbinic interpreters suggest that God actually rewards those who obey the mitzvot of the Torah. Rabbi Joshua of Siknin, in the name of Rabbi Levi, teaches that as a reward

God hears the prayer of those who carry out the commandments. Others suggest that the reward is success in business. Rabbi Jonathan holds that performing the mitzvot leads to the blessing of having children, the guarantee of rain in its season, and life after death (resurrection). Rabbi Abba ben Kahana speaks for many of the early rabbinic commentators when he declares: "If the people of Israel live by the laws of Torah, God will reward them in the world to come—in the life after death."

The idea of being rewarded in the world to come is a recognition of the harsh realities of human existence. The world we inhabit is imperfect. As biblical authors Job and *Kohelet* note, good people suffer, as well as evil ones. Those who live piously and generously often endure pain with no clear benefits or protection for their loyalty to God. In response to the difficult question of why some good people suffer and some evildoers seem to escape suffering, many rabbinic commentators suggest that God's blessings and curses await us in the world to come—in heaven. It is there we will know the true justice of God.

From the rabbinic interpreters' point of view, that does not mean that human beings have no role in determining their fate in the world to come. On the contrary, the choices we make in life influence God's final decree. The intention of the Torah's list of blessings and curses is to urge us to choose lives filled with mitzvah deeds so we will be assured of an eternity of blessing. (*Deuteronomy Rabbah* 7:1–9)

Rashi offers a significant correction of this early rabbinic position. Noting the double emphasis of the Torah's warning: "If you will listen, really listen [to the commandments] . . ." he explains that the intention is educational. The Torah means to help people understand that the road to performing the commandments may be difficult, especially in the beginning. Therefore, the people are promised blessings so they will be encouraged to take the first steps to carry them out. Once they are on the way to fulfilling the commandments and have discovered how pleasant it is to live by them, they will more easily embrace God's law. (Comment on Exodus 19:5)

Rashi's point seems to agree with that of Simeon ben Azzai: "Be as quick to obey a minor mitzvah as a major one and flee from transgression, for one mitzvah performed leads to another, and one transgression leads to another. Indeed, the reward of one mitzvah is another mitzvah, and the punishment of one transgression is another transgression." (*Avot* 4:2) Rashi, like ben Azzai, sees the list of blessings and curses as a pedagogic device, a means of urging the people to comply with the commandments of Torah.

Moses Maimonides agrees but points out that the Torah specifically promises relief from serious disabilities for those who carry out the commandments because "it is impossible for people to perform the service of God when they are sick, hungry, thirsty, or in trouble." The reward of good health enables people to move toward the great purpose of Torah, "the attainment of perfection of knowledge and becoming worthy to enter the world to come." The rewards are not simply incentives. They bring major benefits, allowing frail human beings the strength of good health and a long life in which to achieve knowledge and earn an entrance into heaven. (*Mishneh Torah, Teshuvah* 9)

Is it appropriate, however, to argue that rewards and blessings are guaranteed to those who observe the mitzvot and that punishment and curses are destined to fall upon those who refuse to follow the commandments of Torah? As we have seen, this appears to be the intent of the Torah text and many of its most important interpreters.

Contemporary Jewish philosopher Rabbi David Hartman explains Maimonides' view with a story about his father, a traditional Jew. Each year the family built a beautiful *sukah*, inviting friends to share the joy of the festival. One year, writes Hartman, "a sudden rainstorm forced our family to leave the *sukah*," and "I cannot forget my father's explanation to his children as we left the *sukah*." He told us, "God must be displeased tonight with the community of Israel. He does not welcome us into His 'canopy of peace.'" The rain, continues Hartman, "was seen as a sign of divine anger and rejection."

Hartman disagrees with his father's explanation that God deliberately sends curses and blessings upon human beings as a result of their observance or nonobservance of the commandments. As an alternative, he argues that the world in which we live is imperfect. Human beings make mistakes; they begin with a motive to help and sometimes end up hurting one another. They struggle to bring trust, justice, mercy, and love into human relationships but often fail. Best intentions crash into misunderstandings. Blessings turn to curses and plunge us into confusion.

That is reality, says Hartman. Jewish tradition teaches us to "be sober and careful when performing a mitzvah. God," he asserts, "will give you the protection needed to perform mitzvot, but belief in God's protection should not make you oblivious to real dangers. You must combine your trust in God's protective love with a healthy respect for reality," for a recognition that our best intentions sometimes are twisted into curses.

Does that mean we should not expect rewards for carrying out the mitzvot? Not so, says Hartman, believing that such expectations are critical. "To give up anticipation of reward in this world for mitzvot could destroy the vitality of the sense of personal relationship with God that animates covenantal religious life. . . . If we are taught to expect rewards for mitzvot also in this world, then sometimes we may be disappointed, but we will also attach greater significance to the joyful moments in our lives by seeing them as signs of divine approval." (*A Living Covenant*, pp. 184–194)

Rabbi Hartman's position is that the curses and blessings mentioned in our Torah portion are useful because they add urgency to our relationship with God. They help define the consequences of our actions although there are times when such consequences are beyond our understanding. Most of the time, however, the curses function as warning signs. They signal what we should not do. On the other hand, the blessings we enjoy remind us that God is pleased with our partnership.

Rabbi Abraham Joshua Heschel approaches the subject of our Torah portion from a very different point of view. The purpose of the Torah, he cautions, "is not to substitute for but to extend our understanding." It is meant "to extend the horizon of our conscience and to impart to us a sense of the divine partnership in our dealings with good and evil and in our wrestling with life's enigmas. Clearly one of these serious questions is: What does God want of me?"

Heschel answers that God wants our mitzvah deeds. "It is in *deeds* that human beings become aware of what life really is, of their power to harm and to hurt, to wreck and to ruin; of their ability to derive joy and to bestow it upon others; to relieve and to increase their own and other people's tensions. . . . The deed is the test, the trial, and the risk. What we perform may seem slight, but the aftermath is immense. An individual's misdeed can be the beginning of a nation's disaster. The sun goes down, but the deeds go on. . . ."

For Heschel, deeds have serious, sometimes unknown, and long-range consequences. They possess enormous power to bring blessings or curses, rewards or punishment, fulfillments or despair. But they are also the means through which human beings celebrate or reject their partnership with God. "With a sacred deed goes more than a stir of the heart. In a sacred deed, we echo God's suppressed chant . . . we intone God's unfinished song. God depends upon us, awaits our deeds."

So, says Heschel, does the future of our planet and species. "We stand on a razor's edge. It is so easy to hurt, to destroy, to insult, to kill . . . life." For that reason we must regard ourselves as "half-guilty and half-meritorious." If we perform one good deed, we move the scale toward blessing. One transgression and we move the scale into the realm of curses. "Not only the individual but the whole world is in balance. One deed of an individual may decide the fate of the world."

Heschel places the burden for rewards and punishments, blessings and curses, upon each individual. The long list of blessings and curses mentioned in the Torah is not there as a warning, as an incentive to action, or as a promise of eternal joy in heaven. The blessings and curses, says Heschel, define the harsh consequences of choices made by human beings who hold in their hands not only the fate of their personal lives

but also the fate of the world. Through their mitzvah choices, human beings either banish God's Presence from their midst or become sacred instruments through which God's power for justice, goodness, mercy, and love enters and transforms the world. (*God in Search of Man*, chaps. 28, 34)

Moses places before the ancient Israelites a covenant with consequences. They have choices to make. By following the mitzvot, they can assure themselves of blessings; by rejecting them, they will reap a whirlwind of destruction. Their future does not depend upon blind fate. It depends upon them, upon their choices. We might say that God waits for their answer. Today, we might add, God waits for our answer.

QUESTIONS FOR STUDY AND DISCUSSION

1. Lawrence A. Hoffman, a modern scholar on ritual, explains that prayer is a form of art through which individuals bring order, integrity, hope, and vision into their lives. "When worship works, we are artists in the finest sense of affirming wholeness through the power of our traditional images of time, space, and history." (*The Art of Public Prayer*, Pastoral Press, Washington, D.C., 1988, pp. 148–151) Review the various interpretations of the pilgrim's prayer. How does the prayer fulfill Hoffman's definition of ritual?

2. In her book, *Choosing Judaism* (UAHC Press, New York, 1981), Lydia Kukoff, a convert to Judaism, offers this advice to those entering Jewish life: "Sometimes as I sit in our decorated *sukah*, or as I march around the synagogue on Simchat Torah carrying a Torah scroll, I think back to the time when I walked into those services 'cold.' I am so glad I didn't give up. Don't you give up either. Today it is all new to you. For now, just try to participate as much as you can. In time, you will find that it all belongs to you. You won't get there in a year, but twelve months later you'll be further along, and certainly

even further with each succeeding year." (p. 66) Compare this advice to that offered by Maimonides to the convert Obadiah.

3. Review the interpretations of blessings and curses for observance or nonobservance of the commandments. Are there contemporary consequences (blessings and curses) for observance or nonobservance of the ethical mitzvot of Torah?

4. Several commentators suggest that the enjoyment and personal satisfaction derived from doing a mitzvah leads to the doing of other mitzvot. As examples, the joy and love shared while observing Shabbat may inspire us to acts of charity, and the delight of celebrating a Pesach seder may lead to working for the liberation of people still oppressed. What are some other benefits (blessings) that may be derived from observing the mitzvot? What impact can the observance of ritual commandments have upon observance of ethical commandments?

PARASHAT NITZAVIM-VAYELECH
Deuteronomy 29:9–31:30

Parashat Nitzavim-Vayelech is one of seven designated Torah portions that, depending upon the number of Sabbaths in a year, is either read as two separate portions or combined to assure the reading of the entire Torah. While this volume will combine them, it will present an interpretation on each of their most important themes.

Parashat Nitzavim continues Moses' speeches to the Israelites just before they enter the Land of Israel. He tells them that God is making a covenant with them and, through them, with all future generations, fulfilling the promise made to Abraham, Isaac, and Jacob. The covenant will last, he warns, only if they do not worship other gods. If they forsake the Torah's commandments, devastation, plagues, and curses will afflict them. However, Moses promises that they will not be entirely forsaken. If they return to *Adonai* and take the blessings and curses seriously, God will forgive them and restore them to their land, allowing them another opportunity to conduct their lives according to the laws of Torah. God, says Moses, is setting the choice of life and death before them. They are told: "Choose life."

Parashat Vayelech begins with Moses' announcement that he is one hundred and twenty years old and no longer able to lead the people. He assures them that they will be successful in reconquering the Land of Israel and calls upon Joshua to succeed him as leader, promising that God "will not fail you or forsake you." He transmits the Torah to the priests, instructing the people to gather every seven years at the festival of Sukot to hear the reading of the Torah, which they are to study. Forecasting that the people will nonetheless abandon the laws of Torah, God gives Moses a poem to "confront them as a witness" to all they have been taught. (See Deuteronomy 32: 1–43.) Moses transmits the Torah to the Levites, asking them to place it in the Ark of the Covenant. Moses then calls the people together to hear the poem.

OUR TARGUM

·1·

Parashat Nitzavim opens with Moses' announcement to the people: "You stand this day, all of you, before *Adonai* your God . . . to enter into the covenant of *Adonai* your God . . . as God swore to your ancestors, Abraham, Isaac, and Jacob. I make this covenant . . . both with those who are standing here with us this day . . . and with those who are not with us here this day."

Recalling the forbidden idolatry of other nations, Moses warns the Israelites that they must not turn to "fetishes of wood and stone, silver and gold." Those who do will be punished, especially those who say: "I shall be safe, though I follow my own willful heart." God will punish those who serve other gods with the misfortunes of disease, plagues, and devastation, like those brought upon Sodom and Gomorrah. Moses tells the people that when later generations ask, "Why were they punished with such terrible curses?" they will be told of Israel's unfaithfulness to the covenant.

Foreseeing such a time, Moses speaks of the Israelites' exile from their land, but he promises that God will ultimately restore them. God will open their hearts to the Torah's commandments, and they will be given "abounding prosperity" in all they do.

·2·

"This commandment that I place before you," declares Moses, "is not too difficult for you, nor is it beyond reach. It is not in the heavens, that you should say, 'Who among us can go up to the heavens and get it for us and teach it to us, that we may observe it?' Neither is it beyond the sea, that you should say, 'Who among us can cross to the other side of the sea and get it for us and impart it to us, that we may observe it?' No, the Torah is very close to you, in your mouth and in your heart to observe it."

Lifting his voice, Moses pleads with the people. "See, I set before you this day life and prosperity, death and adversity. For I command you this day to love *Adonai* your God, to walk in God's ways, and to keep God's commandments. . . . I call heaven and earth to witness against you this day: I have put before you life and death, blessing and curse. Choose life . . . by loving *Adonai* your God and observing God's commandments."

·3·

Parashat Vayelech opens with Moses informing the Israelites that he is one hundred and twenty years old and no longer capable of leading them. "Joshua will lead you," he says, calling upon the people to be strong and resolute against their enemies when they go forth to reconquer their land.

Speaking to Joshua before all the Israelites, Moses publicly transfers his authority to him, declaring: "Be strong and courageous, for it is you who shall go with this people into the land that *Adonai* swore to their ancestors to give them, and it is you who shall divide it among them. God will go before you. . . . Fear not. . . ."

·4·

Moses writes the Torah and gives it to the priests and to the elders of Israel. He instructs them to read it to the people every seven years at the time of the fall harvest of Sukot.

·5·

Moses is told by God that he will soon die and that he and Joshua should come to the Tent of Meeting. God tells them that after Moses dies, the people will forsake the Torah and worship false gods. God will abandon the people and punish them with evils and troubles. In the midst of all their sorrow, they will understand why they are suffering. "Surely," they will say, "it is because our God is not in our midst that these evils have befallen us." Moses informs them that he is giving them a poem to be read and studied at such a time. (See Deuteronomy 32:1–43; also *Parashat Ha'azinu*.)

About to die, Moses hands the Torah to the Levite priests, who place it in the Ark of the Covenant. He then speaks to the people, complaining that they are stiffnecked, and he asks that all the elders come forward so he can share with them the words of his poem.

THEMES

Parashat Nitzavim-Vayelech contains two important themes:

1. The meaning of *teshuvah,* or "repentance."
2. Passing leadership from one generation to the next.

PEREK ALEF: *Seeking and Achieving Teshuvah, "Repentance"*

The setting of our Torah portions, *Nitzavim* and *Vayelech,* is dramatic. Moses, grown old and weary, speaks for the last time to the people he has led for forty years through the desert. They are at the parting of the ways. The people will enter the Land of Israel, led by Joshua; Moses will die on Mount Nebo. What can Moses say in his final speech to the Israelites? What final message can he leave them with?

He decides to challenge them with the covenant they have made with God. It is a covenant, he reminds them, that is made not only with them but with all Jews for all times. Its conditions and commandments, he assures them, are accessible. These are not impossible to carry out. Moses urges them to be loyal to the covenant, warning that they will suffer great hardships and punishment if they reject it. "See, I set before you this day life and prosperity, death and adversity," he tells the people, pleading, "Choose life . . . by loving *Adonai* your God."

Woven into this moving appeal is a central theme of Jewish tradition: *teshuvah,* or "repentance." Moses encourages the Israelites to carry out the commandments of their covenant with God. While he warns them of the painful consequences of rejecting the commandments, he also leaves the door open for them to correct their mistakes or wrong decisions. Should they deliberately plunge into wrongdoing or err accidently, says Moses, they can seek forgiveness. Human errors, selfish and harmful acts, shameful behavior—all can be rectified and will be forgiven by God.

Moses explains that even an arrogant person who believes he can break the law with impunity because God will protect him will be punished for abandoning the commandments but will also be given another chance. God does not abandon human beings. God wants human beings to right the wrongs they do, to feel regret for hurting others, and to improve their behavior. God, explains Moses, wants every human being to make *teshuvah,* or "repentance," returning to a life of performing mitzvah deeds defined by the Torah.

Many commentators point out that Moses uses a form of the verb *shuv,* or "turn," seven times within this last speech to the Israelites. (Deuteronomy 30) The repetition of the verb emphasizes Moses' message that *teshuvah* is desirable and possible. Failure to observe the commandments of the covenant may lead to punishment but not to God's abandonment. God does not turn away from any human being nor forsake any sinner. Instead, God waits for the repentance or return of every person. One can always make *teshuvah*, always "return" to God.

This view that the person who rejects God's commandments can seek forgiveness through *teshuvah* is also voiced by the prophets of Israel. For example, Isaiah declares, "Let the sinner give up doing wrong and . . . return to God." Jeremiah suggests that those who turn away from God's commandments will realize their mistakes and seek a new sensitivity for doing good. "Amend your ways and your doings," he instructs the people. Ezekiel speaks of "making a new heart and a new spirit" and doing God's will. Hosea tells his generation, "Return, O Israel, to *Adonai* your God." (Isaiah 56:6; Jeremiah 7:3, 26:13; Ezekiel 18:21; and Hosea 14:2)

It is not surprising, therefore, to find the concept of *teshuvah* as a central theme in Jewish thought and practice. Both the Torah and the prophets share the conviction that our mistakes, even our deliberate wrongs, should be forgiven through repentance. Most rabbinic interpreters agree. Rabbi Samuel ben Nachman, one of the renowned teachers of the third century C.E. in the Land of Israel, speaks for many when he observes, "The gates of repentance are always open." Another rabbinic teacher declares, "Just as a soiled garment can be made white again, so can the people of Israel make repentance and return to God." (*Lamentations Rabbah* 3.44. 9; *Exodus Rabbah* 23:10)

Great is teshuvah
Rabbi Hama ben Hanina taught: "Great is repentance for it brings healing to the world."

Rabbi Yonatan ben Eleazar taught: "Great is repentance for it prolongs life." (Yoma 86b)

The test of teshuvah
Rabbi Judah ben Ezekiel taught: "The test of repentance is refraining from sin on two occasions when the same temptation returns." (Yoma 86b)

The rabbinic tradition, however, adds a further dimension to correcting our errors through repentance. It claims that "if we begin to incline toward regretting the wrongs we have done, God moves within us, pushing us toward admitting and correcting our errors." Another interpreter claims that "God rushes toward all those who make repentance with compassion, mercy, and love." Rabbi Jassa agrees, arguing: "God says to us, 'Make an opening for repentance as large as the eye of a needle, and I will make it large enough for wagons and carriages to pass.'" These rabbinic teachers believe that God is not passive but active in encouraging us to recognize our transgressions and to correct our behavior. (*Midrash* on Psalms 120:7; *Numbers Rabbah* 2:10; *Song of Songs Rabbah* 5:2)

This emphasis by Moses, the prophets, and rabbinic interpreters that *teshuvah*, or "repentance," is possible raises significant questions. Does the opportunity for *teshuvah* mean a person can deliberately hurt or wrong others, say a few prayers, and be forgiven? Is returning to God accomplished by piously proclaiming on Yom Kippur, "*Avinu Malkenu*, inscribe us in the Book of Forgiveness," or by confessing our errors with *Al Chet*, "For the sin we have sinned against You . . ."?

Fourteenth-century Spanish philosopher Joseph Albo confronts these questions about *teshuvah*, explaining that the improvement of our behavior through the process of *teshuvah* is neither automatic nor easy. It requires a careful, painstaking process of "correcting thought, speech, and behavior." By "correcting thought," he means that a person "should feel regret for the wrongs he has done to others." By "correcting speech," he means that a person "should confess his wrongs." By "correcting behavior," he means that a person "pledges never to repeat the wrong again and takes on deeds meant to rectify any damages done, intentionally or unintentionally." For Albo, repentance is more than a pious expression of regret. It moves a person toward a change of heart, mind, and behavior. (*Sefer ha-Ikkarim* 4:26)

In his discussion of *teshuvah*, Moses Maimonides stresses the difficulty of achieving such personality transformation or "true repentance." He points out at least twenty-four different things that hinder human beings from dealing with their mistakes: (1) deliberately misleading others to sin; (2) enticing others to wrongdoing; (3) allowing your children to sin; (4) saying "I will sin and then repent"; (5) standing aloof from the community; (6) opposing the authority of community leaders; (7) making a mockery of the laws of Torah; (8) insulting one's teachers; (9) refusing to hear criticism; (10) cursing others; (11) sharing with a thief; (12) failing to return lost property; (13) robbing from the poor; (14) taking bribes and tampering with justice; (15) taking food from those in need; (16) making profit from a poor person's property; (17) looking lustfully at those of the opposite sex; (18) elevating oneself at the expense of others; (19) condemning others with suspicions, not proof; (20) gossiping; (21) slandering others; (22) acting out of anger; (23) nurturing designs for wrongdoing; and (24) keeping company with those who might influence you to evil ways.

Rambam (Maimonides)

All the above "hinder" but do not "prevent" us from achieving *teshuvah*. Maimonides points out that human beings can achieve repentance by "reviewing and confronting their evil traits" and by "seeking to get rid of them." He argues that none of us is "completely righteous." Every person sins, commits errors, and makes mistakes. "If a person is sincerely remorseful about them and repents, he can achieve full repentance."

Repentance, however, is important not only for individuals but also for society. "Human beings," says Maimonides, "should see themselves and the world as always balanced delicately on scales, hovering between half-guilty of evil and half-innocent of evil." If we think constantly in such terms and measure our every action on such scales, then each action will be seen as either tipping the scales of the world to evil or to good. Our choices of action may either do harm to society or improve the lot of all human beings. Quoting Proverbs 10:25, Maimonides con-

cludes: "A righteous person is the foundation of the world." (*Mishneh Torah, Teshuvah* 4:1–6; 7:2–4, 8)

Cheshbon ha-nefesh
In discussing the harm of sin and the power of repentance, modern philosopher Israel Knox calls attention to the rabbinic concept of cheshbon ha-nefesh, *"taking stock of one's soul, an inner accounting, a sitting-in-judgment upon oneself." He regards this as the essence of teshuvah. "As we make our* cheshbon ha-nefesh, *we confess our failure to span the gap between conscience and conduct, between the standards we profess and the actions we perform. . . . This chasm between* believing *and* living *may or may not always be surmountable, but the refusal to try to span it is* sin *and the will to bridge it, at least to narrow it, is* atonement [repentance]." *(The Jewish Spectator,* vol. 27, no. 7, September 1963, pp. 7–9)*

Steinsaltz

Reaching out
Repentance does not bring a sense of serenity or of completion but stimulates a reaching out in further effort. Indeed, the power and the potential of repentance lie in increased incentive and enhanced capacity to follow the path even farther. The response is often no more than an assurance that one is in fact capable of repenting, and its efficacy lies in growing awareness, with time, that one is indeed progressing on the right path. In this manner the conditions are created in which repentance is no longer an isolated act but has become a permanent possibility, a constant process of going toward. It is a going that is both the rejection of what was once axiomatic and an acceptance of new goals. (Adin Steinsaltz, The Thirteen Petalled Rose, *Basic Books, New York, 1980, pp. 131–132)*

On the basis of these views of Moses Maimonides, modern interpreter and philosopher Rabbi Joseph B. Soloveichik elaborates on another important aspect of *teshuvah*. He claims that struggling with our failures and errors and seeking forgiveness for them leads us to *taharah,* or "purification." Through the process of admitting our sins, asking God and those we have hurt to forgive these sins, and correcting them, we "strive to convert them into a spiritual springboard for increased inspiration and evaluation."

This, Soloveichik points out, is the other benefit of *teshuvah*. It allows us to use our mistakes and selfish behavior as building blocks for human growth. The memory of our wrongdoings has the potential of transforming us into more generous, kind, and loving human beings. Our sins, observes Soloveichik with sharp psychological insight, "become part of our ego . . . awaking a creative force that shapes a new and loftier personality." In other words, confronting our sins forces us to improve ourselves, and remembering them helps us change our behavior for the good.

"When a person stumbles and falls . . . he should not despair . . . but should cultivate hope . . . 'gaining' by his experience new visions and vistas. Our ideal," Soloveichik concludes, "is not repetition but re-creation on a higher level. *Teshuvah* contains hope and purification." It motivates us to mature and develop positive aspects of our personalities. (*Gesher,* vol. 3, no. 1, June 1966, pp. 5–29)

Soloveichik's view is in harmony with another modern interpreter, Rabbi Mordecai M. Kaplan, who argues that *teshuvah* "stands for nothing less than the continual remaking of human nature." It is a form of "introspection," a means of achieving "progressive self-realization." Kaplan claims that repentance has the potential for repairing "three types of failure."

The first type is the failure "to integrate our impulses, habits, social activities, and institutions in harmony with those ethical ideals that make God present in the world." For example, we may busy ourselves with feeding strangers but be careless and hurtful in our family relationships. Through *teshuvah* we can examine honestly and critically what we are doing and close the gap between our "aspirations" and behavior.

The second type of failure is "fixation," ceasing to change and grow as human beings. Kaplan points out that at various stages in our lives we develop different responses and habits. They may work while we are children but are inadequate, even dangerous, in adulthood. As children we depend on our parents and teachers and what the community provides for us. As we mature, we realize we can no longer "depend on others." We must not only take care of ourselves but also contribute to the welfare of the entire community. Repentance, Kaplan claims, helps us "recognize the inadequacy of our acquired personality to do justice to the demands of a new situation." It spurs our ethical growth.

The third type of failure *teshuvah* helps us confront is the failure to realize "to the fullest degree the potentialities inherent in our natures and in the situations in which we find ourselves." Kaplan points out that "we all have latent powers for good, powers we do not summon to active use." For example, we will plunge into petty arguments with others or refuse to cooperate because of jealousy, rather than build friendship and enjoy the benefits of trust and mutual support. Through the introspection of *teshuvah,* we examine how we waste our potentials and discover how we should use them creatively and constructively, not only for ourselves, but for our society. The act of repentance, Kaplan concludes, is meant "for the reconstruction of our personalities in accordance with the highest ethical possibilities of human nature." (*The Meaning of God in Modern Jewish Religion,* Reconstructionist Press, New York, 1962, pp. 178–187)

Jewish tradition places great emphasis upon the importance of *teshuvah*. While various interpreters offer different points of view about its meaning, process, and potential, none doubts its power to transform human behavior. Rabbi Simeon ben Lakish summarizes the overwhelming agreement of our commentators. "Great is repentance," he writes, "for it turns sins into incentives for right conduct." It is through *teshuvah* that human beings find forgiveness for their mistakes and summon the strength to repair their faults and errors. Repentance leads to renewal and to new opportunities for ethical and personal growth. (*Yoma* 86b)

PEREK BET: *Moses Passes on Leadership to Joshua*

On two occasions the Torah speaks of Moses' retirement and of his responsibility to pass on his leadership to the next generation. In *Parashat Pinchas*, Moses is told he will not be allowed to enter the Land of Israel but, like Aaron, will die in the wilderness because of his excessive anger in striking the rock and damning the people at the Waters of Meribath-kadesh. (Numbers 27:12–14)

Moses responds by asking God to "appoint someone over the community who shall go out before them and come in before them, and who shall take them out and bring them in, so that *Adonai's* community may not be like sheep that have no shepherd." God answers Moses: "Single out Joshua son of Nun, an inspired man, and lay your hand upon him." Moses then confirms the appointment publicly before the priests and the entire people. (Numbers 27:15–19)

In *Parashat Vayelech*, Moses has reached the age of one hundred and twenty years and is about to die. He calls Joshua and "in the sight of all Israel," transfers the powers of leadership to him. Moses tells him, "Be strong and resolute, for it is you who shall go with this people into the land . . . and it is you who shall apportion it to them. . . . Fear not and be not dismayed." (Deuteronomy 31:1–8)

Interpreters ask several questions about the Torah's description of the passing of leadership by Moses to Joshua: Why doesn't Moses choose one of his sons to succeed him? What is special about Joshua? Why does Moses *publicly* confer his leadership powers upon Joshua?

Some of the first rabbinic commentators seek to explain why Moses' sons, Gershon and Eliezer, do not inherit the leadership from their father. Because the Torah does not contain any direct information about the decision, rabbinic interpreters use their imagination. They portray Moses as a concerned father, worried about the rights of inheritance of his sons. Arguing with God, Moses says, "Whoever keeps the fig tree should

have the right to eat its fruits. Let them succeed me." But Moses is told, say the rabbis, that Gershon and Eliezer are not worthy of leadership. "They idle away each day. They do not study Torah or put it into practice. Joshua does. Furthermore, Joshua honors you. He cleans and arranges the room where students gather to learn from you, and he has protected you from harm. For those reasons he is more worthy to succeed you than your own sons." (*Numbers Rabbah* 21:16)

In their imaginative reconstruction of a conversation between Moses and God about the succession, rabbinic commentators highlight the criteria for leadership of the Jewish community. The accident of birth, as in the case of Gershon and Eliezer, is insufficient; character is all important. Moses' sons are unworthy because they waste their energies and talents, and they are not dedicated to growing intellectually and spiritually through study. Nor are they committed to putting their knowledge into practice.

Joshua, on the other hand, is worthy of inheriting the leadership from Moses. Rabbinic commentators note not only his inquiring mind devoted to learning but his willingness to work hard and serve as an apprentice to Moses, honoring and protecting him. Joshua is chosen because of his demonstrated commitment to Moses and his loyalty to the Israelites.

 Rashi

Agreeing with this assessment, Rashi adds another reason for the choice of Joshua as successor to Moses. Rashi points out that Joshua's competition was neither Gershon nor Eliezer but Pinchas, Aaron's son. Pinchas had demonstrated loyalty to both Moses and God when he rushed forward to murder an Israelite who had, in violation of the law of Torah, taken a Midianite woman into his tent for sexual pleasure.

Pinchas's action, however, revealed his propensity for quick, careless, and violent action. Instead of consulting with Moses, Pinchas took matters into his own hands, acting rashly and self-righteously. Rashi reasons that Moses' successor could not be impulsive or tend to act in anger. The Israelites required a person who would understand their diverse nature and regard each individual with patience. Leadership demanded tolerance and a temperament of careful and cautious judgment.

Pinchas was not such a person. He acted before he questioned. He was a single-minded zealot and, therefore, unworthy of leadership. Joshua, on the other hand, is seen by Rashi as judicious, careful, slow to act, and sensitive to differences of opinion. While forming his own conclusions, Joshua is a person who listens and learns from others. Rashi implies that only a person with such characteristics deserves to succeed Moses and lead the people into the Promised Land. (Comments on Numbers 27:16)

Peli

Fair and firm
As the future leader, Joshua is described as "a man in whom there is spirit." Here Rashi comments: "A man who knows how to stand up against the spirit of each one of them" [and who knows how] to teach us that to be tolerant does not necessarily imply passivity or spinelessness. A good leader must know his own mind; he must be able to stand up for his views; and he also must be capable of changing his mind, of freeing himself from preconceived ideas. He must not be the type who declares: "My mind is made up—don't confuse me with facts." (Pinchas H. Peli, Torah Today, p. 186)

Leading
Leaders who truly lead their people will raise them to their own level. They have a chance to "lead them out" of corruption and to "bring them in" to holiness. Leaders who trail behind their people will finally be dragged down by them to their own low level. (Avnei Ezel, from A. Z. Friedman, Wellsprings of Torah, p. 337)

Modern interpreter Pinchas H. Peli points out that Joshua is chosen by Moses because of his bravery and courage. In his prayer for a successor, Moses asks God to "appoint someone over the community who shall go out before them and come in before them, and who shall take them out and bring them in." Joshua is chosen, says Peli, because Joshua is "not like leaders of other nations who send their troops into battle while they themselves stay behind." Instead, he is a person "who goes before his troops."

Moses, explains Peli, is concerned about the great task of leading the people in the many battles that will be necessary to conquer the land. "He knew well that it is one thing to take a people out to war and another to get them out of war and bring them back home. The second task is much harder. A true leader has to be capable of both." Joshua had collaborated with Moses for years. The old leader had confidence in his determination and courage. Joshua was a man who would "go before them," bravely shouting, "Follow me." (*Torah Today*, pp. 186–187)

Philosopher and commentator Martin Buber offers another perspective. He says Moses chooses Joshua as his successor because of Joshua's personal loyalty and for his "physical and instinctive interest in everything connected with fighting." Buber speculates that young Joshua proves himself to Moses by helping put down the many revolts against Moses by the Israelites. He silences the opposition against Moses and defends Moses against his critics. Moses entrusts him with guarding his tent against those who might come to do him harm; Joshua demonstrates his total commitment. When the spies return with their fearful report, doubting the Israelites' ability to conquer the Land of Israel, it is Joshua who contradicts them, boldly telling the people: "Have no fear . . . *Adonai* is with us." It is all this evidence of enthusiasm, determination, courage, and faith that leads Moses to choose Joshua as his successor. (*Moses*, pp. 197–198)

Aaron Wildavsky agrees with Buber. He points out that Moses at times is a guide for Joshua's enthusiasm and leadership skills. For example, when two men, Eldad and Medad, are overheard speaking in a prophetic manner in the camp,

Joshua immediately reports the matter to Moses. Believing they represent a dangerous challenge to Moses' authority, Joshua urges Moses to stop them. Instead of acting rashly against the men, Moses calms Joshua's fears, telling him: "Do not be concerned about me. Would that all of God's people were prophets." (Numbers 11:26–29)

Moses' lesson to Joshua is twofold. A leader must not make quick decisions. Taking counsel with others, a good leader can allow other voices, even dissenting ones, a place in the community. Leading is not silencing or repudiating the opinions of others. It is providing an atmosphere where all views flourish and where even diverse decisions are made, still maintaining the unity of the community. Moses, Wildavsky maintains, seeks to train Joshua with such wisdom. (*Moses as a Political Leader*, pp. 143–44)

Ramban (Nachmanides)

Nachmanides appears to agree when he stresses the educational role Moses played in preparing Joshua for succession. In his commentary, Nachmanides observes that Moses' instruction of Joshua was not private. It was not a closed-door tutorial with student and teacher sharing information and wisdom. Instead, says Nachmanides, it was, as the Torah indicates, "before the eyes of the community."

In other words, Nachmanides maintains that Moses taught Joshua before the entire community. Moses *publicly* "instructs him in his duties as a leader and judge." Moses emphasizes Joshua's role as the one who should go out before them, care for them, be concerned about bringing them back safely from battle, and be careful in all matters of judgment. Every direction and explanation of the law Moses gives to Joshua is open for all to hear and discuss.

The reason for such a public, open process of leadership education and transition, concludes Nachmanides, has to do with the morale of the people. Hearing all Moses' instructions to Joshua and witnessing everything being taught to him, the people are encouraged to trust him. They

come to believe he would treat them honestly and fairly. The prospect of change appears less traumatic. Moses wants a smooth shift in power and authority from him to Joshua. Building up the confidence of the people in Joshua is critical for that smooth transition. (Commentary on Numbers 27:19)

Although Moses prepares Joshua to succeed him, loving him as a disciple, the reality of retirement and death is difficult for Moses to accept. Leading the people for forty years, making all the decisions, interpreting the law, and fighting off detractors and enemies, Moses must have become accustomed to power and responsibility. Giving up such responsibilities and power must have resulted in personal pain.

The rabbis capture Moses' feelings in those transition moments between retirement and death. They call attention to the deal Moses seeks to make with God. "Please let me live," the rabbis imagine him saying. "Let Joshua take over my office, but allow me to live by his side." God grants Moses' wish, and the next day he goes with Joshua to the sanctuary. They enter, and a pillar of cloud separates them. When it departs, Moses asks Joshua, "What did God tell you?" Joshua, looking at the aged leader, responds, "When God spoke to you, did you tell me what was said?" Stunned, Moses realizes that authority has shifted to Joshua. The transition is complete, and Moses is deeply jealous. "Better to die than to experience such envy," he mutters to God. Now Moses is ready for death. (*Deuteronomy Rabbah* 9:9)

This rabbinic tale about Moses makes the point that retirement is not easy. Giving up authority, power, position, status, and office is difficult, even if you have trained your successor. Envy and jealousy, bewilderment and resentment are natural feelings surrounding the loss of one's position. So, too, is fear—especially fear about the unknown future, about the end of one's career, and possibly about impending death. Will others forget me? Will I die unnoticed, alone?

These fears must burden Moses as he prepares to pass on to Joshua the mantle of leadership. Nonetheless, Moses turns his concerns to the future of his people, rising above his envy and anxiety, urging Joshua to go forward and reconquer the Land of Israel. He inspires his successor with the promise, "God will be with you. God will not fail you or forsake you." Moses transforms his retirement and death into a legacy of courage and love.

QUESTIONS FOR STUDY AND DISCUSSION

1. How is *teshuvah,* or "repentance," a process for healing? Can it repair relationships? Can it bring inner peace? Can it bring world peace?

2. Are there some acts for which there can be no *teshuvah?* What about abandoning a friend in time of need? What about failure to speak out when injustice is being done?

3. According to the commentators, what character traits did Moses find in Joshua? Are these qualities still important for leadership today? How?

4. At the moment of passing on his authority to Joshua, Moses assembles all the people and says to Joshua, "Be strong and resolute, for it is you who shall go with this people into the land that *Adonai* swore to their ancestors . . . it is you who shall apportion it to them." Why does Moses choose to say those words "in the sight of all Israel"? Why did he not choose to voice them in a private ceremony?

PARASHAT HA'AZINU
Deuteronomy 32:1–52

Parashat Ha'azinu is a prayer-poem that Moses presents to the people of Israel just before he ascends Mount Nebo, where he will die. In these verses, Moses declares that God's "deeds are perfect . . . and just," and God is "never false" but always "true and upright." He warns against those who act dishonestly against God. He tells the Israelites to "remember" their history and their special relationship with God, who guided their ancestors and cared for them despite the many times they turned to idolatry. God, Moses declares, could have obliterated the Israelites many times for their disloyalty but decided against doing so lest their enemies assume Israel's destruction was their doing rather than God's punishment. Indeed, says Moses, it is God who constantly saves Israel from destruction. It is God "who deals death and gives life." God, Moses concludes, will bring vengeance upon Israel's enemies. Moses warns the people to "take to heart" all of the Torah and its laws and to teach the laws to their children. "The Torah is your very life," he tells them, and "through it you shall long endure. . . ." Moses is then told to climb Mount Nebo from which he will be able to see the Land of Israel. There he will die, without entering the land, punishment for his anger at the Waters of Meribath-kadesh.

OUR TARGUM

·1·

Moses prays that his words of poetry will be heard by all the Israelites. "Give glory to our God," he tells them, for "God's deeds are perfect . . . all God's ways are just. God is faithful, never false, always true and upright. . . . God creates and sustains" all human beings and the people of Israel.

·2·

He urges them to "remember your history" and advises them to ask their parents to inform them

about their past and their relationship as a nation to other peoples. He then recounts how God found the Israelites in a desert region, "guarded [them] as the pupil of God's eye," and cared for [them] as an eagle cares for its young.

God, Moses says, "set the Israelites on the highlands to feast on the yield of the earth, fed them honey and the milk and meat of the best herds." The people "grew fat" and spoiled, and they turned against God and worshiped idols.

God threatened to forsake them, to punish them by sending enemies against them. But God, explains Moses, did not do so lest their enemies conclude that "our own hand has prevailed; none of their defeat was brought about by God."

Moses declares that God alone will punish the people for turning away and bring them back so they understand "there is no God beside Me. I deal death and give life; I wounded and I will heal."

· 3 ·

After reciting his poem, Moses declares: "Pay attention to all I have told you today. Teach it to your children that they may observe faithfully all the terms of the Torah . . . for it is your very life, the guarantee that you will endure on the land that you will occupy across the Jordan River."

Moses is then told to climb Mount Nebo from where he can view the Land of Israel. This is where he will die.

THEMES

Parashat Ha'azinu contains two important themes:

1. God and evil.
2. The importance of history.

PEREK ALEF: *If God's Ways Are Just, What about Evil?*

Moses stands before the people of Israel as an old man. He has led them for forty years; he has been their liberator and their teacher. Now, he is about to die. The people will follow Joshua, his successor, into the Land of Israel. One can imagine Moses' agony as he ponders the question: What shall be my final message to my people?

The Torah presents his answer in a powerful poem. It begins with a plea that his thoughts be heard.

> Give ear, O heavens, let me speak;
> Let the earth hear the words I utter!
> May my discourse come down as the rain,
> My speech distill as the dew,
> Like showers on young growth,
> Like droplets on the grass.
> For the name of *Adonai* I proclaim;
> Give glory to our God!
>
> (Deuteronomy 32:1–3)

Moses continues his poem, offering within it his understanding of God. His words are carefully chosen. They portray God in a number of significant ways. He tells the people:

> The Rock!—God's deeds are perfect,
> Yes, all God's ways are just;
> A faithful God, never false,
> True and upright is God.
>
> (Deuteronomy 32:4)

> God is the Source who created you,
> Fashioned you and made you endure!
>
> (Deuteronomy 32:6)

> . . . God wounds and heals. . . .
>
> (Deuteronomy 32:39)

> . . . Those who reject God will be punished.
>
> (Deuteronomy 32:41)

> Those who harm Israel will be punished.
>
> (Deuteronomy 32:43)

Moses' portrait of God is complex and raises a number of important questions: What does Moses mean when he calls God "perfect," "just," "faithful," "true," and "upright"? Can God be "just" and "faithful" and "wound and heal" at the same time? How can we understand God's justice?

Interpreters of Torah have constantly struggled with such questions. From ancient to modern times, human beings have asked in the midst of their pain and suffering, "Where is God? If God is 'perfect,' why is the world that God created so imperfect? Why do people hurt one another? Why does a God of justice allow hunger, war, and disease? Why does God permit loving and generous human beings to be tortured by disease or cruelty or innocent children to be abused, starved, or killed? Can we really say that 'God's deeds are perfect . . . just . . . never false, true and upright'?"

Despite the anguish they have experienced, many Jews like the prophet Isaiah maintain the faith expressed by Moses that *Adonai* is a God of justice. (Isaiah 5:16) In his time, the Psalmist articulates the same determination: "Your righteousness is like the mighty mountains; Your judgments are like the great deep. . . ." (Psalms 36:7) For centuries, even in the darkest times of persecution, many Jews have declared their faith in the ultimate justice of God.

Others go even further. For them, God's justice is tempered with the equally powerful claim of God's mercy and love. They, too, base their view on Moses' experience and testimony within the Torah. Just before receiving the Ten Commandments at Mount Sinai, Moses experiences and defines God as "compassionate and gracious, slow to anger, rich in kindness and faithfulness, extending kindness to the thousandth generation, forgiving iniquity, transgression, and sin." (Exodus 34:6–7) Reflecting this view of God, the Psalmist (Psalms 119:64) comments that "the earth, *Adonai,* is full of Your mercy," underscoring the conviction that while God may judge the world and all its creatures and even punish them for their sins, God also cares for them and loves them.

Rabbinic commentators teach that God's "power for justice" *(midat ha-din)* and "power for mercy" *(midat ha-rachamim)* are always combined. Without their interconnection, the rabbis argue, the world cannot endure. It will be out of balance and incomplete, resulting in destruction. Only by simultaneously exercising justice and mercy, say the rabbis, can God create and sustain the world. "Mercy or justice alone is insufficient."

 Zugot

This idea that justice and mercy are blended is both suggested and extended by Hillel. He claims that when judging human beings or the world, "God weighs the scale of judgment toward the scale of mercy." God actually favors the "power for mercy" over the "power for justice."

Rab, a later sage, agrees, portraying God at a moment of judgment as saying, "Let My power of love overcome My power of anger." This view that God's powers of mercy and justice are blended with a tendency toward mercy allows rabbinic interpreters to accept Moses' claim that "God's deeds are perfect . . . God's ways are just." *(Genesis Rabbah* 12:15; *Tosefta, Sanhedrin* 13:3 and *Berachot* 7a)

How, then, can we account for the suffering of the innocent, of good people? How does this blending of justice and mercy apply to their situations? How can one maintain that "God's ways are just . . ." when, at times, they appear to be cruel?

Early rabbinic commentators commonly answered these questions by claiming that while righteous human beings may suffer in this world, they will be rewarded by God in the *olam ha-ba,* or the "world to come." Pain in this world is temporary and brief. The righteous may suffer at

the hands of cruel human beings or, in the case of illness or disease, because of the inability of human beings to find a cure. Such pain is identified by the rabbis as *yisurim shel ahavah,* or the "sufferings of love," and God, the *Dayan ha-emet,* or the "Judge of truth," rewards those who endure these sufferings with mercy forever in the *olam ha-ba.* (*Ta'anit* 11a)

This concept of God as *Dayan ha-emet,* balancing justice and mercy in this world and in the *olam ha-ba,* became a standard explanation for the reason bad things happen to good people. For rabbinic commentators it justified Moses' claim that "God's deeds are perfect, and all God's ways are just. God is faithful, never false, true and upright." For them, God's justice and mercy might not be apparent in the lives of victims of pain and evil in this world, but—in the *olam ha-ba*—God's justice and mercy eventually will prevail.

With this belief in mind, the rabbis prescribe that, at the death of a loved one, a person should recite the words: "Be praised, O *Adonai* our God, Ruler of the universe, *Dayan ha-emet,*" affirming that God, the "Judge of truth," will consider each life according to its deeds and dispense the appropriate reward in the *olam ha-ba.*

It is this faith in God's ultimate justice and mercy that strengthened Jews throughout the centuries when they were faced with persecution, torment, and death. It is said that when Rabbi Hananiah ben Teradyon, his wife, and daughter were taken by the Romans to be put to death after the Bar Kochba revolt in 135 C.E., they publicly declared God's justice in the words of Moses: He boldly told his tormenters, "God's deeds are perfect"; she said, "God is faithful, never false!" Their belief that God had not forsaken them, even in the midst of their torture and death, but would reward them in the *olam ha-ba* provided the courage and faith they required to face their enemies with strength and pride. (*Avodah Zarah* 18a)

No good without evil
The Koretzer Rabbi taught that human beings cannot be consciously good unless they know evil. They cannot appreciate pleasure unless they

have tasted bitterness. Good is only the reverse of evil, and pleasure is merely the opposite of anxiety. Without the evil impulse human beings do no evil, but neither can they do good. (Louis I. Newman, The Hasidic Anthology: Tales and Teachings of the Hasidim, *Schocken Books, New York, 1963, p. 97)*

Rambam (Maimonides)

In his book *The Guide for the Perplexed* (3:22–23), Moses Maimonides raises a serious objection to the view that trials and suffering are sent "as an opportunity for achieving great reward" in the *olam ha-ba*. He argues that this is not what Moses had in mind when he declared that "God's ways are just. . . ." Using Job and his loss of wealth, property, and children as an example, Maimonides argues that there are no explanations for the suffering of innocent people. We cannot understand the mysterious and miraculous ways in which God brings the universe to life. "We should not fall into the error of imagining God's knowledge to be similar to ours or God's intention, power, and management comparable to ours."

According to Maimonides, if we appreciate, as Job finally did, that God's ways are not our ways and God's knowledge is not our knowledge, we will find suffering more bearable. "We will not be filled with doubts about God. Instead, our faith will increase our love of God."

Maimonides' view that God's powers of justice and mercy are beyond human understanding is not shared by Jewish mystics. They believe that evil enters the world at creation. Rabbi Isaac Luria teaches that God created the world out of a clash between the powers of mercy and judgment. In that collision, sparks of light and love were lodged into dark shells that make up all the substance of the world. We suffer, Luria maintains, because so much is still locked in such shells. The human responsibility is to liberate the light, to free goodness and healing. God's will is

for justice, truth, and mercy. God, dependent upon human beings, is waiting for them to break the dark shells and release God's power for mercy and love.

Modern philosopher Martin Buber amplifies this mystic insight about evil. He writes: "What we call 'evil' is not merely in human beings; it is in the world . . .; it is the uncleanness of creation. . . . We know what has been proclaimed by the anonymous prophet whose words stand in the second part of the Book of Isaiah: like light and darkness, good and evil have been created by God . . . the abyss of the absence of light and the struggle for light . . . [have been created by God]."

For Buber and for Jewish mystics, evil is real. It is embedded in the "dark shells," the material of the universe. Since God could not create the universe without such "material" or "potentials," human beings, like all other forms of life, must be subjected to evil and its awful consequences. Nevertheless, Buber adds that we have the power to liberate the good and diminish the evil. "Everything wants to be hallowed, to be brought into the holy . . . everything wants to come to God through us. . . . God wills . . . man for the work of completing creation. . . . God waits for us." The task of humanity is to reduce evil and its suffering in the world. God, whose ways are just, true, and merciful, depends upon us. (*The Way of Response: Selections from His Writings,* Nahum N. Glatzer, editor, Schocken Books, New York, 1971, pp. 134, 148, and 151)

Controlling the yetzer ha-ra, or the "evil inclination"
The rabbis tell the story of the people who capture the yetzer ha-ra, *or the "source of evil." They are about to destroy it when they are warned that if they do, they will also destroy the world. Instead, they put it in prison. Three days later, they notice that the world about them is changing in dangerous ways. No eggs are being hatched anywhere. Fearful that the world and they will not survive, they decide to liberate the* yetzer ha-ra *and seek ways to control it. (Yoma 69b)*

God's power against evil

I believe . . . the only intellectually satisfying answer that has been given to the Holocaust: God "allowed" it because God didn't have the power to stop it. God was not strong enough yet to prevent this torment, and we did not use our moral capacity to compensate for God's weakness.

The same may be said of other evils we face. God is doing all the good [that] God now can do. We cannot blame our suffering on a God who, like ourselves, does not have all power. (*Eugene B. Borowitz*, Liberal Judaism, *UAHC Press, New York, 1984, p. 203*)

Evil is chaos

Evil is chaos still uninvaded by the creative energy; [it is] sheer chance unconquered by will and intelligence. . . . In the measure that human beings learn to release their potentialities for good, they transform and transcend evil and associate themselves with the divine energies that inhere in the universe. . . . (*Mordecai M. Kaplan*, The Meaning of God, *pp. 72–79*)

Rabbi Robert Gordis rejects the views of both Jewish mystics and Martin Buber. "The suffering of the innocent in painful disease, the death of a child, the cutting off of genius or talent before its fulfillment—all these categories of evil are too agonizing to yield to such views." Like Maimonides, Gordis argues that there are some forms of suffering and evil we can understand, but many others are "beyond all the resources of the human intellect.

"The universe is a work of art, the pattern of which cannot be discerned if the spectator stands too close to the painting. Only as one moves back a distance, do the scales and blotches dissolve and does the design of the artist emerge in all its fullness. In the world that is our home, we are too close to the pattern of existence, too deeply involved in it, to be able to achieve the perspective that is God's alone. . . . Perhaps the truest word was spoken by a third-century sage, Yannai: 'It is not in our power fully to explain either the well-being of the wicked or the suffer-

ing of the righteous.'" (*A Faith for Moderns*, Bloch Publishing Co., New York, 1960, pp. 187–189)

Not so, says Rabbi Abraham Joshua Heschel. Rescued from Europe when Nazism began to rise, Heschel draws a distinction between the evil of natural catastrophes or diseases and the evil perpetrated by human beings. God, he argues, gives us commandments for justice, truth, goodness, and love. Human beings are unfaithful to them and unfaithful to God. They bring the evil upon themselves, and then they bitterly turn on God like selfish children looking for someone to blame, crying out: "Where are You?"

Quoting the chasidic teacher Ba'al Shem Tov, Heschel observes: "If people behold evil, they may know it was shown to them in order that they learn their own guilt and repent; for what is shown to them is also within them." Continuing, Heschel declares: "We have profaned the word of God, and we have given the wealth of our land, the ingenuity of our minds, and the dear lives of our youths to tragedy and perdition. . . . We have failed to fight for right, for justice, for goodness; as a result we must fight against wrong, against injustice, against evil. We have failed to offer sacrifices on the altar of peace; thus we offered sacrifices on the altar of war." Such evil is done by human beings.

Heschel agrees with Moses' declaration of faith that "God's deeds are perfect . . . all God's ways are just. . . . God is faithful, true, and upright." God, says Heschel, abhors evil and, therefore, demands of us deeds that are *perfect, just, faithful, true,* and *upright.* God "has not created the universe that we may have opportunities to satisfy our greed, envy, and ambition. We have not survived that we may waste our years in vulgar vanities." Our task, concludes Heschel, is to use our energies and gifts to banish all evil from the world. "God will return to us when we shall be willing to let God in. . . . God is waiting constantly and keenly for our effort and devotion." (*Man's Quest for God: Studies in Prayer and Symbolism,* Scribner, New York, 1954, pp. 147–151)

Rabbi Eugene Borowitz offers a philosophy about God and evil slightly different from that of Heschel. "I believe . . . the only intellectually satisfying answer that has been given to the

Holocaust [is] God 'allowed' it because God didn't have the power to stop it. God was not strong enough yet to prevent this torment, and we did not use our moral capacity to compensate for God's weakness."

Borowitz here breaks with traditional Jewish theology, which sees both good and evil as flowing from God. For him, evil emerges because God is limited in power and cannot do anything to stop it. God's will is for goodness, mercy, justice, and peace, but God requires our help and, at times even with our help, may not prevail.

"The same," argues Borowitz, "may be said of other evils we face. God is doing all the good [that] God now can do. We cannot blame our suffering on a God who, like ourselves, does not have all power." God may want a world without anguish and injustice, but, like that of a human being, God's will is limited by the harsh realities of available resources, by the unexpected flurry of opposing forces, and by the failure of human beings to cooperate. Evil happens because God cannot yet prevent it, not because God plans it. (*Liberal Judaism*, p. 203)

Why is there evil in this world created by a God of justice, mercy, and love? Why do some people suffer and others live long lives of happiness and peace? What does Moses mean by his claim that "God's deeds are perfect . . . are just . . . true and upright"?

Jewish commentators offer a variety of views in response to these difficult questions. They challenge us to formulate our own answers and integrate them into our lives. Perhaps the very process of struggling to understand the meaning of evil is the means through which God triumphs over evil. Some debates, say the rabbis, are truly for the sake of God. Confronting the power and temptations of evil in God's world may be one of them.

PEREK BET: *"Remember the Days of Old": The Importance of History*

In his poetic declaration to the people of Israel, Moses tells them: *Zechor yemot olam,* "Remember the days of old,"/*Binu shenot dor va-dor,* "Consider the years of ages past. . . ." Are these the words of an old man fearful of being forgotten

by his people, or is this statement an important piece of wisdom?

Modern historian Yosef Hayim Yerushalmi notes that while "memory is always problematic, usually deceptive, sometimes treacherous," the Torah has "no hesitations" in commanding it. He points out that "the verb *zachar* [remember] appears in its various forms in the Bible no less than one hundred and sixty-nine times." The people of Israel are commanded to remember and are warned not to forget.

Yerushalmi explains that, within the Torah, "remembering" functions within "two channels: ritual and recital." Each of the festivals celebrates a historical event. Pesach and Sukot tell the tale of the people's liberation from Egypt and their wandering through the Sinai desert. Shavuot, during the time of the Temple in Jerusalem, becomes a celebration of the giving of the Torah on Mount Sinai. The recital of history, the encounter with memory, takes place with each ritual. Every Shabbat *Kiddush* over the wine includes the phrase *zecher li-tziat Mitzrayim,* or "a remembrance of the Exodus from Egypt."

Calling the creation of Israel's history "an astonishing achievement," Yerushalmi concludes that while "biblical history has, at its core, a recital of the acts of God, its accounts are filled predominantly with the actions of men and women and the deeds of Israel and the nations. . . . The result was . . . history on an unprecedented scale." (*Zakhor: Jewish History and Jewish Memory,* University of Washington Press, Seattle, 1982, pp. 1–26)

Why recall or study the past? Why recite it at festival times?

Rashi

Rashi suggests that one should "remember" and "consider" history "in order to be conscious of what may happen in the future." He explains that understanding how God created the heavens and earth, spread human beings throughout the world, made a covenant with Abraham, divided peoples into lands, and gave the Torah with its laws to the people of Israel helps to promote an appreciation of God's power and presence in human life. The knowledge of what God has done encourages faith in what God will continue to do. Knowing about the past, says Rashi, promotes the truth that "God has the power to bring good into human life and will one day bring the world to a messianic time of justice and peace." (Comments on Deuteronomy 32:7)

Peli

Modern commentator Pinchas Peli sees another value in "remembering." He quotes a statement by the great chasidic master Nachman of Bratzlav, which is inscribed in huge stone letters at the entrance to the Yad va-Shem Holocaust Memorial in Jerusalem: "In remembering is the secret of redemption." Peli argues that "recalling the past and understanding it help us put events into their proper focus." Retrieving the past, he says, enriches us. "Even though we may think of ourselves as wise, resourceful, and technologically advanced, we are brought to realize that there is still much we can learn from our parents, and even our grandparents have much that is worth sharing with us."

Peli also believes that knowing about our past provides an important source of "constructive pride." Jews emphasize the "pride to be derived from getting to know their roots. This pride was not aimed at inflating one's sense of importance. . . . On the contrary, it was reason for imposing more obligations and restrictions. There is a short but very meaningful Yiddish expression that is invoked on such occasions: *s'pa'ast nisht*. It does not suit a person of distinguished lineage. . . . Being proud and getting to know the roots of one's culture is not just a hobby or pastime," Peli concludes, "but a delicate and sophisticated business." It is the means through which we adopt and absorb ethical values and standards into our behavior. Considering and understanding our past provides a proud set of models, guidelines, and goals. (*Torah Today,* pp. 239–241)

Studying and recalling history, however, can sometimes be very painful, teaching lessons that are often difficult to accept. Holocaust survivor and Nobel Prize-winning author Elie Wiesel points out that people often are resistent to dealing with what the past teaches. After years of writing about the Nazi attempt to destroy the Jewish people, Wiesel feels "discouragement and shame." Society, he says, "has changed so little."

Hatred, prejudice, and anti-Semitism continue. "So many strategists are preparing the explosion of the planet and so many people willingly submit . . . so many still live under oppression and so many others in indifference, only one conclusion is possible: namely, the failure of the black years has begotten yet another failure. Nothing has been learned. Auschwitz has not even served as warning. For more detailed information, consult your daily newspaper."

Why follow Moses' advice: "Remember the days of old,/Consider the years of ages past"?

Wiesel argues that we must study history because we owe it to those who perished and to new generations who will need to know "where they come from, and what their heritage is." Remembering the past is critical in forming the future. "We need to face the dead, again and again, in order to appease them, perhaps even to seek among them, beyond all contradiction and absurdity, a symbol, a beginning of promise."

To demonstrate the importance of passing memories from one generation to another, Wiesel relates how the famed Jewish historian Simon Dubnow encouraged those about him as they walked to their death, telling them: "Open your eyes and ears, remember every detail, every name, every sigh! The color of the clouds, the hissing of the wind in the trees, the executioner's every gesture: the one who survives must forget nothing!"

As a result Jews wrote plays and poems describing the agony, torture, and degradation of those who perished in the death camps. "Jews," says Wiesel, "went without sleep, bartered their food for pencils and paper. They gambled with their fate. They risked their lives. . . . They did not write them for me, for us, but for the others, those on the outside and those yet unborn. There was then a veritable passion to testify for the future, against death and oblivion, a passion conveyed by every possible means of expression."

As Wiesel notes, those writing history under such circumstances recorded it for those in the future. It was their last gift, a testimony of pride and faith, of courage and determination. Those about to die in gas chambers or be shot at the edge of mass graves or be beaten to death sealed their memories in documents so they would live again in those who read about their experiences. This "historic consciousness," writes Wiesel, provides Jews with a solidarity with other Jews "and those who survive within you."

Studying Jewish history, therefore, bonds Jews to a "collective memory," a legacy reaching back to Abraham and Sarah, Isaac and Rebekah, Jacob, Leah, and Rachel, through Moses and all the prophets, poets, philosophers, and Torah commentators. It means, concludes Wiesel, "choosing to be a link between past and future, between remorse and consolation, between the primary silence of creation and the silence that weighed on Treblinka. . . . To be a Jew today means to bear witness to what is and to what is no longer." (*One Generation After*, pp. 9, 11, 38–39, 168–174)

Modern philosopher Emil L. Fackenheim also addresses the importance of memory and history. For him, Moses' command to "remember . . . and consider the years of ages past" is not a suggestion that Jews have the right to accept or reject. Fackenheim points out that, before the Holocaust, Jews sought to live by the 613 commandments (mitzvot) of the Torah. Following the Holocaust, an additional commandment has been added to Jewish practice.

Jews, Fackenheim writes, must "remember" their history. They must study it carefully, know all its details, celebrate their traditions, teach them to their children, and do everything possible to assure their regeneration and growth as a people. That is the only way they will triumph over Hitler whose policy of extermination was designed to put an end to Jewish memory and existence. *"The authentic Jew of today,"* explains Fackenheim, *"is forbidden to hand Hitler yet another, posthumous victory."* (*The Jewish Return into History: Reflections on the Age of Auschwitz and a New Jerusalem*, Schocken Books, New York, 1978, pp. 19–24)

Jewish history and purpose
A robust sense of identity has not prevented this people from sending the repercussions of its influence far and wide into the oceans of universal history. It is when historic Israel is most persistently distinctive that its universal vocation is enlarged. The lesson of history is plain. There is no salvation or significance for the Jew except when he aims high and stands straight within his own authentic frame of values. (Abba Eban, My People, p. 522)

Making history
Human beings make their own history, but they do not make it just as they please; they do not make it under circumstances chosen by themselves but under circumstances directly found, given, and transmitted from the past. (Karl Marx)

Ignoring history
Those who ignore the past are doomed to repeat it. (George Santayana)

The choice of confronting and embracing Jewish history in very personal terms does not apply only to being, in Wiesel's terms, "a witness" or, in Fackenheim's formulation, an instrument in the "triumph over Hitler." For many Jews, "remembering" and "considering" the Jewish legacy is a means of recapturing Jewish identity.

Modern writer Paul Cowan grew up without a Jewish education, without Jewish celebrations, and with almost no experience with his Jewish relatives. He recalls suffering bitter moments of anti-Semitism, while attending a private school where he hid his Jewish identity. "I never told anyone. I felt guilty about it, as if I were personally responsible for my plight."

In his thirties, Cowan began a writing project about Jewish socialism as it had flourished on the Lower East Side of New York. The research led him to questions about his own family, where they had come from, why some bore the name Cohen and others Cowan. Soon he was enmeshed in reclaiming his Jewish heritage. Explaining his motivation, Cowan writes, "For my part, I am reacting to the rootlessness I felt as a child—to the fact that, for all the Cowan family's warmth, for all its intellectual vigor, for all its loyalty toward one another, our pasts had been amputated. We were orphans in history."

Cowan explains that when he met people who made Judaism attractive, "I was faced with a clear choice—a choice, indeed, about history, though I never knew how to articulate it until my sister Holly furnished the words. Should I explore Judaism, the real, living link with my ancestors and the six million? Or should I reject it and be another conscious participant in the obliteration of five thousand years of history? Put that way, of course, it wasn't really a choice." For Paul Cowan, carrying out Moses' commandment to "remember the days of old,/Consider the years of ages past" was the means through which he retrieved his legacy as a Jew. (*An Orphan in History: Retrieving a Jewish Legacy,* Doubleday, New York, 1983, pp. 3–21)

What about a convert to Judaism? Is Moses' command also applicable to Jews-by-choice? If one has not been born a Jew and is, therefore, not related to generations of Jews by birth, how can one feel a part of the Jewish past?

Lydia Kukoff, herself a convert, offers some important insights into such questions. She comments: "When I became a Jew, my husband and I lived far away from our extended Jewish family. Fortunately, however, I found some friends who were quite Jewishly literate. We started a study group and met regularly to learn, to cook together for holidays, and just to be together. These friends gave me a great deal of support. I had a comfortable environment in which to learn and ask questions, while gradually becoming part of a Jewish community. By doing and learning I began to build my own Jewish past."

Creating a "Jewish past" takes time and discipline. Kukoff underscores the importance of Shabbat and festival celebrations in the home and synagogue, constant study, reading cookbooks, history, literature, Jewish religious thought, placing a *mezuzah* on the door, using a Jewish calendar, learning Hebrew, and acquiring synagogue skills. She advises, "Don't be impatient. You won't get it all right away. Nobody does. . . . What you are learning and doing will slowly

become internalized. You will make Judaism your own, and you will feel authentic." Studying, accumulating knowledge about Jewish history, and celebrating the traditions of Jewish life provide a convert with a Jewish memory. It is the means through which a sacred heritage is transfused into the soul. (*Choosing Judaism*, pp. 23–29)

Jewish history carries with it a distinct task, which we encounter in Moses' demand to "remember the days of old,/Consider the years of ages past." The great lawgiver and leader does not stop there. He also declares that "God's portion is the people of Israel." What does such a claim mean? How can it be understood within the context of Jewish history?

Modern interpreter Rabbi Leo Baeck sees in the study of Jewish history an extraordinary explanation for the purpose of the Jewish people. "According to an old saying," he writes, "Israel was called into existence for the sake of the Torah; but the Torah can live only through its people. . . . The Jewish right to existence was dependent upon the Jews retaining their peculiarity. All education was directed to this end: To be different was the law of existence. According to an ancient interpretation, the Jews were exhorted: 'You shall be different, for I *Adonai* your God am different. . . .' The Jew was the great nonconformist, the great dissenter of history. That was the purpose of Jewish existence."

Baeck underscores his view by observing that "often it seems that the special task of Judaism is to express the idea of the community standing alone, the ethical principle of the minority. Judaism bears witness to the power of the idea as against the power of mere numbers and worldly success; it stands for the enduring protest of those who seek to be true to their own selves, who assert their right to be different against the crushing pressure of the vicious and the leveling. . . . If Judaism did not exist," argues Baeck, "we should have to invent it. Without minorities there can be no world historic goal."

For Rabbi Baeck, Israel is "God's portion" because of its unique role in history as a community "standing alone," questioning the power of the multitude, and representing the sanctity of each human being as a child of God. Knowing and understanding that history are crucial for every Jew and for the world. "So long as Judaism exists," Baeck concludes, "nobody will be able to say that the soul of humanity has surrendered." (*The Essence of Judaism,* pp. 260–273)

Is this what Moses has in mind when he emphasizes, "Remember the days of old,/Consider the years of ages past"? Undoubtedly, Moses was concerned with several of the considerations expressed by our interpreters on the significance of Jewish history. He must have sensed the power in reviewing history, realizing that acquiring and confronting one's past is a source of pride and identity that builds a commitment for future survival. The past leads through the present into tomorrow.

QUESTIONS FOR STUDY AND DISCUSSION

1. At the death of a loved one, a Jew says a blessing: "Be praised, O *Adonai, Dayan ha-emet,* Judge of truth." What does this blessing acknowledge about God and human life? How does it relate to Moses' statement that God's "deeds are perfect . . . all God's ways are just"?

2. Some Torah interpreters claim that evil is a necessary part of human existence. What do they mean by this argument? How would you apply their claim to the evils of sickness, dishonesty, murder, child abuse, war, and famine? Which explanation of the relationship between evil and God presented by the Torah interpreters makes most sense to you? Why?

3. In her book *Generation without Memory* (Linton Press/Simon and Schuster, New York, 1981, pp. 99–100), writer Anne Roiphe quotes a friend: "We Jews are molded together like a family; because of our incredible and unique history we have developed our own intellectual modes, the modes of logic and humor that we share with other Jews. We are a single family that traces its history back to before the Flood. Being Jewish is one of the major ingredients of my psyche. I could not live suspended in air. I need my roots, my feelings of belonging." How does a study of Jewish history create a sense of belonging to "a family"? How does such study prevent one from feeling "suspended in air"?

4. For Jews, as Torah interpreters point out, memories of the past, a shared history, are very important in the formation of a proud identity. Today, however, there are many converts to Judaism and many born-Jews who have not accumulated a "memory bank" of Jewish experiences or knowledge. If you were shaping a program meant to help them acquire such a "memory bank," what would you include?

PARASHAT VEZOT HA-BERACHAH
Deuteronomy 33:1–34:12

Parashat Vezot ha-Berachah, meaning "This is the blessing . . .," begins with Moses' blessing of and his farewell to the people of Israel. He blesses each of the twelve tribes, noting that the Torah is "the heritage of the congregation of Jacob." He concludes with the pronouncement: "O happy Israel! Who is like you,/A people delivered by *Adonai,*/Your protecting Shield, your Sword triumphant!" Then Moses climbs Mount Nebo, located in Moab just across from Jericho and the Dead Sea, from whose peak he sees the Land of Israel. He dies there at the age of one hundred and twenty years and is buried in Moab. No one knows the location of his grave. At the end of a thirty-day mourning period, Joshua assumes leadership of the people. "Never again," declares the Torah, "did there arise in Israel a prophet like Moses— whom *Adonai* singled out, face to face. . . ."

OUR TARGUM

·1·

Moses speaks words of poetry and blessing in his last statement to the people of Israel. He recalls how God "came from Sinai . . ./Lightning flashing" at the people, and how they accepted the Torah as their heritage.

·2·

Moses blesses each of the tribes. He prays that "Reuben may live and not die"; that Judah be restored and aided against his enemies; that all the undertakings of Levi be blessed; that Benjamin continue to be protected; that Joseph and his sons, Ephraim and Manasseh, be blessed "with the bounty of earth and its fullness"; that Zebulun and Issachar enjoy the bounty of sand and sea; that Gad be enlarged and rewarded for his leadership and courage in battle; that Dan "leap forth" to victory; that Naphtali be "sated with favor"; that the tribe of Asher "be the favorite of his brothers," dipping "its foot in oil" and enjoying security.

·3·

Concluding his blessing, Moses declares that "there is none like God,/ Riding through the heavens to help you,/ . . . God is a refuge,/ A support . . . /O happy Israel! Who is like you,/ A people delivered by *Adonai*,/ Your protecting Shield, your Sword triumphant!/ Your enemies shall come cringing before you,/ And you shall tread on their backs."

·4·

Moses climbs to the peak of Mount Nebo in Moab just opposite the city of Jericho near the Dead Sea. From there he can see the Land of Israel that is promised by God to the people. Moses, who is forbidden to enter the land, dies in Moab at the age of one hundred and twenty. No one knows the place of his burial.

The Israelites mourn his passing for thirty days. Afterwards, Joshua son of Nun succeeds him as leader of the Israelites.

The Torah concludes by citing Moses' unique-

ness. "Never again did there arise in Israel a prophet like Moses—whom *Adonai* singled out, face to face, for the various signs and portents that *Adonai* sent him to display in the land of Egypt, against Pharaoh and all his courtiers and his whole country, and for all the great might and awesome power that Moses displayed before all Israel."

THEMES

Parashat Vezot ha-Berachah contains two important themes:

1. The significance of Torah to the Jewish people.
2. The role of Moses as prophet and leader.

PEREK ALEF: *Torah: "The Heritage of the Congregation of Jacob"*

In his farewell message to the Israelites, Moses again recites a poem. He recalls the spiritual experience of the people at Mount Sinai, declaring:

Adonai came from Sinai;
God shone upon them from Seir;

Lightning flashing at them from the right.
Lover, indeed, of the people,
Their holy ones are all in Your hand.
They followed in Your footsteps,
Accepting Your pronouncements,
When Moses commanded us with the Torah
As the heritage of the congregation of Jacob.

About to die, the aged leader impresses upon the people their historic relationship to the Torah.

It originates in the "lightning flashing at them" at Mount Sinai. It is proof of God's love for the people of Israel; following the commandments of the Torah is proof of the people's loyalty to God. Torah is the unique "heritage of the congregation of Jacob," of the Jewish people.

Rashi

In commenting on the meaning of Moses' observation on the relationship of the Jewish people to the Torah, Rashi writes: "We have taken the Torah and will not abandon it." For Rashi, the people have chosen to accept the Torah, and they are defined by their attachment and devotion to it. Torah forms the basis of Jewish tradition. There can be no Jewish people without it. Adherence to its wisdom, ethics, and rituals is essential for preserving the people. (Comment on Deuteronomy 33:4)

Rashi's emphasis on defining the Jewish people by its relationship to Torah may be based on earlier comments by Rabbi Eleazar. In a rhetorical question, Eleazar asks, "What was the blessing Moses made before reading the Torah?" He answers his question with the claim that Moses said: "Be praised, O God, who has chosen the Torah and made it sacred and finds pleasure in those who fulfill it."

"Moses," Rabbi Eleazar stresses, "does not say 'those who study it or meditate upon it.' He claims that God 'finds pleasure in those who fulfill it,' who practice it by carrying out its commandments. It is the 'practice' of Torah that transforms it into 'a heritage of the congregation of Jacob.'" (*Deuteronomy Rabbah* 11:6)

Ramban (Nachmanides)

Nachmanides widens Rabbi Eleazar's claim to include both those who are born-Jews and those who convert to Judaism. He points out that Moses does not speak of the Torah as belonging to the "house of Jacob" or to the "seed of Jacob," which could have led to the assumption that Torah is "the heritage" only of those born to Jewish parents. Instead, he emphasizes that the Torah is "the heritage of *kehilat Ya'akov*, or the 'congregation of Jacob.'" It is not an exclusive birthright but a legacy that can be adopted or chosen by any person. (Comment on Deuteronomy 33:4)

Hertz

On the meaning of Torah
The real Torah is not merely the written text of the Five Books of Moses; the real Torah is the meaning enshrined in the text, as expounded . . . and unfolded . . . by successive generations of sages and teachers in Israel. (Rabbi Joseph H. Hertz, Authorized Daily Prayer Book, *p. 35)*

The purpose of the whole Torah is that each person should become a Torah. (Ba'al Shem Tov)

If not for Torah, the people of Israel would not at all differ from the nations of the world. (Sifre Deuteronomy 32:29)

Blessing before reading the Torah
Blessed is the Eternal, our God, Ruler of the universe, who hallows us with mitzvot and commands us to engage in the study of Torah. Eternal our God, make the words of Your Torah sweet to us, and to the house of Israel, Your people, that we and our children may be lovers of Your name and students of Your Torah. Blessed is the Eternal, the Teacher of Torah to the people Israel. (Gates of Prayer, p. 52)

When two people meet to study Torah, God is present. (Hananiah ben Teradyon, Avot 3:6)

Rambam (Maimonides)

Steinsaltz

In his discussion of the importance of Torah to the Jewish people, Moses Maimonides observes that as soon as children begin to talk, parents must teach them the words: "Moses commanded us with the Torah as a heritage of the congregation of Jacob," and "*Shema Yisrael*, 'Hear, O Israel,' *Adonai* is our God, *Adonai* is One." Children must be taught the importance and the lessons of the Torah as soon as they can speak. Teachers, says Maimonides, are to be employed if parents cannot provide education. "Every person is commanded to study Torah, whether poor or rich, in sound health or sick, young or old . . . one must study until the day of death."

Maimonides even suggests how the time for studying Torah should be divided. One-third of the time should be spent on the Torah; one-third on commentaries and the Talmud; and one-third in "thinking and reflecting" upon what has been covered. One subject should be compared to another; questions should be asked; ethical rules should be inferred from the standards found within the Torah. Furthermore, the study of Torah may not be postponed with the excuse that one has no leisure time. "Should such a thought enter your mind," writes Maimonides, "you will never win the crown of Torah. Instead," he concludes, quoting *Avot* 1:5, "make the study of Torah a fixed obligation."

For Maimonides, no commandment "is equal in importance to the study of Torah. Indeed, the study of Torah is equal to all the commandments because it leads to the practice of Torah." He concludes, "Thus the study of Torah takes precedence over practice." In Maimonides' view, the Torah constitutes God's truth, given to the people of Israel. Deciphering that truth and understanding the commandments motivate one not only to fulfill God's will for justice, mercy, and peace but to make the Torah "the heritage of the congregation of Jacob." (*Mishneh Torah, Sefer ha-Madah* 1–5)

Modern commentator Rabbi Adin Steinsaltz builds on Maimonides' emphasis on the importance of Torah study as a means of knowing what God wants from us. Defining Torah as not only the Five Books of Moses but also as all the works of the Talmud and subsequent commentaries, Steinsaltz claims that "the Torah of the Jews is the essence of divine revelation; it is not only a basis for social, political, and religious life but is in itself something of supreme value . . . it is the spiritual map of the universe . . . for the Torah expresses the divine will and wisdom . . . the intellectual study of Torah and the emotional involvement in its contents are a form of identification with the divine will, with what may be called God's dream of the existence of the world and the existence of human beings."

Knowing Torah is more for Steinsaltz than understanding what God wants for the world and its human beings. Torah is not just an "intellectual" document for study. It is also "Law." Torah compels people "to behave in certain ways." It "is a way of life, showing both how to relate inwardly and how to conduct oneself outwardly, practically. . . . One finds the Torah significant in every aspect of community, commerce, agriculture, and industry, in the life of feeling and love, in relations between the sexes—down to the most minute aspects of living, like buttoning one's shoes or lying down to sleep. . . ." Steinsaltz's view of the Torah as a "divine map of the world" and as God's Law, which "directs the conduct of one's daily business from waking to sleeping," represents a widely held view within Jewish tradition. (*The Thirteen Petalled Rose*, pp. 87–98)

The evolving Torah
Torah results from the relationship between God and the Jewish people. The records of our earliest confrontations are uniquely important

to us. Lawgivers and prophets, historians and poets gave us a heritage whose study is a religious imperative and whose practice is our chief means to holiness. Rabbis and teachers, philosophers and mystics, gifted Jews in every age amplified the Torah tradition. For millennia the creation of Torah has not ceased, and Jewish creativity in our time is adding to the chain of tradition. (From Reform Judaism: A Centenary Perspective, *CCAR, New York, 1976)*

Differing with Steinsaltz and others who believe that the Torah is the product of a single revelation to Moses at Mount Sinai, Rabbi Mordecai M. Kaplan maintains that the Torah is a sacred document that evolved through many centuries. He argues that "all the basic elements of human culture are represented" in the written Torah and in the later Talmud. As such, the Torah "contains folklore and a world perspective; it outlines a national policy; it prescribes ethical and religious conduct; it lays the foundation of a system of jurisprudence. . . . The Torah, especially as developed in life and interpretation, can, therefore, without exaggeration be regarded as the full equivalent of what we understand by a national civilization."

Kaplan, in terms of this evolving "national civilization," sees the Torah as "the embodiment of Israel's quest through the ages for the moral law that expresses the will of God." The Torah, therefore, "is not infallible." It contains errors and deals with matters that are no longer relevant, such as the dress of the priests or the sacrifices offered on ancient altars. At times, as in the case of capital punishment or the treatment of women, it presents ideas that are questionable. However, Kaplan maintains that, as the Jewish people quest for an understanding of what is morally right, the Torah, even with its errors, "when submitted to study and analysis, may prove instructive and enlightening. We learn the moral law, as we learn natural law, by trial and error."

Kaplan adds an important element to his view of Torah as an evolving, imperfect record of the Jewish people's search for what is morally right. He believes that while God did not present the whole Torah to Moses on Mount Sinai, God is the power continuing to urge the Jewish people in an ethical quest for love, justice, purity, and peace. For him, the Torah is a record of God's continuing influence upon them. "The Torah reveals the working of God in the life of our people, in that it articulates the earliest striving of our people to live up to the highest potentialities of human nature." (*The Meaning of God,* pp. 311–318; also *Questions Jews Ask,* pp. 167–168)

As the "heritage of the congregation of Jacob," the Torah holds the secret of Jewish survival. The people's devotion to and study of Torah guarantee the Jewish future. It has never become a static "literature" or "tradition." Commentators have constantly applied its ethics to the challenging realities of their times. Mystics and philosophers have explored its views of God, history, and the nature of human life. The rituals and festivals first described in its chapters have nurtured the flowering of Jewish celebrations. The Torah has evolved with the Jewish people and has remained its main source of historical identification and moral teachings. Jews are the people of an ever-expanding Torah.

Rabbi Leo Baeck captures the meaning and challenge of the Torah "as the heritage of the congregation of Jacob." He observes that "Judaism did not affix itself to any particular period so as to finish up with it; never did it become complete. The task abides but not its solution. The old revelation becomes a new revelation: Judaism experiences a *continuous renaissance.*" The ancient Torah of Moses continues to unfold.

PEREK BET: *Moses "Whom Adonai Singled Out, Face to Face"*

Parashat Vezot ha-Berachah refers to Moses as *ish ha-Elohim,* or a "man of God" (Deuteronomy 33:1), and as *eved Adonai,* or a "servant of God." (Deuteronomy 34:5) We are told also that, unlike all other prophets, Moses knew God with a special intimacy that is described as "face to face." Within rabbinic tradition, Moses is called *Moshe rabbenu,* or "Moses, our teacher." These various descriptions and names for the leader whose life fills the books of Exodus, Leviticus, Numbers, and Deuteronomy and who is known in Jewish tradition as the bearer of *Torat Moshe,* the "Torah of Moses," dramatize his central place in both Jewish and world history. Today, his religious teachings and powerful political image continue to influence millions. Yet, this great man, who dies alone on Mount Nebo, outside the Promised Land of Israel, and whose burial place "no one knows to this day," remains an enigma.

Commentators throughout the centuries have sought to uncover his motives, unmask his personality, and reveal the secrets of his greatness. Piecing together the fragments of his life collected from the Torah or using their imagination, interpreters have speculated about his origins, family relationships, complex association with the people of Israel, emotional stability, instincts for leadership, moral sensibilities, and his mysterious connection with God.

Each spark disclosed about this "man of God" brings us nearer to understanding what constitutes a "great" human being, a "servant of God." Taken together, the critical elements become a powerful inspiration and model—a goal for the cultivation of character.

Who, according to our commentators, is Moses? What are the elements of his greatness?

In analyzing Moses within the context of great biblical personalities, early rabbinic commentators assert that he is superior to Adam, Noah, Abraham, Isaac, and Jacob. Adam, they say, is created in God's image but, failing to follow God's command, is banished from the Garden of Eden. Moses' loyalty to God is never diminished. Noah saves himself, but Moses saves himself and his generation. Abraham provides hospitality to passersby, but Moses feeds all Israel in the desert. Isaac glimpses God at the time Abraham is about to slaughter him on the altar, but Moses sees God face to face with eyes that never dim. Jacob wrestles with an angel on earth, but Moses takes on all the angels of heaven!

Moses' greatness, however, is not only a matter of comparing his "powers" with those of others. He is also superior in deeds. Rabbi Isaac speaks for many rabbinic interpreters in underscoring the Torah's portrayal of Moses as honest, pure of motive, selfless, scrupulous about never taking advantage of others or of representing his own needs, and always acting out of justice, in defense of the people of Israel.

Other rabbinic commentators point out that Moses constantly seeks to bring peace between the people of Israel and God. When the time comes for Israel to receive the Torah, Moses willingly climbs Mount Sinai, enduring forty days and nights of hunger, cold, and frightening thunder and lightning. Later, each time God is about to destroy the people because of their complaining and disloyalty, Moses intervenes to save them. When he learns that he is about to die, he immediately selects Joshua to succeed him so there will be no lapse in the leadership of the Israelites. It is this character profile, says Rabbi Tanchuma, that "makes Moses worthy of transmitting blessings to others." (*Deuteronomy Rabbah* 11:2, 3; *Mechilta, Beshalach* 6; *Sifre Deuteronomy, Haʾazinu* 306; and *Sifre Numbers, Pinchas* 138; *Tanchuma, Chukat* 63b)

This rabbinic composite of Moses presents an ideal portrait. It is a Moses without faults, a larger than life "perfect" hero. Rabbinic commentators, however, are well aware that Moses had his faults. He was human and flawed like all people.

According to the Torah, he is forbidden to enter the Land of Israel because of his sins at the Waters of Meribath-kadesh in the wilderness of Zin. There, instead of speaking to the rock and bringing forth water as God requests, he loses his temper at the complaining people, insults them by calling them "rebels," and strikes the rock with his staff. As punishment for his rage and his public demonstration of unfaithfulness to God, he is not allowed to enter the Promised Land. (See discussion in *A Torah Commentary for Our Times, Parashat Chukat,* "*Perek Bet.*")

While Moses is portrayed by rabbinic commentators as a flawed but great hero, Nachmanides believes that the real clue to his unique place in history has nothing to do with his personality. What defines Moses' uniqueness, says Nachmanides, is his relationship to God. Moses, as the last lines of Deuteronomy testify, was "singled out by God" who knew him "face to face."

Nachmanides explains that "when two people

see each other face to face, they become acquainted with each other through that meeting." That, however, was not the kind of acquaintance shared by Moses and God. The Torah says that "God knew Moses face to face"; it does not say that "Moses knew God face to face." In other words, continues Nachmanides, "Moses knew God to the extent that such knowledge is possible." Unlike other prophets or the people of Israel who knew God's power, felt God's hand upon them, sensed God's Presence in the midst of the fire and thunder at Mount Sinai or in the cloud they followed day and night across the desert, Moses was "singled out" for special meetings of intimacy with God. Because of these moments of sharing, the Torah was given to Israel. This constitutes the greatness of Moses. "Never again," concludes Nachmanides, quoting the Torah, "did there arise in Israel a prophet like Moses." (Commentary on Deuteronomy 34:10)

Hirsch

Nachmanides' view is repeated by many interpreters and finds clear expression in the writings of Rabbi Samson Raphael Hirsch. "Moses," explains Hirsch, "stands unique for all time. The direct contact in which God's will is manifest to Moses in raising him out of the rest of humanity for the mission he is to carry out was not attained by any later prophet. . . . Moses alone receives every word of his mission face to face, and no word not received in a similar direct manner can ever shake in the tiniest degree that which is given so directly to Moses." (Commentary on Deuteronomy 34:10–12)

Hirsch's argument is meant not only to etch out the extraordinary quality of Moses but also to "prove" the superiority of his prophetic career over that of all other religious prophets and traditions. Such arguments and claims are common, but they are dangerous because they often lead to unwarranted assumptions about who possesses the authentic truth or word of God. Instead of accepting that God speaks to many prophets and peoples, that all human beings and nations are precious to God, and that there are many equally sacred and wise ways for fulfilling God's will, human beings have often gone to war to establish the preeminence of their faith.

Hirsch's intimation of the exclusivity and superiority of God's relationship to Moses misses a very important point that the Torah text itself corrects. The Torah does not say "never again did there arise a prophet like Moses," but it says "never again did there arise *in Israel* a prophet like Moses." With that special emphasis, the Torah avoids a dangerous arrogance and remains open to God's revelation to other prophets and other peoples.

Psychologist and biblical interpreter Erich Fromm sees Moses as a person "who, in spite of his extraordinary talents and genius, is aware of his inadequacy for the task he is supposed to accomplish." Nonetheless, because of his experience with the suffering of his own people, Moses acquires "the necessary impulse for liberation." As the first of the prophets, writes Fromm, Moses fulfills a fourfold function: (1) He announces that there is a God and that our human goal "is to become fully human; and that means to become like God"; (2) he demonstrates the alternatives that human beings can choose and the consequences of these alternatives; (3) he expresses his dissent and protest when Israel chooses the wrong road but never abandons the people; and (4) he does not "think in terms of individual salvation only but believes that individual salvation is bound up with the salvation of society."

It is this unique role of first prophet that makes Moses so important a figure in history. He sets the standard for future Jewish prophets. It is Moses, Fromm emphasizes, who articulates the common themes of the prophetic tradition, especially "the establishment of a society governed by love, justice, and truth"; it is Moses who insists "that politics must be judged by moral values and that the function of political life is the realization of these values." (*You Shall Be as Gods*, Holt, Rinehart and Winston, New York, 1966, pp. 94–95, 117–118)

Sarna

Nahum M. Sarna perceives other dimensions of Moses' greatness. Noting that "the advent of Moses marks a radically new development in the religion of Israel," Sarna underscores and defines his innovations. They include: "the concept of a national covenant between God and an entire people, the insistence on the exclusive worship of one God, the thoroughgoing ban on representing God in any material or corporeal form, and the emergence as a national institution of the messenger-prophet." Taken together, says Sarna, these innovations constitute nothing less than "a revolutionary religious phenomenon, a sudden and new monotheistic creation the like of which had not hitherto existed. . . ."

Sarna maintains that this revolution is the work of the outstanding creative genius of Moses. He is the powerful personality transforming his people. "Moses must be seen as the towering figure behind the . . . religious developments that took place in Israel . . . his role as the first and greatest leader of Israel, as the spiritual titan, the dominating personality that powerfully informed for all time the collective mind and self-consciousness of the community, is unassailable." (*Exploring Exodus: The Heritage of Biblical Israel,* Schocken Books, New York, 1986, pp. 61–62, 148–157)

Loyalty to Israel
Author Elie Wiesel singles out Moses' loyalty to the people of Israel as a sign of Moses' greatness. While he occasionally became enraged with them, he constantly rose to rescue them. "If others spoke ill of Israel, he was quick to come to its defense, passionately, fiercely. . . . Moses defended them not only against their enemies but, at times, even against God. . . . In spite of his disappointments, in spite of his ordeals and the lack of gratitude he encountered, Moses never lost his faith in his people. Somehow he found both the strength and the courage to

---

remain on Israel's side and proclaim its honor and its right to live." (Messengers of God: Biblical Portraits and Legends, translated by Marion Wiesel, Summit Books, New York, 1976, pp. 199–201)

Peli

A mentsh
Many were the epithets and titles given to Moses in the course of his long career. Now, close to his death, he is referred to as ish ha-Elohim, "man of God." I believe that he was called this not to emphasize his relationship to God but rather to underscore his remaining a "man" even now. Being closer to God than ever before and about to leave this mundane world to embrace eternity, Moses was not concentrating only on himself, pondering his life in preparation to meet his Maker. His attention, even at this moment, was given to blessing the children of Israel. Intoxicated with godliness, he remains, to his very last breath, a man among men, a human being preserving that precious quality represented by the untranslatable Yiddish expression—to be a mentsh. (Pinchas Peli, Torah Today, p. 243)

Welding Israel together
I believe there was a Moses, that he played a central role in the life of the tribes that escaped from Egypt, and that his major achievement was not so much getting them out but the far more difficult task of welding a disparate group of tribes, a motley riffraff by the Torah's own account, into a community over the course of a long, punishing wilderness trek. . . . (Rabbi Daniel Jeremy Silver, Images of Moses, Basic Books, Inc., New York, 1982, p. 16)

Yeshayahu Leibowitz agrees with Sarna's evaluation of Moses. He goes on to point out, however, that "the greatest deed that Moses accomplished was not the deliverance from Egypt nor transmitting the Torah but that he shatters the tablets that had been engraved by God, when the people worshiped idolatry, and the holy words given on these tablets might have been desecrated."

Leibowitz refers to the moment when Moses, on Mount Sinai, is receiving the tablets with the Ten Commandments. Below, the people, led by Moses' brother Aaron, build and then worship a golden calf. Hearing their shouts and wild enthusiasm for the idol they have molded out of gold, Moses throws the tablets against the jagged rocks of the mountain. He refuses to tolerate idolatry. His demonstration of faith in that crisis, argues Leibowitz, is the true mark of his greatness. For him, not even the tablets on which the Ten Commandments are inscribed are sacred. They are to be broken if the situation demands such radical behavior.

"To break idolatry, not to sanctify values that stem from human drives and interests—that is faith. The main thing in faith in God is not to believe in anything that is not divine, not to sanctify things that stem from the drives and interests and plans and ideals and visions of man, even if, in human terms, they are the most lofty of matters." Moses teaches us that "when things are made into something holy, they are to be smashed."

Applying the lesson to our times, Leibowitz warns against setting up false gods; of worshiping nation, land, leaders or cult, any thing or any object. Idolatry of any kind is forbidden, including the idolatry of stones containing the words of God! "The holiness of God alone—that is the content of faith. If one adds to it the holiness of the nation and the holiness of the land, in one breath and in the same context, the holiness turns into its opposite. And this great thing was shown to us by Moses when he smashed this counterfeit and distorted holiness." (*Weekly Parashah,* pp. 206–208)

Rabbi Abba Hillel Silver singles out this same strength and genius of Moses. "With Moses," he reflects, "religion entered the nonrepresentational world, the inner world of thought, will, quest, and motivated conduct. It was one of the few radical shifts in the religious history of humanity—a new enlightenment that opened up roads to new horizons. Religion became boundless and dynamic, a progressive revolution in humanity's quest for security in God. Moses, in his radical monotheism, and his uncompromising opposition to any form of material embodiment of the idea of God, not only spiritualized the concept of the divine for all time, but negated all forms of worship known to the heathen world of his day."

Moses' contributions, however, go beyond his smashing of the idols of his time and his giving birth to a pure spiritual understanding of God. Silver also points out that it is Moses who transforms the tribes of Israel into the people of Israel. Though centuries elapse before they "would become a *people* in the true sense of the word . . . the events of liberation and escape into a new life had transformed them into a community of shared interests and a single purpose." Moses, Silver insists, gives the people a soul; binds them together; and endows them with a pioneering spirit, task, and goal. Under his leadership, they become a "whole community" fused "to a spiritual and ethical purpose."

And it is to that "whole community" that Moses devotes his life. Despite all the disappointments and rebellions, Moses never abandons his people. He battles for them, constantly arguing their case before God. As Silver points out, he endures unflinchingly . . . "ingratitude, rebellion, vilification, feuds, and rivalries. . . . He felt the gibes and stings to which all leaders come to be subjected. . . . Yet, compact of firmness and compassion, his heart was always full of concern for the people that so often failed him. It was the people that was at all times uppermost in his mind." (*Moses and the Original Torah,* Macmillan, New York, 1961, pp. 16–38)

Aaron Wildavsky also emphasizes Moses' loyalty to his people, but his perspective is different from that of Rabbi Abba Hillel Silver. He maintains that Moses' unique leadership of Israel marks his greatness. "The genius of Moses lies in joining revolution with evolution. He leads the people out of Egypt, introduces them to new values, creates new institutions, yet he does so gently and with patience. He urges them to accept the commandments, but when they fail to do so, or fall into complaining about conditions on the desert, he supports them, even defends them when God is ready to destroy them.

Moses the leader, Wildavsky points out, understands that change does not come easily to society. It requires patience, the willingness to risk new ideas and to fail. He stresses in his leadership "the ongoing necessity of learning from error" and the wisdom of "discovering new coalitions of interests" that can bring about desired ends. In Moses we see a leader using strength when the people require judgment, mercy when they fall into despair, and anger when they need to be punished for their selfishness and lack of patience. He demonstrates an ability to be both critical and constructive, to uplift and inspire with visions of a Promised Land, even to accept his death and the need to transfer leadership to another. Moses, concludes Wildavsky, "is politically productive. . . ." It is as a model of leadership that he achieves his extraordinary place in history. (*Moses as a Political Leader*, pp. 211–212)

The character of Moses continues to fascinate those who search for the secrets defining human greatness. Was it his humility, compassion, moral sensibility, defense of his people, organizing skills, ability to accept criticism, anger, articulation of law, formulation of monotheism, belligerence under attack, vindictive punishment of enemies, political leadership, or some special combination of all these traits?

No one answer or theory seems to satisfy our curiosity. Perhaps that alone is a clue to his greatness. There is a mystery residing in the human soul. It is beyond our understanding. We barely sense it or comprehend its power. We encounter and know its presence in the lives and unique contributions of human beings who, like Moses, are said to have known God "face to face."

QUESTIONS FOR STUDY AND DISCUSSION

1. Rabbi Meir teaches that every Jew should take time from business to study Torah. Moses Maimonides writes that every Jew, rich or poor, healthy or sick, young or old, is obligated to study Torah. Given the variety of meanings associated with Torah in Jewish tradition, why is the study of Torah considered critical to the survival of the Jewish people and its traditions of celebration and ethics?

2. Which view on what constitutes Moses' greatness makes the most sense to you? Why?

3. Rabbi Nachman ben Jacob teaches that "a leader must always show respect for the community." In what ways does Moses fulfill this qualification for leadership? In what ways does he fail?

4. Select four modern leaders, two of whom you respect for their successes and two of whom you judge as failures. How do their strengths and weaknesses compare with those of Moses?

Glossary of Commentaries
and Interpreters

(For further information on those entries followed by an asterisk, see Introduction II in A Torah Commentary for Our Times, *Volume One: Genesis.)*

Abravanel, Don Isaac.*

Adani, David ben Amram (13th century). (See *Midrash ha-Gadol.*)

Akedat Yitzhak. A commentary to the Torah by Isaac ben Moses Arama. (See Arama, Isaac ben Moses.)

Alshekh, Moshe ben Chaim (1507–1600). Lived and taught in Safed in the Land of Israel. His commentary to the Torah contains his Sabbath sermons.

Arama, Isaac ben Moses (1420–1494). Author of the Torah commentary *Akedat Yitzhak.* Spanish rabbi. Known for his sermons and allegorical interpretations of Torah. Defended Judaism in many public disputes with Christians and settled in Italy after the expulsion of Jews from Spain in 1492.

Ashkenazi, Eliezer ben Elijah (1513–1586). Lived in Egypt, Cyprus, Venice, Prague, and Posen. Died in Cracow. Emphasized the gift of reason and in his commentary, *Ma'aseh ha-Shem,* urged students to approach the Torah with care and independence. Worked as a rabbi, Torah interpreter, and physician. (See *Ma'aseh ha-Shem.*)

Ashkenazi, Shimon (12th century). (See *Yalkut Shimoni.*)

Ashkenazi of Yanof, Jacob ben Isaac (13th century). Author of *Tze'enah u-Re'enah.* (See *Tze'enah u-Re'enah.*)

Astruc, Anselm Solomon. (See *Midrashei Torah.*)

Attar, Chaim ibn (1696–1743). Born in Morocco and settled in Jerusalem, where he opened a school. His Torah commentary, *Or ha-Chaim,* combines talmudic and mystical interpretations. (See *Or ha-Chaim.*)

Avot or *Pirke Avot,* "Sayings of the Fathers." A book of the *Mishnah,* comprising a collection of statements by famous rabbis.

Avot de-Rabbi Natan (2nd century). Compiled by Rabbi Nathan, sometimes called "Nathan the Babylonian." Based on *Pirke Avot.*

Ba'al Ha-Turim, Ya'akov (1275–1340). Born in Germany. Fled persecutions there in 1303 and settled in Spain. Author of the very important collection of Jewish law *Arba'ah Turim,* "Four Rows," the basis for the later *Shulchan Aruch,* "Set Table," by Joseph Karo. His Torah commentary known as *Ba'al ha-Turim* often includes interpretations based on the mathematical meanings of Hebrew words.

Bachya ben Asher (14th century). Lived in Saragossa and Aragon. Known for his Torah commentary.

Bachya ben Joseph ibn Pakuda (11th century). Lived in Spain as poet and author of the classic study of Jewish ethics *Hovot ha-Levavot,* "Duties of the Heart." (See *Hovot ha-Levavot.*)

Bamberger, Bernard J.*

Berlin, Naphtali Zvi Judah (1817–1893). Head of the famous yeshivah at Volozhin. Supporter of early

Zionism. His Torah commentary, *Ha-Emek Davar,* is a record of his lectures on the weekly portions. (See *Ha-Emek Davar.*)

Bin Gorion, Micha Joseph (Berdyczewski) (1865–1921). Though a Russian citizen, spent most of his years in Germany. A Hebrew writer, his collection of Jewish folktales, *Mimekor Yisrael,* is considered a classic. (See *Mimekor Yisrael.*)

Biur. *

Buber, Martin Mordecai (1878–1965). Born in Vienna. Became renowned as a twentieth-century philosopher. With Franz Rosenzweig, translated the Bible into German. His *Moses* is a commentary on Exodus.

Caspi, Joseph ben Abba Mari (1280–1340). A philosopher and commentator who lived in France. His commentary seeks to blend reason with religious faith.

Cassuto, Umberto. An Italian historian and biblical scholar. Accepted chair of Bible Studies at Hebrew University, Jerusalem, in 1939, when Italian racial laws made continuation of his work impossible. Wrote famous commentaries on Genesis and Exodus.

Da'at Zekenim mi-Ba'alei ha-Tosafot. A thirteenth-century collection of Torah commentaries by students of Rashi who sought to resolve contradictions found within the talmudic discussions of the rabbis.

De Leon, Moses. (See *Zohar.*) *

Deuteronomy Rabbah. One of the early collections of *midrashim.* *

Dubno, Solomon. (See *Biur.*) *

Ecclesiastes Rabbah. One of the early collections of *midrashim.* *

Edels, Shemuel Eliezer ben Yehudah Halevi (1555–1631). One of the best-known and respected interpreters of Talmud. Born in Cracow. Also known as the *Maharsha.*

Epstein, Baruch (1860–1942). Murdered by the Nazis in the Pinsk ghetto. (See *Torah Temimah.*)

Exodus Rabbah. One of the early collections of *midrashim.* *

Genesis Rabbah. One of the early collections of *midrashim.* *

Gittin. A tractate of Talmud that discusses the laws of divorce.

Guide for the Perplexed. A philosophical discussion of the meanings of Jewish belief written by Moses Maimonides. (See Maimonides, Moses.)

Ha-Cohen, Meir Simcha (1845–1926). (See *Meshekh Hochmah.*)

Ha-Emek Davar. A Torah commentary written by Naphtali Zvi Judah Berlin. (See Berlin, Naphtali Zvi Judah.)

Ha-Ketav ve-ha-Kabbalah. A Torah commentary written by Jacob Zvi Meklenburg. *

Halevi, Aharon (1230–1300). Born in Gerona, Spain. Served as rabbi and judge in Barcelona, Saragossa, and Toledo. Lecturer in Montpellier, Provence, France, where he died. While *Sefer ha-Hinuch* is said to have been written by him, many doubt the claim. (See *Sefer ha-Hinuch.*)

Halevi, Isaac ben Yehudah (13th century). (See *Paneah Raza.*)

Halevi, Yehudah (1080–1142?). Born in Spain. Poet, philosopher, and physician. His book *The Kuzari* contains his philosophy of Judaism. It is a dialogue between the king of the Kazars and a rabbi who convinces the king of the superiority of Judaism.

Hallo, William W. *

Ha-Midrash ve-ha-Ma'aseh. A commentary to Genesis and Exodus by Yehezkel ben Hillel Aryeh Leib Lipschuetz. (See Lipschuetz, Yehezkel ben Hillel Aryeh Leib.)

Heinemann, Yitzhak (1876–1957). Born in Germany. Israeli scholar and philosopher. His *Ta'amei ha-Mitzvot,* "Reasons for the Commandments," is a study of the meaning of the commandments of Jewish tradition.

Hertz, Joseph Herman. *

Hirsch, Samson Raphael. *

Hirschensohn, Chaim (1857–1935). Born in Safed. Lived most of his life in Jerusalem. Supported the work of Eliezer ben Yehuda's revival of Hebrew. (See *Nimmukei Rashi.*)

Hizkuni. A Torah commentary by Hizkiyahu (Hezekiah) ben Manoah (13th century) of France.

Hoffman, David Zvi (1843–1921). A leading German rabbi. His commentary on Leviticus and Deuteronomy is based on lectures given in the 1870s, seeking to refute biblical critics who argued that the Christian New Testament was superior to the Hebrew Bible.

Hovot ha-Levavot, "Duties of the Heart." A classic study of Jewish ethics by Bachya ben Joseph ibn Pakuda. Concerned with the emphasis on ritual among the Jews of his times, Bachya argues that a Jew's highest responsibility is to carry out the ethical commandments of Torah. (See Bachya ben Joseph ibn Pakuda.)

Hullin. A tractate of Talmud that discusses laws dealing with killing animals for food.

Ibn Ezra, Abraham.*

Jacob, Benno.*

Kasher, Menachem. (See *Torah Shelemah.*)

Kelei Yakar. A Torah commentary written by Solomon Ephraim ben Chaim Lunchitz (1550–1619) of Lvov (Lemberg), Poland.

Kiddushin. A tractate of Talmud that discusses laws of marriage.

Kimchi, David (RaDaK).*

Leibowitz, Nehama.*

Lekach Tov. A collection of *midrashim* on the Torah and the Five Scrolls (Song of Songs, Ruth, Lamentations, Ecclesiastes, and Esther) by Tobias ben Eliezer (11th century C.E.).

Lipschuetz, Yehezkel ben Hillel Aryeh Lieb (1862–1932). Lithuanian interpreter of Torah and author of *Ha-Midrash ve-ha-Ma'aseh.* (See *Ha-Midrash ve-ha-Ma'aseh.*)

Luzzato, Moshe Chaim (1707–1746). Known also as *Ramhal.* Italian dramatist and mystic whose commentaries were popular among chasidic Jews. His textbook on how to become a righteous person, *Mesillat Yesharim,* became one of the most popular books on the subject of Jewish ethics. (See *Mesillat Yesharim.*)

Luzzato, Samuel David.*

Ma'aseh ha-Shem. A commentary by Eliezer ben Elijah Ashkenazi, published in 1583. (See Ashkenazi, Eliezer ben Elijah.)

Maimonides, Moses, Rabbi Moses ben Maimon (1135–1204). Known by the initials RaMBaM. Born in Cordova, Spain. Physician and philosopher. Wrote the *Mishneh Torah,* a code of Jewish law; *Guide for the Perplexed,* a philosophy of Judaism; *Sefer ha-Mitzvot,* an outline of the 613 commandments of Torah; and many other interpretations of Jewish tradition. Famous as a physician. Served the leaders in the court of Egypt.

MaLBIM, Meir Lev ben Yechiel Michael.*

Mechilta.

Megillah. A tractate of Talmud that discusses the biblical Book of Esther.

Meklenburg, Jacob Zvi. (See *Ha-Ketav ve-ha-Kabbalah.*)*

Mendelssohn, Moses.*

Meshekh Hochmah. A Torah commentary published in 1927. Written by Meir Simcha Ha-Cohen, rabbi of Dvinsk. Combines insights from the Talmud with a discussion of the philosophy of Judaism. (See Ha-Cohen, Meir Simcha.)

Mesillat Yesharim, "Pathway of the Righteous." A discussion of how one should pursue an ethical life. Written by Moshe Chaim Luzzatto. (See above.)

Messengers of God. A study of several important biblical personalities by Elie Wiesel. (See Wiesel, Elie; also Bibliography in this book.)

Midrash Agadah. A collection of rabbinic interpretations. (See discussion of *midrashim.*)*

Midrash ha-Gadol. A collection of rabbinic interpretations dating to the first and second centuries by David ben Amram Adani, a scholar living in Yemen. (See Adani, David ben Amram.)

Midrash Sechel Tov. Compiled by Menachem ben Solomon in 1139. Combines selections of *midrash* and *halachah* on every Torah portion.

Midrash Tanchuma. Known also as *Tanchuma Midrash Yelamedenu.* A collection said to have been collected by Rabbi Tanchuma (427–465 C.E.). Many of the *midrashim* begin with the words *Yelamedenu rabbenu,* "Let our teacher instruct us. . . ."*

Midrashei Torah. A Torah commentary by Anselm Solomon Astruc, who was murdered in an attack on the Jewish community of Barcelona in 1391.

Mimekor Yisrael. A collection of folktales from Jewish tradition by Micha Joseph Bin Gorion (Berdyczewski). (See Bin Gorion.)

Mishnah.

Mizrachi, Eliyahu (1440–1525). A Chief Rabbi of Turkey during the expulsion of Jews from Spain. Helped many immigrants. Wrote a commentary to Rashi's Torah interpretation.

Morgenstern, Julian.*

Nachmanides.* (See RaMBaN.)

Nedarim. A tractate of Talmud that discusses vows or promises.

Nimmukei Rashi. A commentary on Rashi's Torah interpretation by Chaim Hirschensohn. (See Hirschensohn, Chaim.)

Numbers Rabbah. An early collection of *midrashim.**

Or ha-Chaim. A Torah commentary by Chaim ibn Attar. Combines talmudic observations with mystical interpretations. (See Attar, Chaim ibn.)

Paneah Raza. A Torah commentary by Isaac ben Yehudah Halevi, who lived in Sens. (See Halevi, Isaac ben Yehudah.)

Peli, Pinchas Hacohen (20th century). Jerusalem-born scholar, poet, and rabbi. His "Torah Today" column in the *Jerusalem Post* seeks to present a contemporary view of the meaning of Torah.

*Pesikta de-Rav Kahana.** A collection of *midrashim* or early rabbinic sermons based on Torah portions for holidays of the Jewish year. *Pesikta Rabbati* is similar in both content and organization.

*Pesikta Rabbati.** (See *Pesikta de-Rav Kahana.*)

*Pirke de-Rabbi Eliezer.** A collection of *midrashim* said to have been written by the first-century C.E. teacher Rabbi Eliezer ben Hyrkanos. Contents include mystic interpretations of creation, early human life, the giving of the Torah at Mount Sinai, comments about the Book of Esther, and the Israelite experience in the Sinai.

Plaut, W. Gunther.*

RaDaK, Rabbi David Kimchi.*

RaMBaM, Rabbi Moses ben Maimon. (See Maimonides.)

RaMBaN, Rabbi Moses ben Nachman.* (See Nachmanides.)

RaSHBaM, Rabbi Shemuel (Samuel) ben Meir.*

RaSHI, Rabbi Shelomoh (Solomon) Itzhaki.*

Reggio, Yitzhak Shemuel (1784–1855). Known also as YaSHaR. Lived in Italy. Translated the Bible into Italian. Created a Hebrew commentary that sought to harmonize science and religion.

Rosenzweig, Franz (1886–1929). German philosopher. Worked with Martin Buber in translating the Bible into German. Best known for book *The Star of Redemption,* which seeks to explore the meanings of Jewish tradition.

Sa'adia ben Joseph Ha-Gaon.* (See Introductions I and II of *A Torah Commentary for Our Times, Volume One: Genesis.*)

Sanhedrin. A tractate of Talmud that discusses laws regulating the courts.

Sarna, Nahum M.*

Sefer ha-Hinuch. Presents the 613 *mitzvot,* "commandments," found within the Torah. Divided according to weekly Torah portions. Said by some to have been written by Aharon Halevi of Barcelona. (See Halevi, Aharon.)

Sforno, Obadiah.*

Shabbat. A tractate of Talmud that discusses the laws of the Sabbath.

*Sifra.** A *midrash* on Leviticus. Believed by scholars to have been written during the fourth century C.E.

*Sifre.** A *midrash* on Numbers and Deuteronomy. Believed to have been composed during the fifth century C.E.

Simeon (Shimon) ben Yochai.* (See *Zohar.*) *

Solomon, Menachem ben. (See *Midrash Sechel Tov.*)

Sotah. A tractate of Talmud that discusses laws concerning a woman suspected of adultery.

Speiser, Ephraim Avigdor.*

Steinsaltz, Adin (20th century). An Israeli Talmud scholar. His book *Biblical Images* contains studies of various biblical characters.

Ta'amei ha-Mitzvot. (See Heinemann, Yitzhak.)

Ta'anit. A tractate of Talmud that deals with the laws concerning fast days.

*Talmud.** Combines the *Mishnah* and *Gemara.* Appears in two versions: the more extensive *Talmud Bavli,* "Babylonian Talmud," a collection of discussions by the rabbis of Babylonia from the second to the fifth centuries C.E., and *Talmud Yerushalmi,* "Jerusalem Talmud," a smaller collection of discussions from the second to the fourth centuries C.E.

Tanna Debe Eliyahu. A *midrash* and book of Jewish philosophy and commentary believed by scholars to have been composed during the third to tenth centuries. Author unknown.

*Targum Onkelos.**

*Targum Yerushalmi.**

Toledot Yitzhak.

Torah Shelemah. A study of each Torah portion, which includes a collection of early rabbinic interpretations along with a commentary by Rabbi Menachem Kasher of Jerusalem, Israel.

Torah Temimah. A Torah commentary by Baruch Epstein. Includes a collection of teachings from the Talmud on each Torah portion. (See Epstein, Baruch.)

Tosafot. "Supplementary Discussions" of the Talmud. Collected during the twelfth and thirteenth centuries in France and Germany and added to nearly every printing of the Talmud since.

Tzedeh Laderech. An interpretation of Rashi's Torah commentary by Issachar Ber ben Israel-Lazar Parnas Eilenberg (1550–1623), who lived in Italy.

Tze'enah u-Re'enah. A well-known Yiddish paraphrase and interpretation of the Torah. First published in 1618. Written for women by Jacob ben Isaac Ashkenazi of Yanof. Divided by weekly Torah portions. One of the first texts developed to educate women. (See Ashkenazi of Yanof, Jacob ben Isaac.)

Wessely, Naftali Herz. (See *Biur.*)*

Wiesel, Elie (1928–   ). Nobel Prize-winning novelist. Author of *Messengers of God,* among other books. (See *Messengers of God.*)

Yalkut Shimoni. A collection of *midrashim.* Believed to be the work of Shimon Ashkenazi. (See Ashkenazi, Shimon.)

Yevamot. A tractate of Talmud that deals with laws concerning sisters-in-law.

Yoma. A tractate of Talmud that deals with laws concerning Yom Kippur.

*Zohar.**

Bibliography

Abbott, Walter M.; Gilbert, Arthur; Hunt, Rolfe Lanier; and Swain, J. Carter. *The Bible Reader: An Interfaith Interpretation*. New York: Bruce Publishing Co., 1969.

Adar, Zvi. *Humanistic Values in the Bible*. New York: Reconstructionist Press, 1967.

Adler, Morris, *The Voice Still Speaks*. New York: Bloch Publishing Co., 1969.

Aharoni, Yohanan, and Avi-Yonah, Michael. *The Macmillan Bible Atlas*. New York: Macmillan, 1976.

Alshekh, Moshe ben Chaim. *Torat Moshe,* Vols. I and II, Eliyahu Munk, trans. Jerusalem: Rubin Mass Ltd. Publishers, 1988.

Alter, Robert. *The Art of Biblical Narrative*. New York: Basic Books, 1981.

Asimov, Isaac. *Animals of the Bible*. Garden City, New York: Doubleday, 1978.

Avi-Yonah, Michael, and Malamat, Abraham, eds. *Views of the Biblical World*. Chicago and New York: Jordan Publications, Inc., 1959.

Bachya ben Asher. *Kad ha-Kemach*. Charles B. Chavel, trans. New York: Shilo Publishing House, Inc., 1980.

Baron, Joseph L., ed. *A Treasury of Jewish Quotations*. New York: Crown Publishers, Inc., 1956.

Ben-Gurion, David. *Israel, a Personal History*. New York: Funk and Wagnalls, Inc., and Sabra Books, 1971.

Blumenthal, David R. *God at the Center*. San Francisco: Harper and Row Publishers, Inc., 1987.

Borowitz, Eugene B. *Liberal Judaism*. New York: UAHC Press, 1984.

———. *Renewing the Covenant*. Philadelphia: Jewish Publication Society, 1991.

Braude, William G., and Kapstein, Israel J., trans. Author unknown. *Tanna Debe Eliyahu*. Philadelphia: Jewish Publication Society, 1981.

Buber, Martin. *Moses: The Revelation and the Covenant*. New York: Harper and Row Publishers, Inc., 1958.

Bulka, Reuven P. *Torah Therapy: Reflections on the Weekly Sedra and Special Occasions*. New York: Ktav, 1983.

Cassuto, Umberto. *A Commentary on the Book of Exodus*. Jerusalem: Magnes Press, 1951.

Chavel, Charles B., trans. *Ramban (Nachmanides) Commentary on the Torah*. New York: Shilo Publishing House, Inc., 1974.

Chiel, Arthur. *Guide to Sidrot and Haftarot*. New York: Ktav, 1971.

Chill, Abraham. *The Minhagim: The Customs and Ceremonies of Judaism, Their Origins and Rationale*. New York: Sepher-Hermon Press, 1979.

Cohen, Philip. *Rambam on the Torah*. Jerusalem: Rubin Mass Ltd. Publishers, 1985.

Culi, Ya'akov. *The Torah Anthology, Yalkut Me'am Lo'ez*. Aryeh Kaplan, trans. New York and Jerusalem: Maznaim Publishing Corp., 1977.

Danby, Herbert, trans. *The Mishnah*. London: Oxford University Press, 1933.

Deen, Edith. *All of the Women of the Bible*. New York: Harper and Brothers, 1965.

Doria, Charles, and Lenowitz, Harris, trans. and eds. *Origins, Creation Texts from the Ancient Mediterranean.* New York: Anchor Press, 1976.

Dresner, Samuel H., and Siegel, Seymour. *The Jewish Dietary Laws.* New York: Burning Bush Press, 1959.

Efron, Benjamin. *The Message of the Torah.* New York: Ktav, 1963.

Epstein, Baruch Halevi. *The Essential Torah Teminah.* Shraga Silverstein, trans. Jerusalem: Feldheim Publishers, 1989.

Epstein, I., trans. and ed. *The Babylonian Talmud.* London: Soncino Press, 1952.

Fields, Harvey J. *Bechol Levavcha: With All Your Heart.* New York: UAHC Press, 1976.

Freedman, H., and Simon, Maurice, trans. *Midrash Rabbah: Genesis,* Vols. I and II. London: Soncino Press, 1961.

Friedman, Alexander Zusia. *Wellsprings of Torah.* Compiled and edited by Nison Alpert. Gertrude Hirschler, trans. New York: Judaica Press, 1986.

Friedman, Richard Elliott. *Who Wrote the Bible?* New York: Summit Books, 1987.

Fromm, Erich. *You Shall Be as Gods.* New York: Holt, Rinehart and Winston, 1966.

Frye, Northrop. *The Great Code: The Bible and Literature.* New York: Harcourt Brace Jovanovich Publishers, 1981.

Gaster, Theodor H. *Festivals of the Jewish Year.* New York: William Morrow and Co., Inc., 1953.

Gilbert, Martin. *Jewish History Atlas.* New York: Macmillan, 1976.

Ginzberg, Louis. *Legends of the Jews.* Philadelphia: Jewish Publication Society, 1968.

Gittelsohn, Roland B. *Man's Best Hope.* New York: Random House, 1961.

Glatzer, Nahum N., ed. *Hammer on the Rock: A Midrash Reader.* New York: Schocken Books, 1962.

———. *On the Bible: 18 Studies.* New York: Schocken Books, 1968.

Goldman, Solomon. *In the Beginning.* Philadelphia: Jewish Publication Society of America, 1949.

Gordis, Robert. *A Faith for Moderns.* New York: Bloch Publishing Co., 1960.

Graves, Robert, and Patai, Raphael. *Hebrew Myths: The Book of Genesis.* New York: Greenwich House, 1983.

Greenberg, Moshe. *Understanding Exodus.* New York: Behrman House, 1969.

Hartman, David. *A Living Covenant.* New York: The Free Press, 1985.

Herford, R. Travers. *Pirke Aboth, The Ethics of the Talmud: Sayings of the Fathers.* New York: Schocken Books, 1971.

Hertz, J.H., ed. *The Pentateuch and Haftorahs.* London: Soncino Press, 1966.

Heschel, Abraham J. *The Prophets.* Philadelphia: Jewish Publication Society, 1962.

———. *God in Search of Man: A Philosophy of Judaism.* New York: Farrar, Straus and Cudahy, 1955.

Hirsch, Samson Raphael, trans. *The Pentateuch.* London, England: L. Honig and Sons Ltd., 1959.

———. *Horeb: A Philosophy of Jewish Laws and Observances.* I. Grunfeld, trans. 4th ed. New York: Soncino Press, 1981.

The Interpreter's Bible. 12 vols. Nashville: Abingdon, 1951–1957.

Jacobson, B.S. *Meditations on the Torah.* Tel Aviv: Sinai Publishing, 1956.

Kahana, S.Z. *Heaven on Your Head.* Morris Silverman, ed. Hartford: Hartmore House, 1964.

Kaplan, Mordecai M. *Questions Jews Ask: Reconstructionist Answers.* New York: Reconstructionist Press, 1956.

———. *The Meaning of God in Modern Jewish Religion.* New York: Reconstructionist Press, 1962.

Katz, Mordechai. *Lilmod Ul'lamade: From the Teachings of Our Sages.* New York: Jewish Education Program Publications, 1978.

Korn, Lester. *The Success Profile.* New York: Fireside, 1988.

Kushner, Harold S. *When Bad Things Happen to Good People.* New York: Schocken Books, 1981.

Lamm, Maurice. *The Jewish Way in Death and Mourning.* New York: Jonathan David Publishers, 1975.

Leibowitz, Nehama. *Studies in Bereshit.* Jerusalem: World Zionist Organization, 1980.

———. *Studies in Shemot.* Jerusalem: World Zionist Organization, 1980.

———. *Studies in Vayikra.* Jerusalem: World Zionist Organization, 1980.

———. *Studies in Bemidbar.* Jerusalem: World Zionist Organization, 1980.

———. *Studies in Devarim.* Jerusalem: World Zionist Organization, 1980.

Leibowitz, Yeshayahu. *Weekly Parashah.* Shmuel Himelstein, trans. Brooklyn, New York: Chemed Books, 1990.

Levin, Meyer. *Beginnings in Jewish Philosophy.* New York: Behrman House, 1971.

Levine, Baruch A., ed. *JPS Torah Commentary: Leviticus.* Philadelphia: Jewish Publication Society, 1989.

Levine, Moshe. *The Tabernacle: Its Structure and Utensils.* London: Soncino Press, 1969.

Maimonides, Moses. *The Book of Knowledge: Mishneh Torah.* Moses Hyamson, trans. Jerusalem and New York: Feldheim Publishers, 1974.

Matek, Ord. *The Bible through Stamps.* New York: Hebrew Publishing Company, 1967.

Milgrom, Jacob, ed. *JPS Torah Commentary: Numbers.* Philadelphia: Jewish Publication Society, 1990.

Miller, Madeline S., and Lane, J. *Harper's Encyclopedia of Bible Life.* New York: Harper and Row Publishers, Inc., 1978.

Morgenstern, Julian. *The Book of Genesis.* New York: Schocken Books, 1965.

Munk, Eli. *The Call of the Torah,* Vols. I and II. Jerusalem and New York: Feldheim Publishers, 1980.

Neusner, Jacob. *Meet Our Sages.* New York: Behrman House, 1980.

———. *Tzedakah.* Chappaqua, New York: Rossel, 1982.

Orlinsky, Harry M., ed. *The Torah: The Five Books of Moses.* A New Translation. Philadelphia: Jewish Publication Society, 1962.

———. *Understanding the Bible through History and Archaeology.* New York: Ktav, 1972.

Peli, Pinchas H. *Torah Today.* Washington, D.C.: B'nai B'rith Books, 1987.

———. *Shabbat Shalom.* Washington, D.C.: B'nai B'rith Books, 1988.

Peters, Thomas J., and Waterman, Jr., Robert H. *In Search of Excellence.* New York: Harper and Row Publishers, Inc., 1982.

Pfeiffer, Robert H. *Introduction to the Old Testament.* New York: Harper and Brothers, 1941.

Phillips, Anthony. Exodus Commentary. *The Cambridge Bible Commentary: New English Bible.* Cambridge, England: Cambridge University Press, 1972.

Plaut, W. Gunther, ed. *The Torah: A Modern Commentary.* Commentaries by W. Gunther Plaut and Bernard J. Bamberger. Essays by William W. Hallo. New York: Union of American Hebrew Congregations, 1981.

———. *The Case for the Chosen People.* New York: Doubleday, 1965.

Pritchard, James B., ed. *Ancient Near Eastern Texts Relating to the Old Testament.* Princeton, New Jersey: Princeton University Press, 1955.

Quick, James C., and Jonathan D. *Organizational Stress and Preventive Management.* New York: McGraw-Hill, 1984.

Rabbinowitz, J., trans. *Midrash Rabbah* (Genesis, Exodus, Leviticus, Numbers, Deuteronomy). London: Soncino Press, 1961.

Rabinowitz, Louis I. *Torah and Flora.* New York: Sanhedrin Press, 1977.

Rad, Gerhard von. *Deuteronomy.* Commentary and translation by Dorothea Barton. Philadelphia: Westminster Press, 1966.

Reed, Allison. *The Story of Creation.* New York: Schocken Books, 1981.

Rosenbaum, M., and Silbermann, A.M., trans. *Pentateuch with Targum Onkelos, Haphtaroth and Rashi's Commentary.* Jerusalem: Silbermann Family Publishers, 1973.

Rosenberg, David, ed. *Congregation: Contemporary Writers Read the Jewish Bible.* New York: Harcourt Brace Jovanovich Publishers, 1987.

Samuel, Maurice. *Certain People of the Book.* New York: Alfred A. Knopf, Inc., 1955.

Sandmel, Samuel. *Alone Atop the Mountain: A Novel about Moses and the Exodus.* New York: Doubleday, 1973.

Sarna, Nahum M. *Understanding Genesis*. New York: Schocken Books, 1966.

Schneerson, Menachem M. *Torah Studies*. London: Lubavitch Foundation, 1986.

———. *Likutei Sichot*. London: Lubavitch Foundation, 1975–1985.

Sheehy, Gail. *Pathfinders*. New York: William Morrow, 1981.

Silbermann, A.M., ed. *Pentateuch with Rashi Commentary*. Jerusalem: Silbermann Family Publishers, 1933.

Silver, Abba Hillel. *Moses and the Original Torah*. New York: Macmillan, 1961.

———. *The World Crisis and Jewish Survival*. New York: Richard R. Smith, Inc., 1931.

Silver, Daniel Jeremy. *Images of Moses*. New York: Basic Books, Inc., 1982.

Silverman, Hillel E. *From Week to Week*. New York: Hartmore House, 1975.

Simon, Solomon, and Morrison, David Bial. *The Rabbis' Bible*. New York: Behrman House, 1966.

Speiser, E.A., trans. *The Anchor Bible: Genesis*. New York: Doubleday, 1964.

Steinberg, Milton. *Basic Judaism*. New York: Harcourt Brace, 1947.

Steinsaltz, Adin. *The Thirteen Petalled Rose*. New York: Basic Books, Inc., 1980.

Van Doren, Mark, and Samuel, Maurice. *In the Beginning . . . Love*. Edith Samuel, ed. New York: John Day Company, 1973.

Weinstein, Jacob J. *The Place of Understanding*. New York: Bloch Publishing Co., 1959.

Wiesel, Elie. *Messengers of God*. New York: Random House, 1976.

Zakon, Miriam Stark, trans. *Tze'enah u-Re'enah: The Classic Anthology of Torah Lore and Midrashic Commentary*. Brooklyn, New York: Mesorah Publications Ltd./Hillel Press, 1983.

Zeligs, Dorothy F. *Psychoanalysis and the Bible*. New York: Bloch Publishing Co., 1974.

Zlotowitz, Meir, trans. *Bereishis*. Art Scroll Tanach Series. New York: Mesorah Publications Ltd., 1977–1981.